Critical Essays on Mark Twain, 1867–1910

Critical Essays on Mark Twain, 1867–1910

Louis J. Budd

G. K. Hall & Co. ● Boston, Massachusetts

Library of Congress Cataloging in Publication Data
Main entry under title:

Critical essays on Mark Twain, 1867–1910.

  (Critical essays on American literature)
  Includes index.
  1. Twain, Mark, 1835–1910—Criticism and interpretation—
Addresses, essays, lectures. I. Budd, Louis J. II. Series.
PS1338.C73   818'.409   81–20031
ISBN 0–8161–8619–7   AACR2

This publication is printed on permanent/durable acid-free paper
MANUFACTURED IN THE UNITED STATES OF AMERICA

CRITICAL ESSAYS ON AMERICAN LITERATURE

This series seeks to publish the most important reprinted criticism on writers and topics in American literature along with, in various volumes, original essays, interviews, bibliographies, letters, manuscript sections, and other materials brought to public attention for the first time. Louis J. Budd's volume on Mark Twain is the most comprehensive collection of criticism ever assembled for the period from 1867 to 1910, the year of Twain's death. It covers not only Twain's books but also his periodical publications and lecture performances, aspects of his career too often neglected. Among the writers and critics represented in this volume are William Dean Howells, Oliver Wendell Holmes, George Ade, Brander Matthews, Hamilton W. Mabie, Henry Van Dyke, and Josh Billings. We are confident that this collection will make a permanent and significant contribution to American literary study.

JAMES NAGEL, GENERAL EDITOR

Northeastern University

CONTENTS

INTRODUCTION

Between 1955 and 1974 eight surprisingly different collections of reprinted essays offered to demonstrate the literary reputation of Mark Twain.[1] In part the differences follow from the high selectivity imposed by a diverse body of commentary that itself often engages the question of Twain's ultimate standing. Only Walt Whitman arouses as keen an interest in how a writer's contemporary critics received him and, in the process, created evidence by which we can judge them and their encompassing values. But in Twain's case the emphasis on his reputation springs not from his experimentalism but from his immense popularity then and now, the sharply, even bitterly opposed judgments on the quality of his books, and the puzzles of his mixed goals. The urge to classify him goes finally beyond the literary historians' liking for order and the critics' instinct to set up a hierarchy of prestige even while professing that any great artist is unique. If only grudgingly both guilds realize that Twain's career questions their standard criteria, perched on assumptions about the superiority of elitist tastes. Because of the wealth of materials and because his death significantly changed the dynamics of the situation, this latest collection stops with 1910. A second volume can center on the patterns in evaluation that was increasingly escaping the impact of his personality while narrowing toward his major books and, as it turned out, formalist analysis.

The most striking overt feature of the criticism during Twain's lifetime is the regular discovery of his serious qualities that starts before his visibility blazed beyond his western circle. Prematurely, a friend's introduction to *The Celebrated Jumping Frog of Calaveras County and Other Sketches* (1867) tried to establish that discovery as the guiding principle. However, *The Innocents Abroad* (1869) made a firm base for those who wanted to insist that even much of Twain's clowning leaves a sober point. In a minority verdict on *The Prince and the Pauper* (1881) that was both revealing and farsighted, a disappointed reviewer complained that Twain had tried to prove he was more than a "humorous story-teller and ingenious homely philosopher"—though Twain still doubted he stood that high. The reviewer went on to scold:

1

It was not necessary for the author to prop his literary reputation with archaic English and a somewhat conventional manner. His recent humorous writings abound in passages of great excellence as serious compositions, and his serious nervous style is the natural expression of an acute mind, that in its most fanciful moods is seldom superficial in its view. Indeed, it is because Mark Twain is a satirist, and in some measure a true philosopher, that his broadly humorous books and speeches have met with wide popular favor.[2]

Confusingly for Twain himself, this spokesman for a genteelist monthly respected him more when he was blithely following his instincts rather than straining to satisfy the current literary norms. Still, though *The Prince and the Pauper* chafes most of his adult admirers today it may have repaid the sacrifice. The dominant note of the reviews applauded the unexpected solemnity of its intentions,[3] and the next few years brought his first sizable recognition as at least a force on the cultural scene. Self-consciously the public notice of his fiftieth birthday in 1885 marked the turning point, if not for the anxious need of his admirers to keep affirming his depth, then for the awareness of his eminence because of or else despite his humor. Evidently he had to pile up a case first of all for having a wide appeal on whatever grounds.

The second striking feature, implicit in the review just quoted, is that Twain's relative standing was likewise discussed from the start and not just as his career built up toward its awesome peak. Almost pathetically this approach betrayed the guilt of Anglophiles over enjoying native humor that gloried in brashness and exuberance. That guilt surfaced most starkly in Twain's case because of his excellence. While his own stated opinions accepted the pecking order for genres that was handed down by the ruling literary clique, his work kept challenging it. Reviewers, without grasping why they showed such a passion for forecasting, could seldom gauge his latest book without generalizing about how it would change his rating. Today, we can excuse them as trying to account for a genius when they stood too close for a rounded perspective. That handicap also helps to explain the third revealing feature of their criticism—a frequent tone of puzzlement because the achievement, even when made quasi-conventional by a row of expensively bound books, did not justify the acclaim that swirled to gale force during the 1890s. *Adventures of Huckleberry Finn* (1884), we tend to forget, got off to only a moderate popularity; Twain himself needed at least ten years to realize how well it was lasting. But by 1897 his personality had risen to the status of a revered American institution, truly the "living legend" that journalists of our own time announce so often. After that the biases toward him must be corrected more for overpraise than for owlish hostility. Ironically, the Oxford degree in 1907 stampeded the Anglophiles into superlatives that some soon regretted, even if pre-World War I orthodoxy made a secular prayer out of intellectual growth or, more broadly, self-development that could be held up as a model for the young.

The underlying fact is that Twain's reputation has been charted from the wrong coordinates, that is, from reviews and essays in the magazines and the occasional chapter before entire books started coming, very slowly at first, with Archibald Henderson's authorized hymn of praise (1911). But as the introductory essays for the volumes in the Iowa/California Edition of *The Works of Mark Twain* are proving, his books, published mostly by the subscription method which depended on door to door selling rather than bookstores or ads in the mainline periodicals, got reviewed far more often in the daily newspapers. The first exception to this pattern came as late as 1896 with *Personal Recollections of Joan of Arc*. Even for his writings after that, the scattered magazine reviews have been put to much heavier use than they deserve without a corrective factor for each author's purpose—which was, usually, to raise the taste of the lower-middle class—and the size of his (or rarely her) readership.[4] Furthermore, for the earlier decades the opinion of British critics has figured too prominently because they met and treated his books through regular channels. Among American critics William Dean Howells, because he so loyally praised Twain's every volume, has been credited with greater importance than he could have had for his crony's finally stunning eminence. In fact, after 1900 Howells may have gained more than he granted through their public relationship though neither of them cared to size it up that way. He did help significantly during the 1870s when Twain's educated admirers felt defensive, but on his own he could not have made Twain so popular outside the unexpanding *Atlantic* audience, which received him as a brash immigrant from the marketplace. Mostly anonymous and happy to quote Howells, the newspaper critics often compounded any praise through columns with much higher circulation.

Moreover, to emphasize Howells puts the focus on individual critics rather than the shared attitudes which a reviewer supposedly expresses while also shaping them. Twain aimed the promotion as well as the contents of his books at the broadest literate public. To the extent which the public wanted to make sure it was buying "good literature," it looked primarily to the metropolitan newspapers for standards and concrete verdicts. It was served better than we might now assume. The *New York Evening Post* rightly took pride in its reviews throughout Twain's lifetime, the *World* presumed to match their quality during the 1870s, the *Times* had periods of excellence, the *Tribune* considered itself second to none intellectually, the *Herald* kept struggling to elevate its image, and the *Sun* claimed a patent on stylistic polish and taste—to survey the pacesetters of just one group of metropolitan dailies. On his part Twain customarily—for him a term that allows many changes of mind—thought of "working" the newspapers as the prime way to push his latest volume.

Because of that motive for a cordiality amplified by his sincerely feeling an insider's bond woven by almost ten years as a reporter and free-lancer, his camaraderie with the press corps grew warmer than that enjoyed by any other major author, more mutual than that sustained by Walt Whitman or Stephen Crane, both former working journalists too. To base Twain's critical reputation on the magazines is to poll only the first-class passengers of a 747 while ignoring, furthermore, the advice of the cabin crew.

Even when including some newspapers, the range of essays previously reprinted sticks far too close to Twain's books as the cruxes for opinion.[5] Yet many readers have judged that, except for *Huckleberry Finn*, his shorter works hit his best stride. A later critic who rated the 1890s "singularly barren" for Twain did not, evidently, know enough of his essays and stories, still not fully collected, that the mass-circulation monthlies kept bidding for. Likewise, now that travel writing has lost its permit as a genre of belles lettres, too much weight falls on his novels. "It is easy to forget," warns Jay Martin, "how little of Twain's work was in fiction."[6] Since 1945, moreover, the succeeding varieties of the New Criticism have fastened on those qualities of his fiction most pliable for reflexive analysis. At one recent extreme an admiring reapproach to *Huckleberry Finn* concludes that it is "almost a nihilistic book. It is certainly a very sad book."[7] No matter what comes after postmodernist tastes, no survey of criticism should ever blur the fact that humor dominated the effect of Twain's writings, that the tributes to his seriousness never elevated it into his controlling quality instead, and that some of his funniest sketches, topped of course by "The Celebrated Jumping Frog," had greater impact during his lifetime than all but one or two of his novels.

Most misleading of all, analyses of Twain's reputation, even those that respect every genre he tried and give his sketches a fair hearing, have depended too much on his written work. The situation or, rather, process was far more complex and intriguing. Before *The Innocents Abroad* reached its subscribers he made a hit in the East as a lecturer, mainly and outrageously humorous but steadied by passages of eloquence and seasoned wisdom. Though his lectures often plugged his books, especially the one forthcoming, his success on the platform had its independent force before the process became as solidly reciprocating as the modern engines he admired. In between the peak bursts a flywheel of activities kept up enough momentum for his next book to set off another phase of reassessing his power. As newspaper stories increasingly played up his business and publishing deals, his crammed family life, his travels abroad, his quickness to plunge into current fads or social questions, and his spontaneous prominence in any context, he came to seem like either more or less than an author—like a personality lavishly gifted beyond the composing of books or a jack of many interests who did some writing. Spilling over any single channel his public image developed verve early and steadily gained richness. His extra-literary bustle alienated the genteelists then, and many a formalist critic still resents his hurly-burly career. Still, even those determined to consider only his literary art react to vibrations from the total range of his presence. Of course the masses welcomed his dazzling repertoire of roles and carelessly awarded aesthetic honors he did not deserve.

Besides the best-selling author and the comic lecturer Twain's kaleidoscope of images included at least eight others long-running enough to achieve general recognition: those of surefire public speaker, reponsibly activist citizen, investor and businessman, freewheeling American beyond any pull of routine, celebrity and candid self-promoter, colorful subject of interviews, living gallery of photographic and other portraits, and willing victim of cartoons and caricatures. To a slowly ebbing degree these patterns still affect those many readers who seldom see, much less hang on through an analytical essay, who do not strain at verbalizing a response but act on it in ways that cumulatively shape the academics' sense of how Twain is received at his most popular level. Trying to comprehend the vertical range of his career leads into troubling questions about the hierarchy of taste and, ultimately, about the validity of the literary canon that is handed along. Less dramatically they also apply to his contemporaries, not only Howells but once prestigious figures like Bayard Taylor and Charles Dudley Warner. Those questions deserve a wider base than the printed record, but we have little else to go on. In offering data about Twain we should realize at least that the term "essay" can fit most of the meanings since the sixteenth century laid out for it in the *Oxford English Dictionary*: from the process of testing or assaying, and through a physical attempt or endeavor, and up to the written composition, presented either as tentative ideas or polished reasoning. For his case it must include interviews, newspaper fillers, anecdotes, the wordless roar of the crowd, and the admirer scrambling just to behold him.

But first his activity as a lecturer should be fully integrated with the effects on his writings. It helped to characterize him as a humorist through not only the long excerpts in the newspapers but also the details on his stage antics; as late as the tour with George Washington Cable in 1884–1885 he engaged in physical clowning, particularly for entrances and exits. Aside from offending the hopelessly staid his levities stamped him as a rebel against the expectations that a lyceum program would dispense ethical pap and reinforced the impression from his choosing the subscription way of publishing that his books courted an audience instead of pretending to uplift it. When his lectures changed to reading from his written work an air of belles lettres started to gather, but he acted out the scenes with uninhibited éclat while careful to include broadly amusing passages. The world tour of 1895–1896 drew heavily on his shorter pieces and especially anecdotes, gilding his fame as a raconteur. Furthermore, the reports of his "at homes" carried off in faraway places made him look cosmopolitan back home, obviously many social cuts above a Huck Finn. After 1900 he was known as too prosperous to need gate receipts, buoyantly quick in helping a cause with his stage appeal, and so consistently topnotch as to guarantee a packed house. Though the swatches that the press supplied to millions of readers make a scrappy display now, they cumulated to coherent patterns at the time. If nothing else his forty years of triumph as a lecturer-entertainer thickened the aura of a success that billowed beyond all his printed words.

He filled his overlapping role as a public speaker just as expansively. Frederick Anderson, literary editor of the Mark Twain Estate for fifteen years, decided: "Although Mark Twain employed newspaper clipping services, he preserved primarily copies of his public interviews and speeches rather than reviews of his books. When he did collect literary reviews, he seemed usually to have intended them for use in advertising."[8] Anxious about how print chilled his oral magic he studied the newspapers to gauge the secondhand reactions that eventually, one contemporary believed, formed the strongest pillar of his prestige.[9] As dusty but ornate tomes in the library testify, oratory was then ranked as one of the many arts in both content and delivery. Besides redoubling Twain's fame as raconteur, the decades of applause underscored his versatility in rising to staggeringly different occasions, his daring twists of idea, and his ripened skill at dipping just long enough into pathos, as on his seventieth birthday or with his *Begum of Bengal* farewell to England in 1907. His willingness to regale banquets, large and small, further enlarged his air of generosity; the flood of invitations raised him above the suspicion of merely loving the sound of his voice, as the *New York Times* explicitly reassured him when he declared a "farewell" appearance in 1902. After his acclaim as a speaker grew beyond any doubt he began to build a careening text on that or toy breathtakingly with the compliments heaped on him by the chairman of the evening. More generally, during his last ten years the public learned to expect unique candor about himself when he sauntered to the rostrum. Because he could sense and smooth away a false step, his speeches took wilder risks than his late sketches and essays. None of his contemporaries could judge his writings entirely apart from this highwire act though some who knew him up close did wonder how much it dazzled their view of the author. The veteran editor of *Harper's Monthly* concluded, "There are no impressions of Mark Twain that are not personal."[10]

Many of Twain's speeches plunged into current affairs too provocatively for friend or foe to enjoy them as mere entertainment. We now examine his politics, if at all, to understand his fiction better, but he literally never proposed that the arts should avoid social or moral values. After working out from under his job as a journalist to harp on topical questions, he still showed just as vigorous a concern from the local to the international level—from streetpaving in Hartford to lifeboats for ocean liners, from female suffrage to world disarmament. His chest-covering array of do-gooder, honorary vice-presidencies surprised nobody who had watched Twain's career or heard his repeated calls to the ideal of citizenship, needed of course for elections but also for declaring taxes honestly or filing a complaint against a dishonest cabman. In 1893 his "Travelling with a Reformer," he gloated to his wife, stirred more response than any other piece of his for years. In 1901 his anti-imperialism raised a barrage of headlines, editorials hotly pro and con, and newfangled newspaper cartoons. After that his pen name carried for many a guarantee of political integrity and boldness in expressing it. Today, a sophisticated commonplace insists that the aesthetic and the political cannot blend, but Twain's admirers, whether as simply readers or as literary judges, maintained that humanitarian fervor had inspired some his finest eloquence.

Any taint of radicalism, however, was swept away by his activities as inventor, businessman, would-be financier, and publisher. They balanced his bursts of madcap comedy with a record for practicality, validated by huge profits. Rich and poor respected him as a selfmade man who had earned his luxurious house; his rebound from bankruptcy elevated him into a never-say-die elite who had amassed a fortune twice. His smartest venture of the 1870s, the Self Pasting Scrapbook, later seemed a springboard for the coup of publishing Ulysses S. Grant's *Memoirs*, which brought Twain credit for editorial wisdom, patriotism, benevolence, and push. During the 1890s the fiasco of his typesetter counted much more as a near-miss than now; anyway, he snatched nobility from the jaws of disgrace. The bankruptcy it helped to precipitate brought on the world tour, reams of praise for his standard of honor, and a clichéd pairing with Sir Walter Scott. His various sides looked far more integrated to his contemporaries than to his recent biographers, and he even convinced many captains of industry that an author could coexist with their world. Though the priesthood in the temple of high culture despise their pompous opinions, by any rounded system of measuring reputations they counted too.

Whether illusion or reality the integration of Twain's images testified to the blinding magic of his personality. Likewise, though admirers as much as enemies disagreed as to what lay at its core, he very visibly functioned with a commanding life-style colored by a range of experiences that few could match, socially or geographically. Far more vividly than for most writers just his works, quite aside from his outings in the flesh, conjured up a real-life giant lustier than the mock-author of any particular book or sketch. Only those sunk in some private Egyptian darkness—one of Twain's revealing pet phrases—did not know him for one of their liveliest fellow citizens. Only the emotionally deaf heard no echoes of his élan and especially his playfulness, typified for the 1870s by the "Punch, Brothers, Punch" jingle he took over from a newspaperman's joke. Both the proper minded and the iconoclastic had already registered the iron string of irreverence to which his spirit vibrated. By the 1890s he had added an overtone of wry wisdom, typified by his epigrams or maxims promoted on calendars and even postcards. Yet the solidifying if perplexed consensus on his having a serious side did not raise charges of betrayal, and signs that Mark Twain's candor still did not fully reveal the black moods of Samuel L. Clemens heightened the interest in the puzzle of his psychological vitality. The most sober of the literati finally had to acknowledge the power of his demotic appeal and to start discovering respect-worthy grounds. It was only because the magnetism of his confident and reassuring presence had slackened by 1920 that Van Wyck Brooks dared to argue in terms of an "ordeal."

Such a viewpoint would have seemed perverse to the public that was acclaiming him the quintessence, the throbbing avatar of national virtues. Since Americans hunt for chances to define themselves, there is no mystery in why his era settled on so attractive a model. In hindsight the only question is the timing. While the tributes on his fiftieth birthday in 1885 played up his rough-hewn uniqueness, in 1895 reporters and their editors were saluting him as their superaverage countryman. Historical reasons outside his control can be found to explain the transit, but the effective cause probably lies in the always more richly diversified persona he had learned to project in his writing and speeches, in glimpses on a streetcar or at closely observed occasions like the Grant banquet in Chicago. As Kurt Vonnegut put it recently, "Only a genius could have misrepresented our speech and our wittiness and our common sense and our common decency so handsomely to ourselves and the outside world."[11] The social conquest of Vienna in 1897 entrenched his standing as the most genuine product of New World democracy, recognized as such by the nobility as well as the European masses. Back home nobody of consequence dared to call for proof better than fervent clichés strung out with whatever particulars suited the essayist, reviewer, or a layman inspired to compose a letter to the editor. No doubt, nostalgia for the village past that had sheltered Tom and Huck helped. More explicitly Twain had helped now and then with prose hymns to patriotism, starting with *Innocents Abroad* and *Roughing It,* that rang out louder the further he got from the United States. But his continuing triumphs of so many kinds in so many places, topped with an honorary degree from Oxford University in 1907, probably counted more. During his final years he certainly got revenge for the early contempt from the oracles of respectability, and his instinct for iconoclasm must have twinged at the defensiveness of those few who dared to question the size of his halo.

They must have hoped to make more of his crass streak, which he regularly threatened to keep uppermost. The public had soon got used to meeting his face in handouts by a dry-goods store or a steamfitter. If some businesses chummily borrowed his name without asking, other wares among the Mark Twain tobacco, cigars, and whiskey and the Mark

Twain waltz or mazurka had his endorsement. He evidently set low limits of taste on the merchandizing of his lectures and books too. Starting in 1897, despite his gathering splendor, several series of Mark Twain postcards carried a warning of his copyright. Though we are now hardened to watching eminent actors shill for deodorants and beers, we still do not expect it of authors with any chance of getting assigned for students majoring in English. Twain's patience with, sometimes lust for commercialization kept his stodgier constituents uneasy and encouraged the critics to keep taking his aesthetic temperature. Nevertheless his self-promotion, his open coining of visibility never brought on a fatal roar of outrage or contempt, a mass verdict that he had violated the rules for pretending to honor the Muses above any royalties.

Somehow it became accepted that the litterateur's etiquette for decorum could not apply to him because he had never endorsed it. Since his Nevada years he had mixed genuine spontaneity and posturing in an admitted game with the press corps that the white suit eventually symbolized. When he blossomed out in it to lobby for copyright at the Capitol, the public did not just tolerate it but tried to insist on his wearing it all the time. Far ahead of the wave that crested first in the 1920s, he was admired for having achieved celebrity in itself, merit aside. Editorial opinion complimented his shrewdness at raking in the benefits and chuckled when the Mark Twain Company took full legal shape in 1908, sealing his years of effort to protect his pen name as a trademark—so much of a first that no well-known second has followed as yet. Starting in the late 1890s successive sets of his collected works were advertised with hoopla instead of an austerity implying disinterest. The old guard fretted that he was undermining the dignity of authorship as a profession. Belatedly a few recognized that he was making great writers and high culture look more approachable. Perhaps at least the business-minded respected him for flowing with the fact that under capitalism literature functions as a commodity, sometimes marketed with the soft sell but always subject to profit and loss accounting.

The same pattern of an openness compounded by self-promotion and of mass interest uncowed by disdain from the elite ran through the more than three hundred interviews with Twain that enlivened the newspapers and magazines between 1874 and 1910.[12] That he cooperated so often with reporters added up toward a perception of his eagerness, sometimes made transparent by his forced wit when he had a product or a lecture to ballyhoo. That they hounded him so tenaciously became proof of his fame and their judgment that he generated salable copy. They angled for "just one more question," tagged along after he called a halt, and pumped up a story out of his refusal to talk. Probably assuming he would not mind, a few creative journalists faked an entire item, which can nevertheless show how they thought their clientele saw or wanted to or ought to see Twain. His availability continued to identify him as a democratic author who—unlike Henry James or even modestly reticent Howells—accepted the public's right to know whatever stirred its curiosity, who in fact gave many signs of sharing its tastes. In express content the most sensitive of the interviews reflected his shimmering mind that could focus all of a sudden on a serious idea. The best known of the lot eventually, his talk with young Rudyard Kipling showed him as both magnificently casual and brimming with interests, opinions, and theories.[13] Like Kipling the reporters who appreciated Twain's work managed to draw out more about it or his tastes in reading than he revealed elsewhere. Paradoxically, he came across better as an intellectual through this lowbrow medium than almost any other way. Every few years an interview proved that he held responsible positions on the major problems, economic or political or social. In some instances, usually set up with a veteran journalist, he emerged as painfully concerned, even humorless. When he had learned to dominate the transaction, he rated as at least the coauthor, and reacting to an interview with him therefore came close to passing a literary judgment. During his final years, his prepared comments were sometimes reported so carefully that his stylistic voice as well as his persona overran the question-answer framework. Ultimately, anybody who read the newspapers based his or her notion about Twain partly on the interviews, which got more heavily displayed as they turned up less often.

Twain's willingness to sit for photographs and other portraits, and then to encourage their circulation, also got credited to his democratic side, his air of obliging natural curiosity. Once a newshawk himself and never a hypocrite, he did not join in the complaints that privacy was being riddled by the mass media, which even exploited a face without the owner's say-so. To our eyes the onset of the visual invasion looks strikingly dull. The finest woodcuts and engravings of Twain that the magazines of the 1870s could reproduce differ very little, even in degrees of sternness that custom called for because the shopwork turned smiling faces into circus posters. By the 1880s it could do justice to high quality negatives, and Twain would later groan about reencountering the studio portrait signed by the well-known Napoleon Sarony, which still turns up when a fierce quaintness is wanted. With Olivia Clemens monitoring the choices, smiling or even pleasant versions stayed rare. At best, without any relaxing around the mouth his features expressed mature confidence, and one such pose, arranged for in Sydney, Australia, during the world tour, became a favorite of layout editors though it had close mates in the files that bulged after interviewers started carrying a camera. Since the business office argued that newsphotos raised circulation, Twain's face started to match the renown of his name. Somebody in a crowd gathered by a false rumor reasoned: "Why, we can't miss him. I've seen his picture thousands of times. I could tell him even by his moustache."[14] Starting with the 1890s the renown justified the highly formal dress that showed up often on posed occasions. A profile view at the banquet for his seventieth birthday, ineptly retouched to suggest an overaged matinee idol rather than an immortal author, was used for a frontispiece in the next collected edition of his works. Huck and Jim would have stepped off the sidewalk for that gentleman.

However, Twain had started to allow casual poses for the record, and in 1906 a series with him writing or smoking in bed caught the fancy of editors, aware that no other personage would risk lounging in such full view. Among more conventionally informal shots, his reading the daily paper gratified the press itself, of course, while its subscribers felt another bond of taste with him. But Twain's career seldom laid a fresh trail without doubling back. Since the later 1870s a lengthening gallery of oil portraits had started to signalize eminence, not just notoriety. Eventually busts, medallions, and even a weaving confirmed his rise above the fate of the funnymen who vanished like butterflies after their season. Meanwhile, the competition to get a different angle was leaving posterity a range of photographs contradictory enough to fit any biographical theory.[15]

Twain's admirers had to navigate a deeper gulf between the photographs or portraits and the obviously fanciful drawings. The career of the daily editorial cartoon opened only with the 1890s and had not hit full stride before his death, which did inspire a gamut dominated by patriotic motifs. But from the mid-1870s the new humor weeklies had depended heavily on illustrations. A reprinting of *Life*'s verbal as well as graphic treatment of Twain would furnish a paradigm for the changing response of sophisticates who felt no nostalgia about the deserted village or the brawling frontier. For a much broader audience his own travel books circulated many plates centering on his usually laughable misadventures. This cue was first exaggerated as cartoonists outdid his zaniest posturings, using him for a pretext instead of a subject. By the 1880s their treatment hovered closer to his own slowly quieting terms, noticeable in the illustrations for *Life on the Mississippi*. Though cartoons thrive on distortion, some time during the 1890s he reached the security of his hero in "The £1,000,000 Bank-Note," who "might be joked about still, but reverently, not hilariously, not rudely," who "could be smiled at, but not laughed at." The caricatures got almost apologetic, following his leads such as the flaunted corncob pipe or shock of white hair. The *New York World* had him riding to a speech in a wheelbarrow only after he explicitly encouraged the image. In political cartoons the level of respect naturally correlated with how far the artist's newspaper approved Twain's stand. Nevertheless, the opposition went slow in giving him ugly features. Its typical rebuttal regretted he had wandered beyond his depth with such an issue as imperialism. Lightning quick to acknowledge his support, those cartoons keyed on veneration, particularly for his vigor in still rallying to a good cause. Beyond the cartoons, fully recoverable only by tedious searching, lies an unmapped trail of drawings—some routine, a few revealingly distinctive—with which competing New York dailies spruced up their stories. Finally, as an abstract problem, visual images can justify wider differences of interpretation than ordinary prose.

Faced with so many problems among the riches, a book of selections can merely suggest answers. Yet since this volume has insisted on expanding the field of vision, it should lay out its criteria. We always want the "best" evidence, here bravely defined as those reactions most illuminating for Twain's critical reputation at the time even if the tastes of the 1980s aggressively discredit them. This need not mean the exhuming of tinplated opinions that deserved to molder into library dust. Exhibits of past incompetence are seldom informative, however pleasing to our sense of superiority. Though the "best" should not mean, either, those reviews or essays or interviews that cast the kindest light, it does not prove heroworship to decide that most of the hostile responses betrayed prejudice toward Twain or humorous writing in general. His popularity at every level did keep building up, indicating that the positive judgments were the most representative. Likewise, those declaring he embodied main American attitudes were on track, according to the consensus among later historians of ideas and cultural patterns. Anyhow, his admirers expressed enough doubts and even dismay to make the record balanced, and his volunteer claque sometimes caused worse damage than his enemies by demanding encores from his buffo side.

On the practical level, anthologies that try to demonstrate the windings of Twain's reputation have to cope with redundancies. It changed slowly and erratically—an effect more important to show in any set of selections rather than heightening the variety. Nor should a new set pass over essays because they have already been reprinted, often more than once. Though such repetition could plead the fact that most of the similar anthologies have gone out of print, the revealing point is that the record for the 1870s and 1880s, particularly in American magazines, is so thin as to keep leading to the same sources. The choice here does give weight to the magazines with the biggest audience and, by the same criterion, to the daily press. Moreover, it favors the reviews or essays which themselves attracted comment and even got quoted heavily, though they may fail to please formalist critics now or anticipate some postmodernist position. Above all it favors items Twain encouraged—maybe helped initiate and then place somewhere—or else approved of after they reached print. They have the special virtue of indicating how he wanted to be perceived. They also remind us that he worked aggressively at shaping his reputation—for his immediate times, that is; he worried little about immortality before the notion was forced upon him very late by his worshippers. One reason for stopping this anthology at 1910 is that his death significantly changed the critical scales by removing his thumb from them.

He concentrated on promoting his next book while looking back on his published volumes not as stepping stones to Valhalla but as an idling engine for royalties. However, the ad hoc reviews, turgid with summary, got less said than the continual attempts to size up his career or at least readjust the perspectives in the light of his latest book. Choosing the broader essays means fewer pages on *Huckleberry Finn* than in preceding collections. Actually, contemporary reviews of it were scarce in the newspapers; more important, so late as the obituaries it had not emerged as his indisputable, isolated masterpiece. Historical roundness is served better by the essays that approached Twain as a conglomerate, a one-man syndicate, and groped for the secret of the personality conducting it. So, bypassing the early stages of Twain's career, this collection starts just before his national impact as a performer who had obviously put in a varied apprenticeship. Fortunately, Edgar M. Branch's preface for *Early Tales & Sketches, volume 1, 1851–1864*, masterfully covers his rise to local notoriety and then to regional fame for a "relaxed, informal kind of humor," for an instinct toward "comic elaboration" that made him a hybrid of journalist and western celebrity whose gift at turning reportage into a "chronicle of his own doings and thoughts" built up a "comic mythology" about his past.[16] Seen in coldest perspective Twain triumphed at what hundreds of newspaper wits tried to do during the last third of the century. This anthology does not merely tolerate but welcomes comparisons with the other popular humorists and would have included more pieces on him by his competitors if space had allowed.

Since the earliest consequential book on Twain came out after 1910, this anthology can stick to self-contained items reprinted without any cuts. That principle brings on two further problems of repetition. First, since it is standard for newspaper stories to recap the background facts, the details of Twain's biography kept turning up. Collectively they exemplify the fascination that his private life generated.[17] Analyzed separately they fill in the shaping of the legends about his village boyhood, nights of trembling and days of glory on the river, risk-taking in the West, panache as a householder, and the underlying, fitfully erupting personality. Garbled facts and judgments repeated doggedly became emblematic of the values behind the wish to believe them; also, if we look ahead, they point to which ones will encapsulate even his prodigious fame ultimately. Second, Twain criticism indulges heavily in quotation. From the start his rolling, breathless style and of course his humor encouraged long excerpts, offered up for mutual, dazzled pleasure—ragging the Italian guides, the weeping at Adam's tomb, Buck Fanshaw and the tenderfoot preacher, whitewashing the fence, reading the surface of the river, Huck's debates with Jim, the Yankee's entrance into Camelot, or the irreverence of the Bombay crows. This anthology follows the principle that any essay worth including can make its full effect only through having its chosen examples in place even when they are familiar or appear in the preceding pages. Eventually, sharing this revolving fund of passages became a circuit of Twain's reputation. Besides indicating at first hand which of his qualities the critics prized, they acquired quintessential meaning for the readers instructed to treasure them.

This collection does not imply that some clean break justifies stopping at 1910. In a good example of how the generations overlap, Brander Matthews (1852–1929) wrote cogently about Twain as late as 1924. Still, the decade from 1910 to 1920 proved clearly transitional for his reputation. The skeptics that pounce after a hero's death ran into an army of loyalists ready to rally around Albert Bigelow Paine's official, three-volume biography in 1912. Then H. L. Mencken boomed out in 1913 with his usual independence, keen on Twain's iconoclasm but unabashed by his renown and happy to shake established judgments about him too. While fundamentally admiring, John Macy's long chapter in *The Spirit of American Literature* (1913) also had a sophistication of tone and criteria new to the writing about Twain. After the further cultural tempering of World War I, *The Ordeal of Mark Twain* (1920) could set off the campaign to delve into his psyche, investigate the censorship it had endured from within and from others, and wring out the essence of his greediness and somehow related despair. Though Brooks never grappled patiently with a text or even a whole paragraph, he invoked aesthetic standards and thus encouraged putting Twain under the formalistic rigor that was developing.[18] Less spectacularly, the chapter in Carl Van Doren's *The American Novel* (1921) marked both a closure and a fresh start, integrating the keenest of the past insights while presenting Twain as a major novelist—and thus simplifying his career. By then, in any case, time had qualitatively reduced two major perspectives of this anthology—the effects of Twain's multifarious, electric presence and of his diligence in enlarging his reputation, not just by welcoming interviewers but by cultivating and then exploiting his friendship with the press.[19]

By our standards the ablest writing about Twain comes well after 1920. It is not naive progressivism to expect that the quality will continue to rise as critics build on the notebooks, letters, and manuscripts issuing through the Mark Twain Papers Edition and on the authoritative texts of the Iowa/California Edition of his previously published work. Nevertheless, as Arthur L. Scott sanely decided, "intelligence and discernment animate much of the earliest criticism. The shrewdest of Twain's contemporaries, indeed, anticipated most of the judgments passed by succeeding generations."[20] The obituary editorial in the *Baltimore Sun* still sounds outstandingly perceptive. By the 1890s the believers in his greatness gathered enough capable disciples so that the discussion had lasting substance. Those convinced they were witnessing the blaze of genius have been proved far sounder than is usual in such cases while the ground for awe has shifted somewhat. For instance they put higher value than we do on Twain's "versatility" as an author.[21] Though his writing is his central gift to us we will receive it more rewardingly if we appreciate the total range of his career. In trying to display that range this collection hopes to convert the historical record into a stimulatory force.

LOUIS J. BUDD

Duke University

Notes

1. We have had, in chronological order, Arthur L. Scott, *Mark Twain: Selected Criticism* (Dallas: Southern Methodist Univ. Press, 1955; rev. 1967); Lewis Leary, *Mark Twain's Wound* (New York: Crowell, 1962); Guy A. Cardwell, *Discussions of Mark Twain* (Boston: Heath, 1963); Henry Nash Smith, *Mark Twain: A Collection of Critical Essays* (Englewood Cliffs, N.J.: Prentice-Hall, 1963); Justin Kaplan, *Mark Twain: A Profile* (New York: Hill and Wang, 1967); Frederick Anderson, *Mark Twain: The Critical Heritage* (London: Routledge and Kegan Paul, 1971); David B. Kesterson, *Critics on Mark Twain* (Coral Gables: Univ. of Miami Press, 1973); Dean Morgan Schmitter, *Mark Twain: A Collection of Criticism* (New York: McGraw-Hill, 1974). At least another seven collections focus exclusively on *Adventures of Huckleberry Finn*; a few others focus on a different book or on a special theme such as the West. Still useful though outdated is Roger Asselineau, *The Literary Reputation of Mark Twain from 1910 to 1950* (Paris: Marcel Didier, 1954).

2. Unsigned review, *Century Magazine*, 23 (March, 1882), 784.

3. See Lin Salamo, "Introduction," pp. 13–19, *The Prince and the Pauper*, Vol. 6 in *The Works of Mark Twain* (Berkeley: Univ. of California Press, 1979).

4. Thomas A. Tenney's splendid *Mark Twain: A Reference Guide* (Boston: G. K. Hall, 1977) outmodes the current collections or even bibliographies of nineteenth-century criticism because he lists many items previously overlooked—and continues to do so with annual supplements.

5. The best collection, Anderson's *Mark Twain: The Critical Heritage*, is organized around reviews of books. As a result British and Canadian critics get too much space.

6. *Harvests of Change* (Englewood Cliffs, N.J.: Prentice-Hall, 1967), p. 167.

7. Alexander Blackburn, *The Myth of the Picaro: Continuity and Transformation of the Picaresque Novel, 1554-1954* (Chapel Hill: Univ. of North Carolina Press, 1979), p. 187.

8. "Introduction," *Mark Twain: The Critical Heritage*, p. 6.

9. Charles Vale, "Mark Twain as an Orator," *Forum*, 44 (July, 1910), 1–13; see also Hamilton W. Mabie, "Mark Twain the Humorist," *Outlook*, 87 (November 23, 1907), 658.

10. "Mark Twain: Personal Impressions," *Book News Monthly*, 28 (April, 1910), 579. The essay is reprinted in this volume.

11. "The Necessary Miracle," *Nation*, July 7, 1979, p. 22.

12. See my *Listing of and Selection from Newspaper and Magazine Interviews with Samuel L. Clemens* (Arlington, Texas: ALR Press, 1977—also as Vol. 10, No. 1, of *American Literary Realism, 1870-1910*). I do not mean to exaggerate; some items are multiple versions; many others are negligible in content.

13. In the United States it first appeared in *New York Herald*, August 17, 1890, p. 5. As Kipling's own fame grew during the 1890s, this interview became well known. Peter Conrad, *Imagining America* (New York: Oxford Univ. Press, 1980), pp. 105–07, interprets its implied content sweepingly.

14. *New York Tribune*, August 1, 1900, p. 4.

15. Reproducing enough of this material for readers to make their own judgments would require an expensive book. A good sampling can be had by combining Milton Meltzer, *Mark Twain Himself* (New York: Crowell, 1960); Justin Kaplan, *Mark Twain and His World* (London: Michael Joseph, 1974); and John Seelye, *Mark Twain in the Movies* (New York: Viking, 1977). Seelye adds provocative commentary; Meltzer has the most cartoons.

16. Edited by Edgar M. Branch and Robert H. Hirst as Vol. 15 (Berkeley: Univ. of California Press, 1979) of the Iowa/California Edition of *The Works of Mark Twain;* see especially "Introduction," pp. 16, 22, 24, 34, 52–54.

17. Leary, *Mark Twain's Wound,* listed in note 1, centers on biography.

18. The collections by Smith and Kaplan, listed in note 1, intend to give the best of this writing.

19. Some of the details are included in my "Color Him Curious about Yellow Journalism: Mark Twain and the New York City Press," *Journal of Popular Culture,* 15 (Fall, 1981), 25–33.

20. "Introduction," p. 3, of his collection listed in note 1.

21. Such is the judgment in Durant DaPonte, "American Periodical Criticism of Mark Twain, 1869–1917," Diss. Maryland 1953, pp. 128–29. Though limited to periodicals this is still the most thorough and dependable survey of Twain's reputation.

ESSAYS, REVIEWS, AND INTERVIEWS

Advertisement

[Charles Henry Webb]*

"Mark Twain" is too well known to the public to require a formal introduction at my hands. By his story of the Frog, he scaled the heights of popularity at a single jump, and won for himself the *sobriquet* of The Wild Humorist of the Pacific Slope. He is also known to fame as The Moralist of the Main: and it is not unlikely that as such he will go down to posterity. It is in his secondary character, as humorist, however, rather than in his primal one of moralist, that I aim to present him in the present volume. And here a ready explanation will be found for the somewhat fragmentary character of many of these sketches; for it was necessary to snatch threads of humor wherever they could be found—very often detaching them from serious articles and moral essays with which they were woven and entangled. Originally written for newspaper publication, many of the articles referred to events of the day, the interest of which has now passed away, and contained local allusions which the general reader would fail to understand; in such cases excision became imperative. Further than this, remark or comment is unnecessary. Mark Twain never resorts to tricks of spelling nor rhetorical buffoonery for the purpose of provoking a laugh; the vein of his humor runs too rich and deep to make surface-gilding necessary. But there are few who can resist the quaint similes, keen satire, and hard good sense which form the staple of his writings.

---

*Reprinted from John Paul, ed., *The Celebrated Jumping Frog of Calaveras County, And other Sketches. By Mark Twain* (New York: C. H. Webb, 1867). "John Paul" was Charles Henry Webb; he signed the "Advertisement" as "J.P."

Mark Twain as a Lecturer

[Edward H. House]*

About a year and a half ago, a communication entitled "Joe Smiley and his Jumping Frog," with the hitherto unknown signature of "Mark Twain," appeared in *The Saturday Press* of this city. The name, though new, was not remarkable, but the style of the letter was so singularly fresh, original, and full of character as to attract prompt and universal attention among the readers of light humorous literature. Mark Twain was immediately entered as a candidate for high position among writers of his class, and passages from his first contribution to the metropolitan press became proverbs in the mouths of his admirers. No reputation was ever more rapidly won. The only doubt appeared to be whether he could satisfactorily sustain it. Subsequent productions, however—most of them reproduced from California periodicals—confirmed the good opinion so suddenly vouchsafed him, and abundantly vindicated the applause with which his first essay had been received. In his case, as in that of many other American humorous writers, it was only the first step that cost. Since that time he has walked easily—let us hope not too easily—over his special course.

His writings being comparatively new to the public, and his position having been so recently established, it might perhaps, have been doubted whether his name would at present be sufficient to attract an audience of any magnitude to witness his debut as a lecturer. But the proof of the general good-will in which he is already held was manifested last Monday evening by his brilliant reception at the Cooper Institute. The hall was crowded beyond all expectation. Not a seat was vacant, and all the aisles were filled with attentive listeners. The chance offering of "The Jumping Frog," carelessly cast, eighteen months ago, upon the Atlantic waters, returned to him in the most agreeable form which a young aspirant for popular fame could desire. The wind that was sowed with probably very little calculation as to its effect upon its future prospects, now enables him to reap quite a respectable tempest of encouragement and cordiality. His

*Reprinted from *New York Tribune*, May 11, 1867, p. 2. Nobody has questioned previous ascriptions of this review to House.

greeting was such as to inspire the utmost ease and confidence, and it is pleasant to add that his performance in every way justified the favor bestowed upon him. No other lecturer, of course excepting Artemus Ward, has so thoroughly succeeded in exciting the mirthful curiosity, and compelling the laughter of his hearers.

The subject of his address, "The Sandwich Islands," was treated mainly from a comic stand-point, although scraps of practical information and occasional picturesque descriptions of scenery and natural phenomena peculiar to that region were liberally interspersed. The scheme of the lecturer appeared to be to employ the various facts he had gathered as bases upon which to build fanciful illustrations of character, which were furthermore embellished with a multitude of fantastic anecdotes and personal reminiscences. The frequent incongruities of the narration—evidently intentional—made it all the more diverting, and the artifice of its partial incoherence was so cleverly contrived as to intensify the amusement of the audience, while leaving them for the most part in ignorance of the means employed. As to the manner of the speaker, it is difficult to write explicitly. It was certainly peculiar and original. Perhaps no better idea of it could be conveyed than by saying it is in almost every respect the exact opposite to that of the late Artemus Ward. It suited that admirable lecturer's humor to exhibit a nervous quickness and a vivacity which always communicated itself to those who surrounded him, and his best "points" were made by the droll affection of complete unconsciousness with which he uttered the most telling jests. Mark Twain's delivery, on the other hand, is deliberate and measured to the last degree. He lounges comfortably around his platform, seldom referring to notes, and seeks to establish a sort of button-hole relationship with his audience at the earliest possible moment. He is even willing to exchange confidences of the most literal nature. Having made an accidental error in figures, last Monday evening, at which there was great laughter, he paused and requested to be informed "what he had said," and was indisposed to proceed until his curiosity should be gratified. Instead of manifesting indifference to his own good jokes, he appears to relish them as heartily as anybody—a characteristic, by the bye, which also belongs to the most eminent "reader" now known to the British public. The only obvious preconcerted "effect" which he employs is a momentary hesitation or break in his narration before touching the climax of an anecdote or a witticism. But his style is his own, and needs to be seen to be understood. A second opportunity for this, we learn, is presently to be afforded, to which, when it approaches, we shall invite particular attention.

[Review of *The Innocents Abroad*]

Anonymous*

If any book of late years has so generally interested the press of the country and received so extensive and favorable an introduction to the public as has Mark Twain's *Innocents Abroad*, since its appearance, we fail to remember the instance. We gave to our readers last week, in a supplementary sheet, some specimens of the notices we have found in our exchanges. Numerous as were the excerpts there collected, they represent but a fraction of what have fallen under our observation, and the notable fact is, that, instead of the mere mention so commonly accorded to a new book, almost every journal has given it an unusually elaborate review, written not in a simple spirit of courtesy, but evidently with an inspiration of interest excited by reading the work. The truth is, we believe, that no one of an ordinary disposition of mind can dip into the volume without being snared by a curious fascination. It is so different from any narrative of travel that ever was written before. The mere tickle of an ever pervading humor is not all that makes it delightful, but that humor is like an atmosphere, in which the old world scenes that so many tourists and travellers have led us into, take on a new and altogether novel appearance, so that we follow our droll excursionist from place to place as eagerly as though we had never been carried to them by any narrative before. It would be a great mistake to suppose that the book is just a big package of Mark Twain's jokes, to be read with laughter, and for the sake of laughter. It is the panorama of Europe and the Holy Land as they were seen by one who went abroad with no illusions; who carried about with him a shrewd pair of American eyes, and used them to get his own impressions of things, as they actually presented themselves, not as he had been taught to expect them; who bore with him, moreover, as acute an appreciation of sham and humbug as his sense of the humorous and ludicrous was keen. What he saw he tells, and we believe there is more true description in his book than in any other of the kind that we have read. What is to be told soberly he tells soberly, and with all the admiration or

*Reprinted from *Buffalo* (New York) *Express*, October 16, 1869, p. [3]. Twain was part owner of the *Express*; there is no evidence that he wrote this review though he may have approved it in advance.

20

reverence that is due to the subject. But he does like to wash off false colors, to scrape away putty and varnish, to stick a pin into venerable moss grown shams—and it is a perpetual delight to his reader to see him do it in his droll, dry way. We have yet to find the person who could open the book and willingly lay it down again, for, certainly, it is not often that more or livelier entertainment can be had in the same compass. The work has been published by the American Publishing Company, at Hartford, and is sold by agents who canvass for subscriptions.

The Josh Billings Papers/
Sum Biographical—Mark Twain

Henry Wheeler Shaw*

Mark Twain iz about thirty years old last May, stands 5 foot 8 and one quarter inches, iz the best deskriptive humorist living, smokes 40 cigars a day, skorns to part hiz hair in the middle, dont show enny dimond ring, haz got a monarchial mustash, loves woman az she iz, hates dogs, and eschews liquor.

He eats rare biled eggs, wears number 7 boots, and can quill a paragraph at a minnits notice, as full of sharp things az a porcupines back.

He iz az genial (whare he loves) az gin and milk, but iz a charming hater.

He iz married, az all good jokers are; they all know there aint no humor in a cot bedsted.

He lives in Buffalo, and what iz most wonderful, and the hardest to understand, iz sed tew be rich. Wealthy humorists are scarce tew be had, they generally invest all ov their money as they go along, in the common occurrences ov the day.

Report sez he wont lektur no more. I hope report lies (for once in its life), for Mark Twain, before an audiance, iz az easy tew understand az strawberries and cream.

Hiz late book, called "Innocence Abroad," iz the most delishus history i ever perused. It haz all the integrity ov the multiplicashun table, and, at the same time, iz az full ov diviltry as "Gulliver's travels."

Mark Twain i dont think iz college larnt, he haz larnt what he knows bi seeing it did, and kan tell what tree will make shingles bi looking at the bark.

He iz like all other genuine humorists, dont do the laffing himself, and really much prefers to say a good thing rather than a funny one.

He haz no more humor in his looks than a fiddle haz.

He dont use profane language, altho i think i once heard him use the

*Reprinted from a photostatic copy in the Mark Twain Papers taken from *Frank Leslie's Budget of Fun*, a now rare periodical. David Kesterson, *Josh Billings* (New York: Twayne, 1973), pp. 30–31, gives *New York Weekly*, October 6, 1870, p. 7, as the original source. Shaw, a leading humorist, used the pseudonym of Josh Billings.

pronoun "dam," but if mi memory reckolekts herself, at that partickular time, the conversashun was about saw mills.

I beleave he iz not a church member, but mi impreshun is that hiz religion lies deep.

All genuine humorists (altho fun iz their game, and altho they beleave that even virtew haz a ridickilus side to her) have in their bottom natur menny places where they kneell down (in private) and say good things in a low tone.

I love a zealous christian, one who hollers virtew, but i hav cum tew the konklushion (in late years) that the Lord aint deaf, and that all the real piety in this world aint kept in rams horns.

But i may be mistaken about this—it iz just like my darn luck.

I am not a buzzom friend ov Mark Twain, bekause he dont kno me well enuff yet to take me into his buzzom. We never met but three or four times, but there want no time wasted in inquiring after each others familys, we both went in to win, and I am certain he won me.

I think now i could endorse Mark (i dont mean his note, for i have quit all kinds ov gambling), he seems tew me to hav (with all the nervous excentricitys ov his natur) a spot for me.

He has told me that he iz mi friend (i hope he wont alter hiz mind), for thare aint nothing on earth (i wont except bears) that i fear more than i do thoze who i think dont love me.

Thare iz grate strength tew sum men, no doubt, in having plenty ov haters, it elaborates hiz gaul, but i am one of thoze unsanguine kritters who sweat eazy, and who had rather hav a lamb foller him home than tew hav frozen recognishun from a rail rode president.

Mark Twain haz grate wit, he haz grate literary pretenshuns, but he iz a poor punster, and he ought tew be thankful for that, for thare aint nothing (unless it iz three cent gin) that iz more demoralizing than punning. It iz full az bad az whistling, and full az often iz a substitute for thought.

Good-by, Mark Twain; let me advise you tew forgive the liberty i hav taken in this sketch, and also let me ask yu (in behalf ov my nabors) tew keep before the world with yure rare bits ov humor, for thare iz grate need ov sich az yu.

But dont expekt too much pay, Mark, for thare iz one thing that kant be explained, and that iz, those who make us laff the most are like fiddlers, paid off grudgingly in the morning, and then kicked out ov doors.

Mark Twain Last Night

[William A. Croffut]*

The entertainment of the season, thus far, was the curious, disjointed, delightfully incoherent talk of Mark Twain (Clemens is his married name), last evening, in the Michigan-avenue Baptist Church, below Twenty-Second Street.

Twain calls this a "lecture," with the euphemistic vanity of his guild, but it would be just as near to call it a sermon, a tale, a panorama, a magic lantern show, a song, or a concert by a brass band. And yet its very novelty made it piquant; and its supreme ridiculousness drew the crowd and held them.

Every seat in the house, four hundred chairs in the aisles, and standing-room for two or three hundred, were crowded full, when the lank, lantern-jawed, the impudent Californian bestrode the stage as if it were the deck of a steamboat, and getting to the middle of the front, rubbed his bony hands, and gazed around. A thin man of five feet ten, thirty-five or so, eyes that penetrate like a new gimlet, nasal prow projecting and pendulous, carrotty curly hair, and mustache, arms that are always in the way, expression dreadfully melancholy, he stares inquisitively here and there, and cranes his long neck around the house like a bereaved Vermonter who has just come from the death-bed of his mother-in-law, and is looking for a sexton. For something like a minute he says not a word, but rubs his hands awkwardly, and continues the search. Finally, just as the spectators are about to break into giggles, he opens his capacious mouth, and begins in a slow drawl,—about three words a minute by the watch.

"Ladies—and gentlemen: By—the request of the—Chair—man of the—Committee—I—beg leave to—intro—duce—to you—the lecturer of the evening—a gentleman whose great learning—whose historical accuracy—whose devotion—to science—and whose veneration for the truth—are only equaled by his high moral character—and—his—ma-

*Reprinted from *Chicago Evening Post*, December 19, 1871, p. [4]; with deletions and changes reprinted in Circular of the Boston Lyceum Bureau dated January 1, 1872. The author can be identified through his autobiography, *An American Procession, 1855–1914: A Personal Chronicle of Famous Men* (Boston: Little, Brown, 1931), pp. 169–71.

jestic presence. [Roars of laughter.] I allude in these vague general terms—to my—self. I—am a little opposed to the custom of ceremoniously introducing a lecturer to the audience because it seems—unnecessary—where the man has been properly advertised! But as—it is—the custom—I prefer to make it myself—in my own case—and then I can rely on getting in—all the facts! [Laughter.] I never had but one introduction—that seemed to me just the thing—and the gentleman was not acquainted with me, and there was no nonsense. He said, 'Ladies and gentlemen, I shall waste no time in this introduction. I know of only two facts about him; 1st, he has never been in State Prison, and 2nd, I can't—imagine why!'"

Mr. Twain then "hedged toward his subject," as he called it, and took his auditors on a flying trip to California and the mountain mining-regions;—giving alternate glimpses of sense and nonsense, of humor, burlesque, sentiment, and satire, that kept the audience in the most sympathetic mood. He never dipped into pathos, and never rose into eloquence, but he kept sledding right along in a fascinating nasal snarl, looking and speaking like an embarrassed deacon telling his experiences, and punctuating his tardy fun with the most complicated awkwardness of gesture. Now he snapped his fingers; now he rubbed his hands softly, like the catcher of the champion nine; now he caressed his left palm with his dexter fingers, like the end minstrel-man propounding a conundrum; now he put his arms akimbo, like a disgusted auctioneer; and now he churned the air in the vicinity of his imperilled head with his outspread hands, as if he was fighting mosquitoes at Rye Beach. Once he got his arms tangled so badly, that three surgeons were seen to edge their way quietly toward the stage, expecting to be summoned; but he unwound himself during the next anecdote.

It is plain to see that Twain's success as a platformer results: first, from his being a genuine humorist with audacity and imagination; secondly, from his slow and solemn speech and his sanctimonious bearing and manner. Then the style of his delivery gives all the effect of spontaneity. The jokes are uttered as if he had just thought of them a minute before, and didn't perceive the point of them quite as soon as the audience.

After the droll narration, concert, or whatever it was, a few of the journalists of the city were pleasantly entertained at the residence of Dr. Jackson, a gentleman Twain immortalized in "The Innocents Abroad." During this supplemental two hours, the guest of the evening was even more quaintly humorous and interesting than during his public talk, developing a strong placer of fun that will stand a great deal of industrious mining before it begins to be exhausted. Mr. Twain talks at the Union Park Congregational Church, West Side, to-night.

[Review of a Lecture on the Sandwich Islands]

Anonymous*

Mark Twain's lecture at the Hanover Square Rooms on the Sandwich Islands will remind many of us of the inimitable lecture delivered by Artemus Ward some six years ago at the Egyptian Hall, Piccadilly, on his adventures among the Mormons and elsewhere. Indeed the two American humorists resemble each other in the complete reticence and apparently straightforward simplicity of manner with which they make their humorous points. Mark Twain himself even carries this nonchalance to excess. He hurries over some few of his points with so little emphasis or significance of air that they are lost upon the audience, who did not catch his joke at all, for instance, when the present writer was in attendance, about "the long, green swell of the Pacific." But though this perfect calm and assumed earnestness of manner is common to the two humourists, there was something much more comically childlike, much more of serious inward embarrassment and bewilderment at the core of the humour of Artemus Ward than in that of Mark Twain, who is the easy man of the world throughout, and whose humour consists in the unconscious, matter-of-fact way in which he habitually strikes false intellectual notes, the steady simplicity with which he puts the emphasis of feeling in the wrong place, with which he classifies in the most unassuming way, as families of the same tribe of things, the most irreconcilable common nouns, and so glides into sarcasm or caricature, while seeming to pursue, without looking to the right or the left, the even tenor of his way. For instance, he began on one of the evenings with referring to the complaints that he had not been well heard throughout the hall, and threw a tone of high moral ardour and resolve into his promise to make himself adequately heard, which, delivered as it was, with the utmost immobility and gravity of demeanour, was irresistibly humorous. And then he glided off into a candid avowal of his wish to gratify the violent temporary and momentary hunger for information about the Sandwich Islands, with as serious an air as if the fame of the Sandwich Islands was really in every

*Reprinted from *Spectator* [London], 46 (October 18, 1873), 1302–03. The review was reprinted in *Every Saturday* [Boston], 4 (November, 1873), 555–56.

26

mouth, and anxiety about them the ruling passion of every heart. The humour in all this was the anxious travesty of the intellectual assumptions of the easy man of the world which it suggested. The ease and frankness of the speaker impressed you with his complete command of all the social currents of the day; and then the oddity of the false notes, touched so easily and in such apparent good faith,—the virtuous ardour about making himself heard,—the resolve either to appease or to stimulate to a still higher level of enthusiasm the assumed thirst for knowledge about the Sandwich Isles,—became in the highest degree grotesque. It was the same when he confessed casually to the audience the kind of problem which had exercised his mind most in connection with this subject; and his belief that it belonged to that region of the unknown and unknowable which it is the mere knight-errantry of reason to attempt to explore. This problem was "why the Sandwich Islands should have been put away out there in the middle of the Pacific Ocean,"—a point which he declared to be not really "open to criticism," so that it would not be "graceful to dwell upon it." This specimen of the kind of transcendental difficulty by which he was haunted, and of the moral extinguisher which he put upon it, carried on the ludicrous conception suggested of a man of the world with a strange topsy-turviness in his intellectual constitution; and the same notion ran through a good part of the lecture, so far at least as it was humorous, the defect in it as a work of art being that several portions,—the descriptive portions, for instance, which were very vigorous and graphic,—had no relation to this main thread of humour, being in fact terse and imaginative descriptions of the scenery such as any man with a keen eye and a good oratorical faculty, might draw. Even the humorous features of the lecture were not all of the same type. There was some good mimicry and anecdote, and not a little rather commonplace fun at the expense of native manners and the old cannibalism, such as the remark that the Kanaka men, not being "proud," used to wear nothing but "a smile, or a pair of spectacles, or any little thing like that;" or the story about the cannibal Kanaká who wanted to try "how Europeans would go with onions," and who, after eating the tough captain of a whaler, died of "the crime on his conscience and the whaler on his stomach." In fact the commoner humour that consists in happy extravagance was no insignificant part of the fun of the lecture,—in that showing its inferiority to Artemus Ward's, whose humour was everywhere penetrated with a moral coherence which very much set off its intellectual incoherence.

Again, some humorous touches of Mark Twain's were mere epigrammatic applications of strong sense to the facts of savage life, as when he said that by the help of the Europeans, the Kanakas had been more completely and universally educated than any people on the face of the earth, and that "if only the Europeans *could have augmented the native capacity*, they would have made that people perfect;" and as when—that augmentation of capacity being assumed as impossible,—he spoke, with more logical consistency than appeared on the surface, of the blessings of European influence to the Kanakas as having consisted in "complicated diseases, education, civilisation, and all sorts of calamities" (whereby their numbers had been reduced from 400,000 to 50,000), and anticipated that Europeans would "start a few more seminaries of learning among the natives,—and finish." This sort of humour, it will be perceived, is quite different in kind from that which consists in playing the quaintest possible variations on the ordinary intellectual and moral assumptions made by a man of the world, for it depends indeed on a stronger and more masculine use of those assumptions than ordinary men ever make. Some touches, too, of Mark Twain's were due to the well-known genius of the American language, which invents such admirable vernacular phrases for moral feelings, and is wont to express the rather rare emotion of surprise with so much of calm equanimity as to multiply tenfold the force of the emotion. What could be better, for instance, than the adjective for native affections contained in the following comment on the generous liberality with which Kanakas *adopt* mothers,—that if a Kanaka's affections are "liberal and *stretchy*," he may have at least a hundred and fifty mothers?—or than the delightful matter-of-factness of the remark supposed to have been made by a sugar-planter to a Kanaka who had asked for three holidays in three weeks, for the purpose, on each occasion, of going and burying a mother,—"It does seem to me that your stock of mothers holds out very well"? The humorous impassiveness in the American speech is, of course, used by Mark Twain to the greatest possible advantage. For instance, after depreciating the dogs of the Hawaiian Islands as a feeble breed whose only strong point is their curly tails, he told his audience, that a friend of his assured him that if he ever had one of these dogs of his own, "he should cut the tail off, and *throw the balance of the dog away.*" That calm treatment of the elements of the dog as if they were elements of a pecuniary transaction, is essentially American, and belongs not to the individual humour of Mark Twain, so much as to the characteristic humour of the country from which he comes. But the humour of the remark that you might have all climates in the Sandwich Islands, from a permanent average of 80 degrees at the foot of the mountains, through every intermediate temperature as you ascend, down to a temperature at the top "so miserably cold *that a man can't tell the truth*," was all his own, and one of the finest illustrations of his curious power of striking, with easy matter-of-fact simplicity, a most grotesquely strange note, in the midst of the calm and business-like statements of an ordinary man of the world. To assume the cold as taking effect, not on the intellect, but on the conscience, is as genuine and real a surprise as the vagaries of humour ever invented; and when given with that perfect composure of easy common-sense with which Mark Twain drops it out, it produces a most telling effect on the audience. On the whole, though Mark Twain cannot be regarded as so remarkable and rare a humourist as Artemus Ward, no one with any appreciation of the great originality of American literature in this direction will hear him without thorough enjoyment, and at least some new memories of the kind which make a man laugh suddenly at unexpected moments as the flavour of a dry saying comes back to him. His higher humour is not sustained, but it is eked out with so much skill of anecdote, so much command of American idiom, and such powers of mimicry, as to furnish an entertainment perhaps even more generally popular than Artemus Ward's inimitable lectures themselves.

Mark Twain

George T. Ferris*

One of the pleasantest offices of cultivated thought is the study of contrasts in the literatures of different peoples. The trained power of the artist-eye derives no greater pleasure in its discriminating observance of landscapes than that resulting from the arrangement and grouping of the recorded forms of national thought and sentiment, considered purely from the picturesque stand-point.

If this be true of poetry, philosophy, and art in general, it is peculiarly so of national humor. For humor is a direct product from the life-blood. It sucks its ingredients from each hidden taint and essential virtue; from intellectual perversity and moral insight; from external environment and from internal fact.

Other forms of thought are the outcomes of single phases, standing together as symmetrical fragments of the individual or the people. Humor comes the nearest to being the one complete revelation, which subtends all the complex secrets of Nature and habit.

The poet sings sweet songs to the world that thrill or soften. But, behind the cloudy forms which his incantations evoke and his genius illumines, the individual fades away. The orator storms, or pleads, or reasons, but the attention slips by the man to fasten on what he says or thinks. The essayist challenges interest for the most part by appeals from the special to the universal.

Not so the humorist, whether the mouthpiece of his age and country, or the mere witness of himself. Harlequin may wear a mask, but under the shallow fold the face plays hide-and-seek in vain. The heart beams out in the mirth that quivers on the edge of pathos, or the grotesque laugh, which needs only a little deeper tone to become melancholy. It is the intense humanity and life-likeness of humor, that set the ultimate stamp on its charm and significance.

Our literary inheritance from the princes of humor is full of finger-marks, index-signs, and marginal notes. We like to query whether Dean Swift, with his terrible scowl and blighting satire, which seem as if in-

*Reprinted from *Appleton's Journal*, 12 (July 4, 1874), 15–18.

spired from some Dantean depth, where devils mock and laugh, ever had the unctuous enjoyment of roast-beef and mighty ale, that shows in Dick Steele, Charles Lamb, and Charles Dickens? It is pleasant to speculate whether Heine, with his acute French wit sparkling on the current of deep German humor, ever recovered from his infatuation for frisky champagne and Parisian grisettes? Or, if Jean Paul, "the only one," whose imagination pirouetted on earth with as much agility and swiftness as it cleft the upper abysses eagle-winged, never had the vertigo?

Would we not have known exactly how Hogarth looked, his grim features softened by a funny twist of the mouth, even had he never painted himself with an exceeding honest-faced but belligerent-looking bull-dog squatted by his side? How we should like to have heard Rabelais, after he had set a nation in a roar of laughter, reading the "Adventures of Pantagruel" to the jolly old abbot!

Or, again, let us overleap the wide abyss of centuries, and stand amid the vast prairies, the gloomy cañons, and the grand forests of the far West. There in mining-camp or squatter settlement we see the figures of Mark Twain, Bret Harte, or John Hay, casting long shadows before them. In the tedious *entr'actes* between fiery whiskey, coffee, and buckwheat "slapjacks," we can hear them make merry over adventures and fancies, which, vitalized by the breath of genius, were soon to ripple the world's face with laughter.

Such whimsical caprices never cease to haunt the students of the humorous in books with a sense of nearness and intimacy in their favorites. We are impertinently curious about them, make them mental bedfellows, as it were, because we love them. The laugh in literature is the "one touch of Nature" (above all others) "which makes the whole world akin."

America has of late years bristled with humorous writers, as does the porcupine with quills. But few of these quills have been pungent in point or well feathered for flight. Yet what persistent jokers! They have sought to offset failures at the lawyer's brief, the doctor's pill-box, the counter-jumper's measuring-tape, the carpenter's plane, or what not. Still, amid a legion of quacks, there are some who have been crowned and anointed with the true "laying-on of hands."

In surveying the distinctive and peculiar American humor, it becomes necessary to banish two highly-gifted men, Holmes and Lowell. The "Hosea Biglow Papers" have all the pungent wit of Pope, the meaty and athletic vigor of Swift. The genial front of the "autocrat" shines like a fixed star. But their passports are not properly *viséd* by the home stamp. In spite of the use of dialect and other forged ear-marks, with which they would cunningly hoodwink us, we say to these magnificent impostors: "Get you gone, you belong to the world, not to America; you are giants truly, but your national angles, prejudices, and crudities, have been so ground down in the social mill, so polished away in the intellectual workshop, that your humor is that of the cosmopolite. It self-registers as much for any other Anglo-Saxon as for the American."

Mark Twain and Bret Harte may, on the whole, be pronounced our most marked types of humorists. Each one has a noble constituency, but in many respects they are at the antipodes from each other. The latter is impelled to create and idealize, even when most faithful to externals. His plummet feels for the deep heart of hidden mysteries, and finds love, sweetness, and self-sacrifice, beneath what is odd, grotesque, and barbaric. True, he deals largely with suffering, crime, and misery, in his most vigorous and characteristic sketches, yet is it with that sunny charity, which is the moral equivalent of searching insight. He has learned a lesson of the mining-camp, and knows where to look for gold in unsightly places. The essentially dramatic spirit, to which his instincts of form in art lead him, is no doubt partly responsible for the vividness of light and shade which intensifies his stories both in prose and rhyme. Yet, underlying form and method, seems to be a subtile feeling for the truth that good and evil are facts that melt and glide into each other imperceptibly, a recognition of which in painting human life is the tap-root of the soundest philosophy and the deepest humor.

Mark Twain, on the other hand, rarely touches the latent springs of human sentiment, nor is his style more than narrative and descriptive. He strolls in the open, breezy sunshine, happy-go-lucky fashion, yet with a keenness of vision that allows nothing in his horizon to escape him. But, before any further study of the author, let us briefly sketch the man, who was generally known to his little circle as SAMUEL L. CLEMENS, before the world coddled and petted him as Mark Twain.

He was born in Missouri in 1835, and got but scanty gleanings of early education. He became a printer's apprentice when his father died, and found that setting type at the case was by no means a bad school. After a few years, most of which were spent in itinerating from one country newspaper to another, young Clemens became a pilot on a Mississippi steamboat running between St. Louis and New Orleans. The picturesque life which he saw in this new business seems to have stimulated his literary faculties, for we soon find him writing for the newspapers. One day while he was pondering as to what *nom de plume* he should attach to his articles, he heard a sailor, who was taking soundings of the river, call out, "Mark twain!" The phrase tickled the fancy of our young literary pilot, and he adopted it for his own.

After seven years of this river-life, in which Mark Twain sedulously cultivated the art of writing, he went to Nevada Territory as private secretary of his brother, who had been appointed Secretary of the Territory. The chance was peculiarly grateful to one who had a keen thirst for adventure, and a vivid appreciation of the ludicrous. Nevada was just then beginning to swarm with reckless and quaint people, who had shot off at a tangent from the established order of society. Bankrupt tradesmen, young college-graduates who, tired of grubbing for Greek roots, would now grub for gold and silver, thieves and murderers escaped from justice—these and a thousand other offscourings of life collided and made frontier society lively. The fashionable toilet consisted of an eight-inch Colt, an Arkansas tooth-pick, jackboots, and an "insectivorous" shirt. The pet amusements were drinking bad whiskey, playing "draw-poker," and practising at human targets. Such paradisiacal conditions were surely enough to make any reasonable man happy. That our hero was so may be deduced from the fact that, what was originally projected as a pleasure-trip, lasted for seven years. During his life in the mining-region he passed through divers experiences, now exploring and prospecting, now editing a newspaper, now working on days' wages in a quartz-mill. Many of the sketches after incorporated in the "Jumping Frog" and "Roughing It" were published at this time in local or Eastern journals. During a considerable time he was city editor of the Virginia City *Enterprise*, and some of the quaintest and brightest things which have appeared under his name originally enlivened its crimson catalogue of brutal murders and "Judge Lynch" executions.

From Virginia City Mark Twain drifted to San Francisco. Bad luck continued to follow him persistently. What money he had made while oscillating between the editor's quill and the gold-digger's pick had been invested in Nevada mining-stock. Wall Street, however, whispered gently to the wilderness, and there was a sudden collapse in values. He then became interested with Bret Harte in the conduct of the *Californian*, and the two humorists hobnobbed for the first time. The nomadic taint, however, ran riot in the blood of both these "imps of Fortune," and they soon deserted the paste-pot and scissors for another delusive experiment in mining for gold. On returning to San Francisco, Mark Twain, his health now being poor, obtained a commission to go to the Sandwich Islands. Here the delicious climate and *dolce far niente* life built him up again in health, and an absence of a few months brought him back again to San Francisco with renewed health and spirits. A short lecturing tour through California and Nevada was successful, and so replenished his pockets as to furnish sufficient funds for a trip to New York. In 1867 he published "The Jumping Frog," a collection of his best fugitive works, and immediately aroused public attention, not only in America but in England.

The peculiar humor was a revelation to the conservative British mind, and the little work was even more talked of across the ocean than at home. The "Quaker City" excursion to the different seaports of Southern Europe and the Orient gave our rising author an opportunity of which he made abundant use. The amusing record of his experiences was presented to the world in a book which made a very remarkable sensation—"The Innocents Abroad." In the second part of this work—"The New Pilgrim's Progress"—readers were made acquainted with the genesis of a Bunyan of a different type from the old Baptist dreamer.

This publication justified the expectations of a public ever on the alert for something to laugh at, and Mark Twain rose on a flood-tide of popularity. When he returned to America, he betook himself again for a short time to journalism, and became connected with the Buffalo *Express*. The confinement of office-work, however, did not suit his free Bohemian spirit, and the swelling results of his literary venture soon put it in his power to break loose from the slavery of the editor's desk and follow his own intellectual caprices. His next book was "Roughing It," published in 1873, recording, in elaborate form, his early experiences in the mining-country and the Sandwich Islands. This was speedily followed by the novel, "The Gilded Age," written in collaboration with Charles Dudley Warner. Our author is now residing at Hartford, and is in the very prime of his life and power. Before dismissing the mere material facts of Mark Twain's life, some allusion to the very remarkable pecuniary success of his books will be of interest. During the five years which have elapsed since the issue of "The Innocents Abroad," the aggregate sale of our author's works has reached two hundred and forty-one thousand copies, representing a money-value of nine hundred and fifty thousand dollars. Though a large sale is by no means the only or even the best measure of literary excellence, the above-mentioned fact is so remarkable as to be almost unparalleled.

The differences between wit and humor have been elaborated by numerous essayists. These have said many bright things and many stupid ones on the subject. But, after all, the essence of it eludes definition and analysis. We see the effects, but fail to reach the ultimate force. This, at all events, we know, that wit is purely intellectual, and that humor is deeper and wider in its sources and powers. Wit sparkles in instantaneous gleams. It is the point of collision and also of union between opposites. Thackeray somewhere says that "humor is wit and love;" that "the best humor is that which contains the most humanity; that which is flavored throughout with the most tenderness and kindness."

Of humor in its highest phase, perhaps Bret Harte may be accounted the most puissant master among our contemporary American writers. Of wit, we see next to none. Mark Twain, while lacking the subtlety and pathos of the other, has more breadth, variety, and ease. His sketches of life are arabesque in their strange combinations. Bits of bright, serious description, both of landscape and society, carry us along till suddenly we stumble on some master-stroke of grotesque and irresistible form. He understands the value of repose in art. One tires of a page where every sentence sparkles with points, and the author is constantly attitudinizing for our amusement. We like to be betrayed into laughter as much in books as in real life. It is the unconscious, easy, careless gait of Mark Twain that makes his most potent charm. He seems always to be catering as much to his own enjoyment as to that of the public. He strolls along like a great rollicking school-boy, bent on having a good time, and determined that his readers shall enjoy it with him. If Bret Harte had remarkable insight, Mark Twain has no less notable *out*sight. And yet perhaps the great popularity of the latter writer is as much the consequence of his defects as of his powerful gifts. He is representative because he embodies, to a striking extent, in his mode of constructing the forms of humor, the peculiar style of the average American journalist. Journalism on this side of the water has two unique types: the professional funny man, and the police-court reporter. Both these are strongly-marked national characters, and the style in which they serve up dishes for the public breakfast is well known. Hardly a newspaper appears but that it contains a variety of such paragraphs as the following:

> John Smith had a beautiful stallion, who was so amiable in his temper that he would always caress the air with an affectionate gesture of his steel-clad hoofs when a stranger approached from behind. Squire Robinson bought the horse. The gorgeous funeral which Deadhead, the undertaker, supplied for the squire a few days after, enabled our respected fellow-citizen, who presides with such dignity in front of the mourners, to fit out his wife and daughter with the latest spring fashions.

It would be unjust to our author to say that he is either one or the other of these types in full flower. And yet how frequently do we see both these gentlemen surreptitiously stealing away out of sight under the cover of Mark Twain's coat-tails! Or perhaps it is only a literary illustration of Darwin's doctrine of rudimentary organs and limbs by which he explains changes in structural type. Mark Twain's early literary training was that of a writer for newspapers, where news was scarce and hard to get, and the public demanded their intellectual fare dressed with the hottest, strongest condiments. Is it not natural that we should see distinct and powerful traces of this method in all his later work?

In spite of this fault, our writer is so thoroughly genial, so charged with rich and unctuous humor, that we forget the lack of *finesse* and delicacy in its breadth and strength. Its tap-root takes no deep hold in the subsoil, and we may not always find a subtile and penetrating fragrance in its blooms. But these are so lavish, bright, and variegated, that we should be ungrateful indeed not to appreciate our author's striking gifts at their full worth. "The Innocents Abroad," and "Roughing It," are the most thoroughly enjoyable examples of Mark Twain's humor. While they are not to be altogether admired as intellectual workmanship, the current of humor is so genuine and fresh, so full of rollicking and grotesque fun, that it is more than easy to overlook fault both in style and method. Like most of the American humorists, Mark Twain depends chiefly on exaggeration as the effective element in his art. This has long been acknowledged the peculiar characteristic in our humorous processes. The clean-cut, sinewy force, so common to foreign writers, and no less evident in such men as Holmes and Lowell, is wanting in our distinctive

Americans of this guild of literature. Their strength, on the other hand, is large, loose-jointed, and clumsy, the vigor of Nature and free exercise, not that of the gymnasium and fencing-school. It is humor which runs abroad with rambling, careless steps, not the humor which selects deliberately a fixed goal, and disembarrasses itself of every superfluity before commencing the race. What we lose, however, in energy, point, momentum, we gain in freshness and spontaneity.

In using exaggeration as a force in art, Mark Twain exaggerates not characters but circumstances. As a consequence, he is never a caricaturist. We recognize, even in his most extraordinary statements and descriptions, therefore, a flavor of reality, which takes strong hold of the imagination. Many of the unique people, whom he delineates, indeed, in his Western scenes, seem to have stepped right out of life into the printed page, veritable photographs in large and showy settings.

Mark Twain's latest book, "The Gilded Age," was written in conjunction with Mr. Warner. Our author contributed to this joint production the career of the Hawkins family, and of Colonel Sellers, occupying the first eleven chapters, and twenty-two other chapters, scattered throughout the book. The rest of the composite story must be credited to the accomplished author of "Backlog Studies" and "Saunterings." We have the word of the authors that there was no intention of making it humorous, the sole purpose being that of bitter satire, true and honest to the core.

Some of the best detached descriptions which have ever emanated from Mark Twain's pen may be found in this book. They show that the author's powers are at their best working capacity, and that the world has a right to look for liberal fruits from them.

[Review of *Mark Twain's Sketches, New and Old*]

William Dean Howells*

It is easy to say that these new and old sketches by Mr. Clemens are of varying merit; but which, honest reader, would you leave out of the book? There is none but saves itself either by its humor or by the sound sense which it is based on, so that if one came to reject the flimsiest trifle, one would find it on consideration rather too good to throw away. In reading the book, you go through a critical process imaginably very like the author's in editing it; about certain things there can be no question from the first, and you end by accepting all, while you feel that any one else may have his proper doubts about some of the sketches.

The characteristic traits of our friend—he is the friend of mankind—are all here; here is the fine, forecasting humor, starting so far back from its effect that one, knowing some joke must be coming, feels that nothing less than a prophetic instinct can sustain the humorist in its development; here is the burlesque, that seems such plain and simple fun at first, doubling and turning upon itself till you wonder why Mr. Clemens has ever been left out of the list of our *subtile* humorists; here is that peculiar extravagance of statement which we share with all sufficiently elbow-roomed, unneighbored people, but which our English cousins are so good as to consider the distinguishing mark of American humor; here is the incorruptible right-mindedness that always warms the heart to this wit; here is the "dryness," the "breadth,"—all the things that so weary us in the praises of him and that so take us with delight in the reading of him. But there is another quality in this book which we fancy we shall hereafter associate more and more with our familiar impressions of him, and that is a growing seriousness of meaning in the apparently unmoralized drolling, which must result from the humorist's second thought of political and social absurdities. It came to Dickens, but the character of his genius was too intensely theatrical to let him make anything but rather poor melodrama of it; to Thackeray, whom our humorists at their best are all like, it came too, and would not suffer him to leave anything, however

*Reprinted from *Atlantic Monthly*, 36 (December, 1875), 749–51. Unsigned originally, but included by Howells in *My Mark Twain* (New York: Harper & Brothers, 1910).

grotesque, merely laughed at. We shall be disappointed if in Mr. Clemens's case it finds only some desultory expression, like Lionizing Murderers and A New Crime, though there could not be more effective irony than these sketches so far as they go. The first is a very characteristic bit of the humorist's art; and the reader is not so much troubled to find where the laugh comes in as to find where it goes out—for ten to one he is in a sober mind when he is done. The other is more direct satire, but is quite as subtle in its way of presenting those cases in which murderers have been found opportunely insane and acquitted, and gravely sandwiching amongst them instances in which obviously mad people have been hanged by the same admirable system.

Nothing more final has been thought of on the subject of a great public, statutory wrong, than Mark Twain's petition to Congress asking that all property shall be held during the period of forty-two years, or for just so long as an author is permitted to claim copyright in his book. The whole sense and justice applicable to the matter are enforced in this ironical prayer, and there is no argument that could stand against it. If property in houses or lands—which a man may get by dishonest trickery, or usury, or hard rapacity—were in danger of ceasing after forty-two years, the whole virtuous community would rouse itself to perpetuate the author's right to the product of his brain, and no griping bidder at tax-sales but would demand the protection of literature by indefinite copyright. The difficulty is, to condition the safety of real estate in this way; but Mark Twain's petition is a move in the right direction.

We should be sorry to give our readers the impression that they are unconsciously to imbibe political and social wisdom from every page of Mr. Clemens's new book, when we merely wished to point out one of his tendencies. Though there is nearly always sense in his nonsense, yet he is master of the art of pure drolling. The grotesque cannot go further than in that Mediaeval Romance of his, where he is obliged to abandon his hero or heroine at the most critical moment, simply because he can see no way to get him or her out of the difficulty; and there is a delicious novelty in that Ghost Story, where the unhappy spectre of the Cardiff giant is mortified to find that he has been haunting a plaster cast of himself in New York, while his stone original was lying in Albany. The Experiences of the McWilliamses with the Membranous Croup is a bit of *genre* romance, which must read like an abuse of confidence to every husband and father. These are amongst the new sketches, though none of them have staled by custom, and the old sketches are to be called so merely for contradistinction's sake. How I once edited an Agricultural Paper, About Barbers, Cannibalism in the Cars, The Undertaker's Chat, The Scriptural Panoramist, To raise Poultry, A Visit to Niagara, are all familiar favorites, which, when we have read them we wish merely to have the high privilege of immediately reading over again. We must not leave the famous Jumping Frog out of their honorable and pleasant company; it is here in a new effect, first as the Jumping Frog in Mark Twain's original English, then in the French of the Revue des deux Mondes, and then in his literal version of the French, which he gives that the reader may see how his frog has been made to appear "to the distorted French eye."

But by far the most perfect piece of work in the book is A True Story, which resulted, we remember, in some confusion of the average critical mind, when it was first published in these pages a little more than one year ago. It is simply the story an old black cook tells of how her children were all sold away from her, and how after twenty years she found her youngest boy again. The shyness of an enlightened and independent press respecting this history was something extremely amusing to see, and we could fancy it a spectacle of delightful interest to the author, if it had not had such disheartening features. Mostly the story was described in the notices of the magazine as a humorous sketch by Mark Twain; sometimes it was mentioned as a paper apparently out of the author's usual line; again it was handled non-committally as one of Mark Twain's extravagances. Evidently the critical mind feared a lurking joke. Not above two or three notices out of hundreds recognized A True Story for what it was, namely, a study of character as true as life itself, strong, tender, and most movingly pathetic in its perfect fidelity to the tragic fact. We beg the reader to turn to it again in this book. We can assure him that he has a great surprise and a strong emotion in store for him. The rugged truth of the sketch leaves all other stories of slave life infinitely far behind, and reveals a gift in the author for the simple dramatic report of reality which we have seen equaled in no other American writer.

A New Book by Mark Twain

[Robert Underwood Johnson]*

It needs no skillful reading between the lines of this last volume by Mr. Clemens to see that it is essentially an autobiography. The experiences of the author, his trials, his failures, and his final success are patent on every page. Even in the illustrations, one may read the story of his eventful career. Though with rare modesty he has suppressed the most sacred facts of his life, it takes but an ordinary imagination to peer through the palings of his father's fence (see cut on page 25) and behold him in the sportive innocence of his childhood, throwing his grandmother's gridiron (see cut on page 27) at the neighbor's cat. How easy to discern in this incident the budding of those distinguished editorial faculties of later years! Here, too (page 97), is a view of the brick-yard in which—though he says it not, we know from other sources—he worked for years. In fact, there is an air of brick-yard throughout the whole of this volume, which it is impossible to attribute to any other literary mood than reminiscence. The volatility of his youth is also plainly to be seen. If we are not at fault, the inference to be drawn from the book is, that for many years the author could stick to nothing; but that, in later years, his power of application has notably increased. Yet, we must frankly admit that we have found but few irregularities in the whole volume. Further on (pages 124–137) are given numerous sketches from the author's life on the Mississippi. The one of the pontoon bridges (p. 126)—which, it may not be generally known, were used at the times of the overflow of Western rivers—seems to us hardly enough to the point. We think we can detect Mr. Clemens's hand in the sketch from which this view was made; it has, in common with the gridiron, already referred to, a certain individuality bordering on mannerism. (Can we be mistaken in supposing that the gridiron must have come from Mr. Clemens's hand?) Nor do we like so well the view of the Hannibal and St. Joe Railroad (page 140), on which Mr. Clemens went to California in '49; if we should be asked to name its

*Reprinted from *Scribner's Monthly*, 13 (April, 1877), 874–75; unsigned but the attribution to Johnson seems clear—see Thomas A. Tenney, *Mark Twain: A Reference Guide* (Boston: G. K. Hall, 1977), item 1877.B6. The "volume" reviewed is Mark Twain's Self-Pasting Scrap-Book.

principal fault, we should have to complain of the perspective. The views of the stratification of gold in the California mines (page 153), as it appeared to the imagination of Mr. Clemens, have a touch of that quaint humor so characteristic of him. We could wish the text were fuller in regard to this part of the author's romantic life, but we must do him the justice to remember that the title of this book only promises fragmentary sketches; though, as the title modestly suggests, they are not easily displaced from the memory.

But we did not mean to follow Mr. Clemens through the whole of the checkered career exhibited in this volume. It is a book to which readers could easily become attached. Many a lesson of patience and moderation may be learned from the parallels he has here drawn. Artists, even architects, will find much in the drawings to encourage them, while, among the quotations, many a scholar will gladly welcome the frequent lines of Arabic, the smoothness and flow of which are quite beyond praise. The style of the book, though occasionally labored, has none of the discursiveness heretofore so noticeable in Mr. Clemens's work, but is evenly sustained throughout. The compositor's work is almost without flaw. We have found a few instances of "wrong fonts," but, so far, not a single error in the leading. We must, however, protest against the insertion by the publishers, at the close, of the cut of the ladder by which Mr. Clemens rose to fame.

It is quite safe to say that no such work has ever been given to the public; the price per copy is from $1.25 to $3.50, according to style of binding, etc.

Mark Twain at Hartford

Edmund H. Yates*

Among those American authors who, because they have had the courage to cut loose from the apron-strings of England, have achieved the greatest success both at home and abroad, Mark Twain is, in point of popularity, *facile princeps*. Those who only know him as the author of *The Innocents Abroad* and *Roughing It* are apt to imagine he is a kind of frontier joker, of the type with which Bret Harte had made us familiar. It may be that there is even yet a vague suspicion of this bent, although his external person certainly shows no trace of it. If you see him in his charming home at Hartford, in the valley of the Connecticut, surrounded with every object which taste and wealth can procure, you feel that such a conception has been erroneous. The mansion with its quaint old English architecture and its exquisite tiles and mosaics, the rich ferneries and half-tropical hothouses, are no mere extraneous accumulations such as any man of wealth might create, but a gradual and organic outgrowth of the owner's mind which gives you a delightful peep into the inner recesses of his character. The main building, as well as the stables, is built of dark-red brick with dark-brown trimmings, interspersed with inlaid devices of scarlet-painted brick and black Greek patterns in mosaic. The whole has a most novel and pleasing effect—nothing gaudy and glaring, but all arranged with a rare artistic taste and a strict regard for harmony in colours and outlines. During the summer the outer window-sills are draped with hanging ferns and bright nasturtiums, and the wood-work of the broad East Indian portico is half-concealed beneath the foliage of clambering vines. But as winter reigns supreme during a good many months of the year in New England, Mark Twain has taken care to provide himself with summer vistas even while Nature does not afford them. His library, the place where the owner is most frequently to be found, opens into a miniature greenhouse, full of tall graceful ferns and blooming tropical plants. In the midst of all these luxuriant exotics a fountain is constantly playing, shedding its spray over the smooth white rocks at its base, and

*Reprinted from E. H. Yates, *Celebrities at Home/Third Series* (London: Office of "The World," 1879), pp. 135–41; originally appeared in *London World* in late 1877 or early January, 1878.

42

under the glass ceiling hangs a large cage in which a pair of California quails of brilliant plumage spend a brief season of happy captivity. Mark Twain cannot endure to see any bird or beast which Nature intended for freedom imprisoned within the narrow bars of a cage, and he bought these quails in the winter from a boy, meaning to set them at liberty in a neighbouring forest as soon as spring should arrive.

In the pleasant city of Hartford he has gathered about him a delightful circle of friends, authors, business men, and lawyers, to whom his hospitable doors are always open. And he is, indeed, the prince of entertainers. Sitting in his richly-furnished library, to whose beauty and artistic completeness half the lands of Europe have contributed, he will tell an anecdote or discuss a literary or social question with a calm directness and earnestness, revealing to you an entirely new side of his character that has nothing in common with that which he is wont to display to the public who throng to his lectures. Even his drollest stories he relates with this same earnest impressiveness, and with a face as serious as a sexton's. His brilliancy has a certain delightful quality which is almost too evanescent to be imprisoned in any one phrase. You have no oppressive consciousness that you are expected to laugh; you rather feel as if the talker had unexpectedly taken you into his confidence, and you feel your heart going out towards him in return. Throughout his house Mark Twain has indulged liberally his taste for wood-tints and quaint carvings. Each of the doors in the library is surmounted with carved cherubs and other biblical and mythical figures, spoils from some European pilgrimage. In his study on the second floor he revels in sphinxes and griffins, whose reclining bodies and capacious wings fashion themselves into luxurious lounges, easy-chairs, and sofas. The mantelpiece, with all its magnificent superstructure, had once adorned an old English or Scottish country seat, and Mark Twain was fortunate enough to pick it up during one of his many sojourns in England. Amid these surroundings Mark Twain spends the time between breakfast and dinner, composing with much serious reflection the sketches, novels, and dramas which have shaken the American public with laughter. After dinner the chances are that you will find him tranquilly smoking a cigar before the fire in the library, and chatting leisurely with some friend, who addresses him plainly as 'Mark,' as his *non de plume* somehow persists in clinging to him both in his private and public relations. His real name is Samuel L. Clemens. He is still a man in the prime of life, being now about forty-four years old. His rich and varied experiences in the past, as a Western editor, gold-digger, and pilot on the Mississippi, have stored his brain with abundant material for future works which have still to be written.

On such occasions as these he will dwell on his experiences while travelling in England. Once, while going by rail from London to Liverpool, he was shut up in a *coupé* with a fellow-traveller, who was deeply absorbed in a yellow-covered book, which, on further inspection, proved to be *Roughing It*. He evidently regarded the thing as a very serious business, for he hardly ever moved a muscle. 'I presently began to feel very guilty,' Mark Twain went on, 'for having subjected a fellow-mortal to this prolonged torture. I gazed anxiously into his face in the hope of detecting some lurking shadow of a smile. But no, his gloom seemed rather to be deepening. With a guilty conscience and a dreadful sense of responsibility I watched him turning the leaves, and slowly and gradually, as he approached the end, my heart began to grow lighter. At last, as he closed the book, I heaved a huge sigh of relief. But my exultation was somewhat premature. The man quietly opened his satchel, and pulled out the second volume. And now the same process was repeated, only with an intenser agony on my part. With deep anxiety I scrutinised his features, in the hope of finding some hidden trace of mirth. I would have been so grateful for the slightest fraction of a smile. But my friend was miserable. Before we reached Liverpool, I had serious thought of jumping out through the window.'

Mark Twain is a man of middle height; solidly built, but not stout; his features are all of a clear massive modelling, and the prevailing expression seems to be resolute courage and determination. His upper lip is covered with a thick brown moustache, and the broad territory of his forehead is usually encroached upon by his brown curly hair. His eyes are small and keen, but are by no means lacking in kindliness and humour. In his whole bearing there is a frank cordiality which is very winning. He is the father of two beautiful little girls, of whom he is very proud; and like the amiable prince of tradition he takes much pleasure, amid the serious business of his life, in playing with these two charming princesses. His library and his conversation testify to the excellence of his literary taste. Mark Twain is a devoted admirer of Macaulay, and has a habit of ever returning to him when the lighter literary pablum of the day begins to pall upon his sense. The much-abused term, 'professional humorist,' can hardly apply to Mark Twain. He is rather a constitutional humorist, because his mind is so fashioned that, in dealing with any subject whatever, the humorous point of view first and most naturally presents itself to him. For all that he is very careful not to rush into publicity with a half-formed or half-perfected thought. His after-dinner speeches, which are probably read by a larger number of men and women in America than any public document, the President's Message not excepted, would no doubt have been very good and very laughable even if they had been entirely *impromptu*; but the careful and critical revision to which he subjects them before their public appearance certainly refines their quality.

When Mark Twain is not writing or making speeches he smokes, and if he feels any further need of recreation, he takes it in playing billiards. In the third story of his house there is an elegantly appointed billiard-room, where he often spends an evening with three or four masculine friends. Though he keeps handsome horses, housing them in a superb stable, and may be seen daily driving through the city with a fine pair of bays, he is not much of a connoisseur of horseflesh or a sportsman.

In politics he at first impresses you as an indifferentist, with perhaps a leaning towards pessimism; but if you happen to touch certain chords which never fail to respond in an American bosom, you soon discover that your first impression was very remote from the truth. The fact is, like many another thoughtful man, Mark Twain sees plainly the gravity of the present and future in the United States, and accordingly has very little patience with the spread-eagleism and cheap declamations of contending politicians. Probably his political creed is not very different from that of the Independents, a new and still unorganised party, which is daily growing among the citizens of the great Republic.

Not Quite an Editor/The Story about Mark Twain's Connection with the Hartford *Courant*

Anonymous*

Hartford, Jan. 25—Wishing to obtain Mark Twain's views on the probability of a war between England and Russia, I went to the office of the *Courant* expecting to find him at his desk. To my surprise, I was told that he had not been seen in the office for nearly a fortnight.

Then I called at the door of his astonishing residence in the outskirts of the city. The domestic informed me that I would find Mr. Clemens in the back yard. When I approached the celebrated humorist he was sitting on an inverted washtub, trying to teach a frowsy little terrier to catch crackers in its mouth. Twain had his hat full of oyster crackers. The dog stood on its hind legs and snapped with much perseverance, but with only a moderate degree of skill, at the bits tossed by the master. To set a good example, Twain tossed every third or fourth cracker up into the air, catching it in his own mouth as it descended, and never missing. I complimented him upon his surprising dexterity.

"Oh," said he, carelessly, "a great deal can be accomplished by long practice. Here, Jo!"

"Is your dog's name Joseph?"

"I call him Jo Cook because I can't quite understand him. There are depths in that dog's nature that I haven't fathomed."

"Don't you consider that you are neglecting your professional duties? They told me at the office that you hadn't been seen there for a fortnight. No journalist can expect to give his paper a consistent tone when he indulges in such protracted absences. Matters at Washington are very interesting just now, and the Eastern question has assumed a new and critical phase; and yet here you are, out in the back yard, tossing oyster crackers to a small dog. I ask you, sincerely, as a friend, can you hope to succeed as an editor if you continue to act thus?"

"Young fellow," said Clemens, with great seriousness of manner, "did *you* swallow that yarn?"

"What yarn?" I retorted, my indignation rising at his question. "When I last saw you in the *Courant* office you certainly gave me to

*Reprinted from *New York Sun*, January 26, 1878, p. 2.

understand that you had undertaken the editorial charge of that excellent newspaper. You were very explicit in your statements, told me about your failure on the Buffalo *Express*, foreshadowed your design of making the *Courant* a humorous publication with the special feature of humorous advertisements, and, in fact, enlarged generally upon your prospects in journalism. Do you mean to say now that you were imposing upon me?"

"Didn't I tell you," said Twain, after a brief pause—"Didn't I tell you just as you were getting up (at last!) to go, that the story was told not for publication, but merely as a guarantee of good faith?"

"Yes, you told me that, but at the same time you took the trouble to wink hard with your left eye, and nobody knows better than yourself the significance of a wink under such circumstances."

"Did I wink?" asked Twain, with great earnestness. "That was very unfortunate. You know I have a nervous affection of the eyelid, caused, my wife says, by too much tobacco, and it sometimes produces a twitching effect that might be mistaken for a wink. I am sorry I winked. It makes the case look bad for me—very bad."

"The best thing you can do," I urged, "is to make a full, free, and frank confession of your motive in starting such an absurd story. A good many newspapers in all parts of the country have taken it seriously. The announcement called out a large number of notices very complimentary to yourself, and you owe it to the public to explain."

"The notices *were* complimentary, weren't they?" asked Twain, looking up suddenly from his boots and speaking with animation. "They did me proud, I'm sure. Come into the house, where no soul can overhear, and I'll do the square thing, young fellow."

He led the way into his study, and carefully locked the door. It is a strange apartment. The floor was littered up with a confusion of newspapers, newspaper cuttings, books, children's toys, pipes, models of machinery, and cigar ends. Twain's method is to drop everything when he's done using it, but he will let nobody else interfere with the arrangements of his study. "I am naturally lazy," he says, "and I wish to conquer the detestable habit by imposing on myself a certain amount of domestic work. I take care of the room myself." In one corner stood a stack of his patent self-gumming scrapbooks. This invention, I am told, is the source of a considerable income to Mr. Clemens. On the mantel, where the bust of Calvin stood until Mark destroyed it with a poker in a moment of religious frenzy, I noticed a pitcher that looked as if it had contained beer. On the table were many manuscript sheets of Mr. Clemens's unfinished historical work, "The Mother-in-Law in All Ages."

Seating me on top of the scrapbooks, and himself in the only chair that happened to be in the room, Mark Twain began his confession.

"I am aware," said he, "that the world regards me as a proud, cold, haughty being, too far above the level of average humanity to be actuated by human weaknesses. This is not so. I am a creature of impulse, sensitive to the opinions of others, and eager for approbation. You look incredulous. You don't believe it?"

There was an earnestness in his tone that inspired confidence, and I told him so.

"Latterly," he continued, "I have been down in the mouth. I began to think my luck was down on me. My speech at the Whittier dinner didn't exactly take. I meant it merely as a cheerful conceit, and yet people wouldn't laugh. My article in the *Atlantic*, containing the joke about the two dying soldiers quarrelling for first choice of coffins, seemed to fall flat. A good many well-meaning people refused to see it in the spirit intended. I got gloomy. I smoked all day and almost all night. I thought that humor was played out in America. I had nearly resolved to go to Constantinople, offer my services to the Sublime Porte, and be a light-hearted Bashi-Bazouk, when it occurred to me to test public sentiment and see whether my fellow citizens cared for me still. Well, I threw out this feeler."

I nodded.

"Perhaps it was weak; perhaps I was rash, thoughtless—but do you blame me? The response of the press of America was astonishing. The kind things they said of me, the encouragement they gave me in my supposed enterprise, their invariably flattering comments upon my genius and personal beauty, renewed and restored me. They are good fellows, after all, these newspaper editors, and really, now, I should like to be one of them, if I thought I had the mental capacity."

Here the famous humorist buried his face in his pocket handkerchief. I felt for him strongly.

"I will communicate your explanation to the public," said I. "No doubt it will be regarded as satisfactory. Then you never had any idea of becoming editor of the *Courant*?"

"Never dreamed of it, my dear fellow," said he, brightening into his old manner. "You must excuse me now," he added, looking at his watch; "it is time for me to begin to gum."

"To begin to what?"

He took from the pile on which I had been sitting an ungummed scrap book, and picking up from the floor a brush and a pot of mucilage, industriously began to apply the cohesive substance to the yellow pages on that beautiful, rectangular system which will long be inseparably connected with his name.

Mark Twain Home Again

Anonymous*

Mr. Samuel L. Clemens, who is much better known to Americans as Mark Twain, the pilgrim who was moved to tears while leaning upon the tomb of Adam, and the nearest surviving kin of the jumping frog of Calaveras, reached this City in the steam-ship *Gallia* yesterday, after an absence of a year and a half in Europe. Mr. Twain was accompanied by his wife, 12 trunks, and 22 freight packages; and the entire party, after a smooth voyage, arrived in good health and spirits, and were met and welcomed down at Quarantine by a number of friends. During his absence he has visited London, Paris, Heidelberg, Munich, Venice, and a number of other cities, spending most of his time on the Continent, and making prolonged stays in Paris, Heidelberg, and Munich. When Mark Twain went away, it was generally believed that his intention was to familiarize himself with German, that he might prepare one or two scientific works that are still lacking in that language. He not only did not deny these reports; but rather encouraged them, and his taking passage in a German steamer added greater probability to them. It is now certain, however, that such was not his object. He did have some designs upon the German language, but not with the intention of producing a scientific work. A very celebrated Professor in Munich, who has since died, wrote him a long German letter, inquiring about the point of one of the jokes in *Innocents Abroad*, and Mr. Twain desired to learn enough of the language to explain away the difficulty. After more than a year of study he says he can read German well enough, but that, when it comes to talking, English is good enough for him.

"Yes," said he, in response to questions asked by a group of reporters who surrounded him on all sides, except that occupied by the saloon table, so thickly that he could not fill out his Custom-house declaration, "I have been writing a new book, and have it nearly finished, all but the last two or three chapters. The first half of it, I guess, is finished, but the last half has not been revised yet; and when I get at it I will do a good deal of rewriting and a great deal of tearing up. I may possibly tear up the first part of it, too, and rewrite that." With all this tearing up in prospect, the

*Reprinted from *New York Times*, September 3, 1879, p. 8.

book seemed in such danger of being entirely destroyed that one of the reporters suggested the production of a few chapters in advance in the newspapers, as samples; but Mr. Twain said that the manuscript was in the bottom of one of his trunks, where it could not possibly be reached. He added, however, that the book was descriptive of his latest trip and the places he visited, entirely solemn in character, like the "Innocents Abroad," and very much after the general plan of that work; and that it has not yet been named. It is to be published by the same company that brought out his other books, and is to be ready in November. "They want me to stay in New-York and revise it," he continued; "but I cannot possibly do that. I am going to start to-morrow morning for Elmira, where we will stay for some time."

On his outgoing voyage, Mr. Twain had for fellow-passengers Mr. Bayard Taylor, the American Minister to Germany, and Mr. Murat Halstead, who started on five minutes' notice, and without any clothes except those he wore. "I did not see Mr. Taylor after we left the ship," he said, "but corresponded frequently with him. His death was a great surprise to me. Oh, no, I did not lend Mr. Halstead any clothes. He could not get into mine; and, besides, I hadn't any more than I wanted for myself."

The age of the author of *Innocents Abroad, Roughing It*, and *The Gilded Age* has not increased, apparently, in the last two years. His hair is no whiter than when he last sailed for Europe. He is very much the same man, except that he went away in a silk cap and came back in a cloth hat. He was particularly well pleased with the steamer. "I don't like some of these vessels," said he; "some of them keep a man hungry all the time, unless he has a good appetite for boiled rice. I know some steamers where they have the same bill of fare they used to have when the company ran sailing packets: beans on Tuesday and Friday, stewed prunes on Thursday, and boiled rice on Wednesday; all were healthy, but very bad. But we are fed like princes aboard here, and have made a comfortable voyage. We have been in some seas that would have made the old Quaker City turn somersaults, but this ship kept steady through it all. We could leave a mirror lying on the washstand, and it would not fall off. If we stood a goblet loose on the shelf at night, it would be there in the morning." Mr. Twain declined positively, however, to say whether a cocktail, left standing on the shelf at night, would be there all safe in the morning. The ship was hardly steady enough for that.

There was a little ponderous silence that no one interrupted for the returning writer was evidently revolving something in his mind. "I want a ride on one of the elevated railroads," said he; "I've never been on one of them yet. I used to be afraid of them, but it's no use. Death stares us in the face everywhere, and we may as well take it in its elevated form. I have a friend who wanted to take a ride on the elevated when the first one was built; but when he looked at it he thought of his wife and children and concluded to walk home. On the way up town a woman who was washing a third-story window fell out, and just grazed my friend's head. She was killed, and he had a very narrow escape. It's no use; there are women washing windows everywhere, and we may as well fall as be fallen upon."

A very large Custom-house officer, with a great deal of handsome gilt work on his cap, and very large, wide pockets in his clothes, occupied Mr. Twain's attention for some time, and the latter pondered over the joke of how to swear that 12 trunks and 22 freight packages contained nothing dutiable. A smile lit up the face of the Customs man when he read about the 22 parcels. He was opening them in advance, in his mind, and taking the contents out of boxes that they would not go into again, and nicking little corners off the statuettes.

"This new book of mine," said he, breaking suddenly off from the Custom-house blanks, "is different from any book I ever wrote. Before, I revised the manuscript as I went along, and knew pretty well at the end of each week how much of the week's work I should use, and how much I should throw away. But this one has been written pretty much all in a lump, and I hardly know how much of it I will use, or how much will have to be torn up. When I start at it I tear it up pretty fast, but I think the first half will stand pretty much as it is. I am not quite sure that there is enough yet prepared, but I am still at work at it." The group of reporters and five or six listening cabin passengers stood by waiting for something stupendous in the way of a joke to follow all this serious talk. Several times Mr. Twain's lips moved, as if about to speak, but he was silent. The upper end of Staten Island was passed, and the joke was still unborn. Governor's Island came alongside, the Battery drew astern, the Cunard pier was reached, and yet the joker by profession and reputation kept his audience in suspense. The landing was made, but the joke still lay locked up, with the manuscript, in the bottom of the trunk.

[Review of *The Stolen White Elephant*]

Anonymous*

This volume contains most of Mr. Clemens's recent humorous contributions to the magazines, some of which are very well known, such as "Punch Brothers, Punch," "The Facts concerning the Recent Carnival of Crime in Connecticut," "On the Decay in the Art of Lying," "An Encounter with an Interviewer." "The Stolen White Elephant," which gives its name to the book, is a very elaborate piece of satire at the expense of the detective force of this city. In looking over the volume, the reader is struck with the fact that Mr. Clemens's humor is of such a universal and comprehensive character that it is very difficult to say in what its peculiarity consists. His eminent forerunner, Artemus Ward, had a certain literary *cachet* which Mr. Clemens lacks. His sketches were sketches of American life and manners, grotesque and absurd as you please, but still having a distinctly national flavor. It is hardly possible to say that Artemus Ward described life as he found it; but there was a definite literary relation between life as he saw it around him and what he wrote which everybody recognized in his books. Mr. Clemens's humor, on the other hand, is American enough; but his inventions, which he uses as a vehicle for it, are of no nationality. There is a kind of monstrosity about them which we remember in no other writer—a wild extravagance which is not simply that of exaggeration. No one but an American humorist would have thought of this termination of "The Recent Carnival of Crime in Connecticut":

> In conclusion, I wish to state, by way of advertisement, that medical colleges desiring assorted traps for scientific purposes, either by the gross, by cord measurement, or per ton, will do well to examine the lot in my cellar before purchasing elsewhere, as these were all selected and prepared by myself, and can be had at a low rate, because I wish to clear out my stock and get ready for the spring trade;

but there is a wildness about it entirely individual. His "Legend of Sagenfeld," again, is a pleasant bit of humor, no more American than it is German, which might have been written by Hans Andersen, except that

*Reprinted from *Nation*, 35 (August 10, 1882), 119.

Andersen would perhaps not have made the sweepingly libellous statement with which, after explaining how the ass came to be the sacred
animal of the kingdom, he adds: "Such is the legend. This explains why
the mouldering image of the ass adorns all these old crumbling walls and
arches; and it explains why, during many centuries, an ass was always the
chief minister in that royal cabinet, just as is still the case in most cabinets
to this day; and it also explains why, in that little kingdom, during many
centuries, all great poems, all great speeches, all public solemnities, and
all royal proclamations always began with these stirring words:
'Wah . . . he!—wah . . . he!—wah-he!—wah-he—wah-he!' "

Mark Twain

W. D. Howells*

In one form or other, Mr. Samuel L. Clemens has told the story of his life in his books, and in sketching his career I shall have to recur to the leading facts rather than to offer fresh information. He was remotely of Virginian origin and more remotely of good English stock; the name was well-known before his time in the South, where a senator, a congressman and other dignitaries had worn it; but his branch of the family fled from the destitution of those vast landed possessions in Tennessee, celebrated in "The Gilded Age," and went very poor to Missouri. Mr. Clemens was born on the 30th of November, 1835, at Florida in the latter State, but his father removed shortly afterward to Hannibal, a small town on the Mississippi, where most of the humorist's boyhood was spent. Hannibal as a name is hopelessly confused and ineffective; but if we can know nothing of Mr. Clemens from Hannibal, we can know much of Hannibal from Mr. Clemens, who, in fact, has studied a loafing, out-at-elbows, down-at-the-heels, slave-holding, Mississippi river town of thirty years ago, with such strong reality in his boy's romance of "Tom Sawyer," that we need inquire nothing further concerning the type. The original perhaps no longer exists anywhere; certainly not in Hannibal, which has grown into a flourishing little city since Mr. Clemens sketched it. In his time, the two embattled forces of civilization and barbarism were encamped at Hannibal, as they are at all times and everywhere; the morality of the place was the morality of a slave-holding community: fierce, arrogant, one-sided—this virtue for white, and that for black folks; and the religion was Calvinism in various phases, with its predestinate aristocracy of saints and its rabble of hopeless sinners. Doubtless, young Clemens escaped neither of the opposing influences wholly. His people like the rest were slave-holders; but his father, like so many other slave-holders, abhorred slavery—silently, as he must in such a time and place. If the boy's sense of justice suffered anything of that perversion which so curiously and pitiably maimed the reason of the whole South, it does not appear in his books, where there is not an ungenerous line, but always, on the contrary, a burning resentment of all manner of cruelty and wrong.

*Reprinted from *Century Magazine*, 24 (September, 1882), 780–83.

The father, an austere and singularly upright man, died bankrupt when Clemens was twelve years old, and the boy had thereafter to make what scramble he could for an education. He got very little learning in school, and like so many other Americans in whom the literary impulse is native, he turned to the local printing-office for some of the advantages from which he was otherwise cut off. Certain records of the three years spent in the Hannibal "Courier" office are to be found in Mark Twain's book of sketches; but I believe there is yet no history anywhere of the *wanderjahre*, in which he followed the life of a jour-printer, from town to town, and from city to city, penetrating even so far into the vague and fabled East as Philadelphia and New York.

He returned to his own country—his *patria*—sated, if not satisfied, with travel, and at seventeen he resolved to "learn the river" from St. Louis to New Orleans as a steam-boat pilot. Of this period of his life he has given a full account in the delightful series of papers, "Piloting on the Mississippi," which he printed seven years ago in the "Atlantic Monthly." The growth of the railroads and the outbreak of the Civil War put an end to profitable piloting, and at twenty-four he was again open to a vocation. He listened for a moment to the loudly calling drum of that time, and he was actually in camp for three weeks on the rebel side; but the unorganized force to which he belonged was disbanded, and he finally did not "go with his section" either in sentiment or in fact. His brother having been appointed Lieutenant-Governor of Nevada Territory, Mr. Clemens went out with him as his private secretary; but he soon resigned his office and withdrew to the mines. He failed as a miner, in the ordinary sense; but the life of the mining-camp yielded him the wealth that the pockets of the mountains denied; he had the Midas-touch, without knowing it, and all these grotesque experiences have since turned into gold under his hand. After his failure as a miner had become evident even to himself, he was glad to take the place of local editor on the Virginia City "Enterprise," a newspaper for which he had amused himself in writing from time to time. He had written for the newspapers before this; few Americans escape that fate; and as an apprentice in the Hannibal "Courier" office his humor had embroiled some of the leading citizens, and impaired the fortunes of that journal by the alienation of several delinquent subscribers.

But it was in the "Enterprise" that he first used his pseudonym of "Mark Twain," which he borrowed from the vernacular of the river, where the man heaving the lead calls out "Mark twain!" instead of "Mark two!" In 1864, he accepted, on the San Francisco "Morning Call," the same sort of place which he had held on the "Enterprise," and he soon made his *nom de guerre* familiar "on that coast"; he not only wrote "local items" in the "Call," but he printed humorous sketches in various periodicals, and, two years later, he was sent to the Sandwich Islands as correspondent of a Sacramento paper.

When he came back he "entered the lecture-field," as it used to be phrased. Of these facts there is, as all English-speaking readers know, full record in "Roughing It," though I think Mr. Clemens has not mentioned there his association with that extraordinary group of wits and poets, of whom Mr. Bret Harte, Mr. Charles Warren Stoddard, Mr. Charles H. Webb, Mr. Prentice Mulford, were, with himself, the most conspicuous. These ingenious young men, with the fatuity of gifted people, had established a literary newspaper in San Francisco, and they brilliantly cooperated to its early extinction.

In 1867, Mr. Clemens made in the *Quaker City* the excursion to Europe and the East which he has commemorated in "The Innocents Abroad." Shortly after his return he married, and placed himself at Buffalo, where he bought an interest in one of the city newspapers; later he came to Hartford, where he has since remained, except for the two years spent in a second visit to Europe. The incidents of this visit he has characteristically used in "A Tramp Abroad"; and in fact, I believe the only book of Mr. Clemens's which is not largely autobiographical, is "The Prince and the Pauper": the scene being laid in England, in the early part of the sixteenth century, the difficulties presented to a nineteenth century autobiographer were insurmountable.

The habit of putting his own life, not merely in its results but in its processes, into his books, is only one phase of the frankness of Mr. Clemens's humorous attitude. The transparent disguise of the pseudonym once granted him, he asks the reader to grant him nothing else. In this, he differs wholly from most other American humorists, who have all found some sort of dramatization of their personality desirable if not necessary. Charles F. Browne, "delicious" as he was when he dealt with us directly, preferred the disguise of "Artemus Ward" the showman; Mr. Locke likes to figure as "Petroleum V. Nasby," the cross-roads politician; Mr. Shaw chooses to masquerade as the saturnine philosopher "Josh Billings"; and each of these humorists appeals to the grotesqueness of misspelling to help out his fun. It was for Mr. Clemens to reconcile the public to humor which contented itself with the established absurdities of English orthography; and I am inclined to attribute to the example of his immense success, the humane spirit which characterized our recent popular humor. There is still sufficient flippancy and brutality in it; but there is no longer the stupid and monkeyish cruelty of motive and intention which once disgraced and insulted us. Except the political humorists, like Mr. Lowell—if there were any like him—the American humorists formerly chose the wrong in public matters; they were on the side of slavery, of drunkenness, and of irreligion; the friends of civilization were their prey; their spirit was thoroughly vulgar and base. Before "John Phoenix," there was scarcely any American humorist—not of the distinctly literary sort—with whom one could smile and keep one's self-respect. The great Artemus himself was not guiltless; but the most popular humorist who ever lived has not to accuse himself, so far as I can remember, of having written anything to make one morally ashamed of liking him. One can readily make one's strictures: there is often more than a suggestion of forcing in his humor; sometimes it tends to horseplay; sometimes the extravagance overleaps itself, and falls flat on the other side; but I cannot remember that in Mr. Clemens's books I have ever been asked to join him in laughing at any good or really fine thing. But I do not mean to leave him with this negative praise; I mean to say of him that as Shakspere, according to Mr. Lowell's saying, was the first to make poetry all poetical, Mark Twain was the first to make humor all humorous. He has not only added more in bulk to the style of harmless pleasures than any other humorist; but more in the spirit that is easily and wholly enjoyable. There is nothing lost in literary attitude, in labored dictionary funning, in affected quaintness, in dreary dramatization, in artificial "dialect"; Mark Twain's humor is as simple in form and as direct as the statesmanship of Lincoln or the generalship of Grant.

When I think how purely and wholly American it is, I am a little puzzled at its universal acceptance. We are doubtless the most thoroughly homogeneous people that ever existed as a great nation. There is such a parity in the experiences of Americans that Mark Twain or Artemus Ward appeals as unerringly to the consciousness of our fifty millions as Goldoni appealed to that of his hundred thousand Venetians. In one phrase, we have somehow all "been there"; in fact, generally, and in sympathy almost certainly, we have been there. In another generation or two, perhaps, it will be wholly different; but as yet the average American is the man who has risen; he has known poverty, and privation, and low conditions; he has very often known squalor; and now, in his prosperity, he regards the past with a sort of large, pitying amusement; he is not the least ashamed of it; he does not feel that it characterizes him any more than the future does. Our humor springs from this multiform American experience of life, and securely addresses itself—in reminiscence, in phrase, in its whole material—to the intelligence bred of like experience. It is not of a class for a class; it does not employ itself with the absurdities of a tailor as a tailor; its conventions, if it has any, are all new, and of American make. When it mentions hash we smile because we have each somehow known the cheap boarding-house or restaurant; when it alludes to putting up stoves in the fall, each of us feels the grime and rust of the pipes on his hands; the introduction of the lightning-rod man, or the book-agent, establishes our brotherhood with the humorist at once. But how is it with the vast English-speaking world outside of these States, to which hash, and stove-pipes, and lightning-rod men and book-agents are as strange as lords and ladies, dungeon-keeps and battlements are to us? Why, in fine, should an English chief-justice keep Mark Twain's books always at hand? Why should Darwin have gone to them for rest and refreshment at midnight when spent with scientific research?

I suppose that Mark Twain transcends all other American humorists in the universal qualities. He deals very little with the pathetic, which he nevertheless knows very well how to manage, as he has shown, notably in the true story of the old slave-mother; but there is a poetic lift in his work, even when he permits you to recognize it only as something satirized. There is always the touch of nature, the presence of a sincere and frank manliness in what he says, the companionship of a spirit which is at once delightfully open and deliciously shrewd. Elsewhere I have tried to persuade the reader that his humor is at its best the foamy break of the strong tide of earnestness in him. But it would be limiting him unjustly to describe him as a satirist; and it is hardly practicable to establish him in people's minds as a moralist; he has made them laugh too long; they will not believe him serious; they think some joke is always intended. This is the penalty, as Dr. Holmes has pointed out, of making one's first success as a humorist. There was a paper of Mark Twain's printed in the "Atlantic Monthly" some years ago and called, "The Facts concerning the late Carnival of Crime in Connecticut," which ought to have won popular recognition of the ethical intelligence which underlines his humor. It was, of course, funny; but under the fun it was an impassioned study of the human conscience. Hawthorne or Bunyan might have been proud to imagine that powerful allegory which had a grotesque force far beyond either of them. It had been read before a literary club in Hartford; a reverend gentleman had offered the author his pulpit for the next Sunday if he would give it as a homily there. Yet it quite failed of the response I had hoped for it, and I shall not insist here upon Mark Twain as a moralist; though I warn the reader that if he leaves out of the account an indignant sense of right and wrong, a scorn of all affection and pretense, an ardent hate of meanness and injustice, he will come indefinitely short of knowing Mark Twain.

His powers as a story-teller were evident in hundreds of brief sketches before he proved them in "Tom Sawyer" and "The Prince and the Pauper." Both of these books, aside from the strength of characterization, are fascinating as mere narratives, and I can think of no writer living who has in higher degree the art of interesting his reader from the first word. This is a far rarer gift than we imagine, and I shall not call it a subordinate charm in Mark Twain's books, rich as they otherwise are. I have already had my say about "Tom Sawyer," whose only fault is an excess of reality in portraying the character and conditions of south-western boyhood as it was forty years ago, and which is full of that poetic sympathy with nature and human nature which I always find in Mark Twain. "The Prince and the Pauper" has particularly interested me for the same qualities which, in a study of the past, we call romantic, but which alone can realize the past for us. Occasionally the archaic diction gives way and lets us down hard upon the American parlance of the nineteenth century; but mainly the illusion is admirably sustained, and the tale is to be valued not only in itself, but as an earnest of what Mr. Clemens might do in fiction when he has fairly done with autobiography in its various forms. His invention is of the good old sort, like De Foe's more than that of any other English writer, and like that of the Spanish picturesque novelists, Mendoza and the rest; it flows easily from incident to incident, and does not deepen into situation. In the romance it operates as lightly and unfatiguingly as his memory in the realistic story.

His books abound in passages of dramatic characterization, and he is, as the reader knows, the author of the most successful American play. I believe Mr. Clemens has never claimed the reconstruction of Colonel Sellers for the stage; but he nevertheless made the play, for whatever is good in it came bodily from his share of the novel of "The Gilded Age." It is a play which succeeds by virtue of the main personage, and this personage, from first to last, is quite outside of the dramatic action, which sometimes serves, and sometimes does not serve the purpose of presenting Colonel Sellers. Where the drama fails, Sellers rises superior and takes the floor; and we forget the rest. Mr. Raymond conceived the character wonderfully well, and he plays it with an art that ranks him to that extent with the great actors; but he has in nowise "created" it. If any one "created" Colonel Sellers, it was Mark Twain, as the curious reader may see on turning again to the novel; but I suspect that Colonel Sellers was never created, except as other men are; that he was found somewhere and transferred, living, to the book.

I prefer to speak of Mr. Clemens's artistic qualities because it is to these that his humor will owe its perpetuity. All fashions change, and nothing more wholly and quickly than the fashion of fun; as any one may see by turning back to what amused people in the last generation; that stuff is terrible. As Europe becomes more and more the playground of Americans, and every scene and association becomes insipidly familiar, the jokes about the old masters and the legends will no longer be droll to us. Neither shall we care for the huge California mirth, when the surprise of the picturesquely mixed civilization and barbarism of the Pacific coast has quite died away; and Mark Twain would pass with the conditions that have made him intelligible, if he were not an artist of uncommon power as well as a humorist. He portrays and interprets real types, not only with exquisite appreciation and sympathy, but with a force and truth of drawing that makes them permanent. Artemus Ward was very funny, that can never be denied; but it must be owned that the figure of the literary showman is as wholly factitious as his spelling; the conception is one that has to be constantly humored by the reader. But the innumerable characters sketched by Mark Twain are actualities, however caricatured,—and, usually, they are not so very much caricatured. He has brought back the expression of Western humor to sympathy with the same orthography of John Phoenix; but Mark Twain is vastly more original in form. Derby was weighed upon by literary tradition; he was "academic" at times, but Mr. Clemens is never "academic." There is no drawing from casts; in his work evidently the life has everywhere been studied: and it is his apparent unconsciousness of any other way of saying a thing except the natural way that makes his books so restful and refreshing. Our little nervous literary sensibilities may suffer from his extravagance, or from other traits of his manner, but we have not to beat our breasts at the dread apparition of Dickens's or Thackeray's hand in his page. He is far too honest and sincere a soul for that; and where he is obliged to force a piece of humor to its climax—as sometimes happens—he does not call in his neighbors to help; he does it himself, and is probably sorry that he had to do it.

I suppose that even in so slight and informal a study as this, something like an "analysis" of our author's humor is expected. But I much prefer not to make it. I have observed that analyses of humor are apt to leave one rather serious, and to result in an entire volatilization of the humor. If the prevailing spirit of Mark Twain's humor is not a sort of good-natured self-satire, in which the reader may see his own absurdities reflected, I scarcely should be able to determine it.

A Day with Mark Twain

John Henton Carter*

The boat that was to convey Mr. S. L. Clemens—Mark Twain—
northward, was to leave St. Louis at four o'clock in the afternoon. It was
now ten in the morning, and he proposed the interval be spent in driving
about the city, and calling on some old time acquaintances. He had
already arranged his toilet, and added an extra overcoat to meet the
demands of a chilly atmosphere, when, running his hand over his face, he
suggested the propriety of visiting a barber shop before entering upon the
day's programme. During the tonsorial performance we carried on a
rambling conversation about his trip south, which Mark declared had
proved a dismal failure, resulting in nothing but some social interchanges.

"I expected," he went on, "to travel incog. and return east loaded to
the guards with solid information about the late flood, and other matters
of interest concerning the people of the Mississippi river and the valley,
but I was discovered the first day I arrived here from the east, and again
when I took passage on the boat for New Orleans, and undertook to interview the boatmen. This confounded speech of mine betrayed me to the
enemy; and just when the pilot on watch began to 'scape out' in the most
beautiful fashion. No, it's all up. I'd have given world to have been permitted to pass unrecognized, and stand around and listen to those matchless lies by the hour. But I'm in the hands of Providence, and I suppose
Providence does not propose to suffer my morals to be corrupted in
that way."

As we emerged from the barber shop, Mark became impressed with
the idea that he needed a pair of suspenders, and we at once sought a furnishing establishment for the purpose of making the necessary purchase.
When a pair had been selected he divested himself of his three coats, and
then removing his vest revealed still another wrap, which he at once
began to describe as a suspender of his own invention, and which he said
was not yet fully perfected in all the intricate minor details, but it soon
would be. There was an ingredient yet lacking which had been for-

*Reprinted from a typescript made by Walter Blair from *Rollingpin's Humorous Illustrated
Annual* (New York: J. H. Carter, 1883); perhaps this interview appeared first in *St. Louis
Times* in May, 1882.

mulated and when supplied would make the suspender come into general use by every sensible man in the civilized and barbarous world.

"That suspender," said Mark, holding it up and viewing it admiringly, "will yet hand my name down to posterity as a benefactor of my race. I'm the first man that ever gave his genius to the creation of a practical article of this kind,—a garment calculated to fill all the requirements of physical health and esthetical culture. All the rest were idiots. I said when I patented my scrap-book, which cost me years of hard study and sleepless nights, that I would confer another blessing on mankind before I got under my monument, and I will. These buttonholes you notice have torn out, causing the pants to drop down and rest upon the hips. This objection is to be overcome by introducing a rubber band, which will yield to the pressure resulting from the various motions of the body, when the suspender will be ready to go before the country on its merits."

The shop keeper suggested that the design was very simple, and reminded him of a primitive garment worn by small children, and called in nursery parlance a "waist."

"The design differs radically," said Mark, warming. "Don't you see here that the shoulder straps are only three inches wide, whereas they reach from the shoulder to the base of the neck in the child's dress. This is one of the points on which I rest my claim for a patent." Here Mark turned a patronizing look upon the vender, folded the garment, placed it in a pocket of one of his layers of overcoats, when we left the store.

By-and-by we called a carriage, and giving the driver his directions, settled into our seats. During the drive the conversation ran on books, authors, and literary topics generally. I suggested that his last book, "The Prince and the Pauper," was his best, and would outlive any of the others that he had written, notwithstanding some of the critics had been rather severe on it as a work of art. Any minor errors or anachronisms that might have unconsciously slipped into the first edition, I urged could readily be eliminated or corrected in a second.

"Not a word will I ever change," was the prompt response. "I never undertake a piece of work until I have thoroughly prepared myself for the task, and when it issues from the press, it is done as well as I can do it, and that's the end of the matter."

We then talked of the "Innocents Abroad," and "The Tramp Abroad," I maintaining that the latter was equally as good a book as the former, though coming after it, could never hope to be so popular.

"A much better book," said Mr. Clemens. "Twelve years ago I could not have written such a book from the same material."

The conversation next turned upon humor generally, and the fatal mistake men of real ability have often made by permitting themselves to express their thoughts in this vein. Oliver Wendell Holmes, I urged, came near swamping a brilliant career by unconsciously falling into this error, and it required years of toil before he could emerge from the unpleasant predicament in which his youthful folly and enthusiasm had placed him; and it was not until the appearance of that matchless work, "The Autocrat of the Breakfast Table," that his true place in literature was acknowledged. Lowell's "Bigelow Papers" stamped him as a man of genius, and the most original of American humorists; but fun and satire, though wielded by a master hand would never have brought him sufficient standing to have sent him as our minister to the courts of Spain or Great Britain. A quarter of a century had to elapse, and the interim filled with solid work and a solemn repentance, before honors such as these could be aspired to. Tom Corwin, one of the most erudite of lawyers, whose wit was as brilliant as his scholarship was profound, and his patriotism undoubted, fell into a similar error, and placed forever a barrier against his advancement to the highest position in the gift of the American people when he condescended to instruct and amuse by the employment of the lighter vein. And so we might run over the long list of brilliant men who have suffered from a like cause. And Mark Twain cannot hope to be made an exception to the general rule. He recognizes the inevitable, and bows to it with the resignation of the true philosopher. With all his vast store of common sense and practical capability, he is expected ever to appear in his cap and bells and do the risible.

Such a fame as that which he enjoys it would seem should be sufficient to gratify the ambition of any reasonable person, but Twain is too sensible a man not to realize that humor, of all things, is the most ephermeral, and that which will convulse the world today, will appear flat and insipid enough tomorrow.

A quarter of a century ago, Doestick's fame was world-wide, and his writings in everybody's mouth; and yet who reads Doestick now. To take up one of his books one wonders why anybody ever did read him. In all his writing there is not to be found a single piece of word painting that cried for recognition and a permanent place in the book stalls. But, Mark Twain is a man of real parts, and much that he has done will live. He is endowed with strong common sense, steadiness of purpose, judgment and insight into human nature, which, if cast in other fields than that which he adopted, would have fitted him for the broader and higher walks of life. No one can read him for an hour without being convinced that while he is a humorist of the first order, that he is something more. There is a breadth and depth of philosophy about his most mirth-provoking pictures, which might be profitably employed in directing the practical every-day affairs of life.

In personal appearance S. L. Clemens is of medium stature, standing rather wide on his legs, and moving about with a careless, swaggering gait. His head is large and well-formed, and may be termed of the massive order of architecture, being well-poised, and having a firm-set chin, which indicates steadiness of purpose and plenty of stay power. The nose is slightly aquiline, thin and pointed at the extreme. The face is smoothly shaven, with the exception of a sandy mustache. Hair slightly gray. He speaks with a drawl and in measured accents, his ideas at times seeming to run into confusion, when all at once his eyes flash with light, when his mind rallies, and he carries his point with vigor.

As an illustration of the peculiar drift which Twain's mind takes when dealing with ordinary subjects, I may cite an incident that occurred on the morning we first met. I had just remarked that the weather was very disagreeable, in fact it was wretched; to which he replied:

"Yes, the weather is bad, and if I were dealing in weather it is not the brand that I'd put up in cans for future use. No, it is the kind of weather I'd throw on the market and let it go for what it would fetch, and if it wouldn't sell for anything I would hunt up some life-long enemy and present it to him. Failing in this, as a last resort I should probably take it out on the big bridge, dump it into the Mississippi and start it to Europe via the jetties. I'd unload it someway, and that quickly, too."

On the trip south on the steamer Gold Dust, Mark went up into the pilot house and entered into conversation with the pilot, for the purpose, as he himself expressed it, of enjoying some good, old-fashioned, unadulterated Mississippi river lying. The pilot answered all interrogatories with an ease which proved his fertility of resources, while Mark's private stenographer proceeded to take down every word for future use. Questions about the late floods, the changes of the river, and all such matters, were put and satisfactorily answered. At length the conversation turned to piloting, when Mark ventured to inquire of the man at the wheel if he knew Sam Clemens, who at one time was reported to be a pilot. "What! Mark Twain?" said the other. "Yes, that's what they call him," was the rejoinder. "Well I should say I did! Sam left here 'bout twenty years ago, an' has been writin' books ever since. He's better at that'n he was steerin', for he wasn't much of a pilot. He'd just as like as not go to sleep on watch and run the boat into the bank, head on, if you didn't keep a watch on him. If there was a snag in the river he'd go miles out of his way to get a shack at it, and was never happy unless he was bouncin' somethin'. Why, you'd think he was gettin' the biggest kind of money from the government to clear the river of snags if you'd seed how he hustled 'em out of the way." "Do you remember his personal appearance?" "Who? Sam Clemens? Yes, I should say so." "What was it?" "Well, sir, to tell you the truth, to look at Sam Clemens, he wasn't worth sweepin' up!"

Mark Twain

C.*

The renowned archaeologist, poet and astronomer, whose portrait appears above, is a lineal descendant of the celebrated Twain who were made one flesh. He was born on Plymouth Rock, April 1st, 1728, on a remarkably cold morning, and the administratrix of the camphor and red-flannel department afterward stated that he was the most remarkable baby she had ever seen. At the early age of seven, Mark—for so he was cruelly christened—was already addicted to science, and his discovery, made one year later, that a spring clothes-pin artistically applied to the continuation of a cat would create in that somnolent animal a desire for vigorous foreign travel, is still used by the aborigines of Connecticut and Massachusetts. When he was 19, Mark went through college. He entered the front door, turpentined the rector's favorite cat, and graduated the same evening over the fence. He then started for California, Milwaukee and other remote confines of the earth, and began those remarkable series of truthful anecdotes for which he is now so justly famed. As an archaeologist, however, he has won most renown, and his collection of Pompeiian, Sanscrit, Egyptian and early Greek jokes, now in possession of Osgood & Co., of Boston, is considered the most complete in the world. Some envious critics have claimed that most of these were painfully carved by Mark himself, and the balance composed of heterogeneous and unrelated parts, but there seems to be no reasonable doubt that they are all genuine antiques.

Personally, Mr. Twain is a remarkably well preserved man. He is short, florid and very corpulent, laughs incessantly, and is a rapid and brilliant speaker. His essay on "Draw-Poker in American politics" is considered to be a masterly treatise on political economy, while his poem entitled, "The Frog Bowed Down by Weight of Shot" will hold its place as one of the most pathetic in the language.

---

*Reprinted from *Life*, 1 (March 22, 1883), 142. C. perhaps stood for Henry Guy Carleton, who was for a while in 1883 the literary editor of *Life*. This piece ran beneath a bizarre cartoon of Twain dressed in a lounging robe and holding a skull.

Mark Twain as Lecturer/How He Feels When He Gets on the Stage before an Audience

Anonymous*

Mark Twain, in a dress coat, patent-leather slippers and white tie, received a reporter of *The World* yesterday afternoon in the cosy waiting-room off the stage at Chickering Hall. Mr. George W. Cable was giving his recital of Creole life, and the sound of his baritone voice as he sang the songs of the sunny South floated into the room where the humorist was pacing up and down, gathering vital force, as he said, for his address, which was to follow that of Mr. Cable. Mark Twain's blond mustache was exquisitely curled, his chestnut-brown hair was done up in ringlets in the highest style of the tonsorial art, there was a slightly hectic flush on his cheeks and his eyes sparkled with a sort of feverish fire. Yet he spoke with his habitual drawl.

"Ah, you are cruel," he said, with an air of utter sadness, "to attempt to interview a man just at the moment when he needs to feel good. You've got to feel good, you know in order to make the audience feel the same way, but to try to be funny after you've been interviewed"—. The thought seemed to overpower him.

"I did not think it was such a physical strain to deliver a humorous lecture."

"Ah, you have never attempted it; you don't know. On a day like this, when we give two performances, I feel like all burnt out after the first performance. As soon as I get back to the hotel I go to bed. I must get some sleep somehow. If I don't I will not be able to go through with the evening performance the way I want to. It's the same thing when you're travelling. The audiences, intelligent, newspaper-reading audiences, are responsive enough. They quickly catch the point you are trying to make; oftentimes they anticipate it. Then you are put on your mettle to give a sudden turn to the story so as to bring out a new and unexpected point. If these things don't happen, don't blame the audience; it is yourself who is at fault. The travelling has exhausted you, as I said before; you're not feeling good."

"All this you can judge of by the effect you produce on the audience?"

*Reprinted from *New York World*, November 20, 1884, p. 5.

"Oh, yes. If you hear a rustle here or there or see a particularly stolid face you can tell that there is something wrong with yourself. The effect, of course, is not general. Heaven forbid! You would then have to stop right off. Audiences have their peculiarities, you know. It is a great inspiration to find a particular individual fairly respond to you as if you were in telegraphic communication with him. You are tempted to address yourself solely to him. I've tried that experiment. Sometimes it is dangerous. Laughter is very infectious, and when you see a man give one big guffaw you begin to laugh with him in spite of yourself. Now, it will not do for the lecturer to laugh. His is a grave and serious business however it might strike the audience. His demeanor should be grave and serious. He should not even smile."

"You have had ample opportunity to average your audiences on their receptive faculties for fun?"

"Audiences are much the same everywhere. I have been delighted with all before whom I have had the honor of appearing. In Boston, where Mr. Cable and I appeared before coming here, the audiences were delighted with our efforts to please them. You should have witnessed the enthusiasm last evening. Oh, I have nothing to complain of my audiences—perhaps they cannot say the same of me. Our entertainment lasts one hour and three-quarters. The fact that Mr. Cable and I alternate makes us able to extend it for that length. Were I lecturing alone one hour and five minutes is as much as I would dare to impose on the audience. The strain on them, all in a humorous direction, would be too much. But now Mr. Cable gently soothes them; then I excite them to laughter, or try to at least; then Mr. Cable has his turn again, and so the change is very healthful and beneficial."

"Your tour will be an extended one?"

"Our agent has booked us to the end of January, and the tour may extend into February. I should like to go to California, if I can manage it. You know this is my farewell appearance. I so intimated to the audience last evening. I told them that I had not practically appeared on the platform for nine years, and that when this tour was over I would not appear again—at least, say, not for nine years. It will do me good—it will do my hearers good. Yet, I've known people to give farewell performances for fifty years in succession. Now, that I would call stretching a thing a little too far. I like to feel good. To sleep after giving a performance is one way; to go into an assemblage of hail fellows, well met, when things are booming is another way. I expected to have such a time at the Press-Club dinner to-morrow evening. I thought we would give a performance in Brooklyn, and that after it was over I would go to the dinner when things had gotten to be rather lively. Unfortunately, however, there's been a change in the programme. We will be at Newburg, and it will be impossible for me to be at the dinner. I'm ever so sorry. I was going to answer the kind invitation sent me by the secretary of the club, but when I'm on a tour I can't write letters. My wife answers all she's able to. The rest—" A burst of applause at this juncture announced the conclusion of Mr. Cable's recital, and that the time had come for Mark Twain to appear on the stage. As the reporter passed out he heard an outburst of laughter. The humorist had made a point.

Such Is Mark Twain

[Frank George Carpenter]*

Mark Twain has a big head stuck on by a long neck to a pair of round shoulders. Recently he came on to the stage at Washington as though he were half asleep, and he looked to me as though nature in putting him together had, somehow, got the joints mixed. He has a big face, a nose large enough to represent any kind of genius, and eyes large, black and sleepy. He has a thick, bushy mane of hair which is now iron gray, and a bushy mustache which over hangs his characteristic mouth. As he stood on the stage he reminded me much of a mammoth interrogation point, and as he drawled out his words with scarcely a gesture his voice made me think of a little buzz-saw slowly grinding inside a corpse. He did not laugh while he uttered his funniest jokes, and when the audience roared he merely stroked his chin or pulled his mustache.

Still he could not help being satisfied, and I do not doubt the contrast of his first day in Washington, when he came here years ago and had hard work making enough money to pay his board bills, came forcibly before him. Though it is not generally known, Mark Twain was once a Washington correspondent. He came here from the west with Senator Stuart, and for a time wrote letters to the Alta Californian and New York Tribune. He used to drink a good deal in those days, and was hardly considered a reputable character. It was shortly before this that he made a trip from which he wrote "Innocents Abroad," and this book he wrote here from the notes he took during his tour. The book made him both famous and wealthy. His manuscript he first sent to several prominent publishers, but they all rejected it, and he was about giving up in despair when a Hartford company took hold of it. The result was they made $75,000 off the book and sold more than two hundred thousand copies of it. It was after this that Mark Twain tried editing the Buffalo Express. A man who worked on the paper at the same time told me today that this venture was not a success. He loafed around the office, guying the office boy, and telling jokes and stories rather than writing, and the only fruit of

*Reprinted from *Rochester* (New York) *Union Advertiser*, December 8, 1884, p. 1; based on a syndicated letter (*Cleveland Leader*, November 30, 1884, p. 9) from Washington, D.C., by "Carp."

69

his Buffalo experience was his marriage, which like "Innocents Abroad," turned out well. His wife brought a pot of gold into the family, and when he got to Elmira he found that his father-in-law had made him the present of a brown stone front, and thrown in a coachman with a bug on his hat. Twain did not remain in Elmira, however, but went to Hartford and began to write "Roughing It." This was also successful and established his fame.

Mark Twain probably makes as much out of his books as any other writer in the country. He has his Hartford firm publish his books for him and he so arranges it that he gets a royalty on those printed in Europe. He is better known in foreign lands than any other American writer, and he is an international character. Many of his scenes are taken from real life and his descriptions of travel are in the main true. He is a hard worker, and while at Hartford he writes in his billiard room in the attic. Like Trollope, he believes that there is nothing like a piece of shoemaker's wax on the seat of one's chair to turn out good literary work, and, like Blaine, he has a fixed amount of writing for each day's duty. He rewrites many of his chapters, and some of them have been scratched out and interlined again and again. Mr. Clemens—everyone knows Mark Twain's name is Clemens—will be forty-nine years old on the 30th of this month. He is a Missouri man by birth, and has taken care of himself ever since he was fifteen. He has been a practical printer, a steamboat pilot, a private secretary, a miner, a reporter, a lecturer and a bookmaker.

Talk with Twain . . . His Comments on Authors, Magazines and General Literature

Anonymous*

Mark Twain is in town. He did not come here to inspect our manufactories, nor on a pleasure trip. He is to lecture with Cable, the novelist, to-night at the Cumberland Church, on Sixth avenue. He was sitting in an easy chair in his room, having his hair cut, when the writer called on him to-day.

"Take off your overcoat and sit down," said he with the air of a man who in his time has overcome many impediments to happiness by courtesy and perseverance.

"Thank you, but I have not time. I merely called to have a five minutes' talk about cosmos."

"Oh indeed!" he retorted gravely. "Well, I am sorry I cannot oblige you but that is a subject I never speak of except at home after a week's preparation. I always treat light subjects in that way; however, sit down and let us talk. You would not care for a discourse on American art, would you, in place of cosmos?"

"Not just at this time."

"Well, I thought you might. I don't know anything about the subject, but of course that would enable me to be more graphic and entertaining. I met a drummer on a train a short time ago who asked me for my opinion on that matter. I knew he was a humbug in asking it, but I was also a humbug, for I proceeded to tell him what I did not know, but what I pretended to know."

"Suppose you tell me something of what you think about recent American magazine literature?"

"I have not an opinion which would be worth having on that subject. It seems to me, however, that there has been a wonderful advance of late years in the general tone of the magazines. There has been no new 'Autocrat of the Breakfast Table,' to be sure, but what do you expect? You do not want more than one 'autocrat' in a century—you cannot hope for more than one. Such men as Holmes, Hawthorne, Longfellow, Fields, and others of that school, upheld the literary reputation of two generations, and made the *Atlantic* so brilliant. Most of these men have gone,

*Reprinted from *Pittsburgh Chronicle Telegraph*, December 29, 1884, p. 1

71

but the general work in magazines is far superior to that of ten years ago. The trouble is that the two or three magazines which are a good market for a writer, and which can aid him in his work for fame, are over-crowded. The *Century* has perhaps $100,000 worth of accepted articles in its vault which may not appear for years. They are pushed aside by articles on timely topics which cannot be delayed. There are other magazines, it is true, but when you send them an article you send a burial permit with it, for you know that it will be entombed even if it is printed. These combinations of newspapers which print stories and sketches once a week will, it seems to me, give rising and capable writers the field they desire as well as the market. Charles Dudley Warner told me of one of these syndicates which is in charge of Thorndyke Rice, of the *North American Review*. He has fifteen of the leading papers of the country which pay liberally for a page of matter either for their Sunday issues or for another day they may select. The idea is, I believe, to give at least one sketch or story by some very well known writer in each issue, and give other articles on the same page by clever people not so well known. This will bring into Mr. Rice's hands about $10,000 a month to pay his corps of writers. He can pay them just as good, if not better prices than any of the magazines, and besides he can handle matters of passing interest before the magazines get at them. Mr. Rice has written to me and has offered me handsome terms for articles. He seems to think I am a magazine writer, but I really am not."

"He has asked Mr. Henry Irving to write for him also."

"Has he? Well, the idea is to have at his command the men who are eminent in all the branches of art, literature, drama, the sciences and professions. There are few good writers of short stories now, and there have never been very many. Such men as Poe and Aldrich stand out so that you can at once recall them. I do not believe in the decrying of the books of the day, which is so common. I admit I am not a careful reader of novels. I read portions of them, but do not read them through with the care some of them deserve. Much of my opinion is based upon what I hear from men and women of sound judgment whom I know intimately and whom I can rely upon. Take Hawthorne as an example of my peculiar literary bent of thought. It has become quite the custom to speak of him as the greatest of all American romanticists. I read him now and then for his style, the exquisite manner in which he writes, but I do not care for his stories, for I do not think that they are as great as many others by American writers. Howells' newspaper man who is brought before the public a second time in 'Silas Lapham.' He is a wonderful creation, a photograph of many such men do exist, not a cheerful, nice sort of man to sit at a communion table perhaps, but still a strong, living man. I was in Europe when Henry James' 'Daisy Miller' reached there. I chanced to be where there were a great many American ladies, and I must confess I never heard a literary production so roundly denounced as was 'Daisy

Miller.' It was called an absurd exaggeration, a gross libel on the American girl, and all sorts of things. Nothing was too bad to say of it. And yet within a few hours I heard these same ladies allude to young American girls as 'perfect Daisy Millers,' and saw them point out to each other girls who just fitted into the description of that irrepressible young lady. The work has been cavilled at and found fault with, but it is true, and just and close to the truth in spite of all that. The blemishes complained of in recent American books are to be found just as readily in English works or those in other countries. The trouble with many authors of books as well as of plays, is that they let their work run too long. The interest dies before the story ends. That is the only fault to be found, for instance, with such an admirable book as 'Lorna Doone.' I read two-thirds of it with keen relish and interest and then stopped. I felt that there was a disposition to—using a New England phrase—'run emptyings' at the close. I have re-read the first of the book many times, but never have gone through it, yet I suppose this book now has as many people who read it over again annually, as has 'Jane Eyre,' which in many households finds a place between the Bible and the prayer book. The fault, perhaps lies in my own taste, which has a strong bent to history and biography."

Mr. Cable made his appearance there for the third or fourth time, and Mr. Clemens, who by this time had come from the barber's hands, "a very proper man, indeed," wished his visitor good morning.

Mark Twain's Head Analyzed

Edgar C. Beall*

Wit and humor are very familiar words and yet, from the difficulty in defining them, or from not distinguishing the particular mental mechanism upon which they depend, the relative merits of many authors are often but vaguely understood.

Wit is primarily an intellectual perception of incongruity, or unexpected relations, but the idea that anything thus apprehended is ludicrous is suggested by the affective faculty of mirthfulness in the same manner that the understanding may perceive a dangerous object and thus arouse the emotion of fear.

The relation between the intellectual faculties and the feelings is reciprocal, so that the sentiment of the ludicrous, when strong, may prompt the intellect to create imaginary scenes or associated ideas adapted to gratify it, or become active as a result of real perceptions. Talent for wit, then, depends upon certain intellectual activities combined with the sentiment of mirth. But humor introduces another element—namely, secretiveness.

This propensity not only creates the desire to conceal one's own thoughts, but gives almost equal pleasure in penetrating the disguises of others. It enables a joker to "keep a straight face" while telling a story, and the secretiveness of the listener is gratified by detecting the absurdity in the narrative beneath the assumed gravity of the speaker. That is, to the amusing incongruity of the events in the story is added the further incongruity between the character of the story and the serious countenance of the narrator.

The English and Italians are more humorous than witty, the reverse of which is true of the French. Mark Twain is excellent in wit, but superexcellent in humor. Secretiveness is very marked in the diameter of his head just above the ears, and is indicated also by the width of his nostrils, the nearly closed eyes, compressed lips, slow, guarded manner of speech, etc. His nose is of the "apprehensive" type in its great length and somewhat hooked point, but it is not thick enough above the nostrils to indicate taste for commerce.

*Reprinted from *Cincinnati Commercial Gazette,* January 4, 1885, p. 8.

This "apprehensive," or cautious, nasal organ, so prominent in Dante, Calvin and other men celebrated for earnestness and gravity, might seem an anomaly in this case but for the explanation that cautiousness and secretiveness are essential ingredients in genuine humor. On this principle we can account for the temperament of our great humorist, which is not the laughing, fat, rotund vital, but rather the spare, angular mental, or mental-motive, which is favorable to hard sense, logic, general intelligence and insight into human nature.

His intellect is well balanced, having a strong foundation of perceptive faculties which gather details with the fidelity of a camera. He has also a large upper forehead, giving philosophical power, ability to generalize, reason, plan, and see a long way ahead. The middle centers, or memory of events, criticism and comparison, are also well developed. His eyes are rather deeply set, and his language is subordinate to his thought. The hollow temples indicate but little music, and mirthfulness, at the upper corners of the forehead, is by no means remarkable. Ideality, or love of beauty, is only fair.

The head measures 22-½ inches, which is half an inch less than the average intellectual giant, but the fiber of the whole man is fine, close and strong, and the cerebral combination is of a very available sort. He has very ardent affections, strong love of approbation, sense of justice, firmness, kindness and ability to read character; with small self-esteem, love of gain, or inclination to the supernatural. Knowledge of the world and interest in humanity are his leading traits, and altogether, he is a phenomenal man of whom Americans may well be proud.

Mark Twain at "Nook Farm" (Hartford) and Elmira

Charles H. Clark*

The story of Mark Twain's life has been told so often that it has lost its novelty to many readers, though its romance has the quality of permanence. But people to-day are more interested in the author than they are in the printer, the pilot, the miner, or the reporter, of twenty or thirty years ago. The editor of one of the most popular American magazines recently alluded to him as 'the most widely read person who writes in the English language.' More than half a million copies of his books have been sold in this country. England and the English colonies all over the world have taken at least half as many in addition. His sketches and shorter articles have been published in every language which is printed, and the larger books have been translated into German, French, Italian, Norwegian, Danish, etc. He is one of the few living persons with a truly world-wide reputation. Unless the excellent gentlemen, engaged in revising the Scriptures, should claim the authorship of their work, there is no other living writer whose books are now so widely read as Mark Twain's; and it may not be out of the way to add that in more than one pious household the 'Innocents Abroad' is laid beside the family Bible and referred to as a hand-book of Holy Land description and narrative.

Off the platform and out of his books, Mark Twain is Samuel L. Clemens—a man who will be fifty years old at his next birthday, November 30, 1885. He is of a very noticeable personal appearance, with his slender figure, his finely shaped head, his thick, curling, very gray hair, his heavy arched eyebrows, over dark gray eyes, and his sharply, but delicately, cut features. Nobody is going to mistake him for any one else, and his attempts to conceal his identity at various times have been comical failures. In 1871 Mr. Clemens made his home in Hartford, and in some parts of the world Hartford to-day is best known because it is his home. He built a large and unique house in Nook Farm, on Farmington Avenue, about a mile and a quarter from the old centre of the city. It was the fancy of its designer to show what could be done with bricks in building, and what effect of variety could be got by changing their color, or the color of

* Reprinted from *Critic*, 6 (January 17, 1885), 25–26, where it ran as the fifth part of an "Authors at Home" series.

the mortar, or the angle at which they were set. The result has been that a good many of the later houses built in Hartford reflect in one way or another the influence of this one. In their travels in Europe, Mr. and Mrs. Clemens have found various rich antique pieces of household furniture, including a great wooden mantel and chimney-piece, now in their library, taken from an English baronial hall, and carved Venetian tables, bedsteads, and other pieces. These add their peculiar charm to the interior of the house. The situation of the building makes it very bright and cheerful. On the top floor is Mr. Clemens's own working-room. In one corner is his writing-table, covered usually with books, manuscripts, letters, and other literary litter; and in the middle of the room stands the billiard-table, upon which a large part of the work of the place is expended. By strict attention to this business, Mr. Clemens has become an expert in the game; and it is a part of his life in Hartford to get a number of friends together every Friday for an evening of billiards. He even plans his necessary trips away from home so as to be back in time to observe this established custom.

Mr. Clemens divides his year into two parts, which are not exactly for work and play respectively, but which differ very much in the nature of their occupations. From the first of June to the middle of September, the whole family, consisting of Mr. and Mrs. Clemens and their three little girls, are at Elmira, N. Y. They live there with Mr. T. W. Crane, whose wife is a sister of Mrs. Clemens. A summer-house has been built for Mr. Clemens within the Crane grounds, on a high peak, which stands six hundred feet above the valley that lies spread out before it. The house is built almost entirely of glass, and is modelled exactly on the plan of a Mississippi steamboat's pilot-house. Here, shut off from all outside communication, Mr. Clemens does the hard work of the year, or rather the confining and engrossing work of writing, which demands continuous application, day after day. The lofty work-room is some distance from the house. He goes to it every morning about half-past eight and stays there until called to dinner by the blowing of a horn about five o'clock. He takes no lunch or noon meal of any sort, and works without eating, while the rules are imperative not to disturb him during this working period. His only recreation is his cigar. He is an inveterate smoker, and smokes constantly while at his work, and, indeed, all the time, from half-past eight in the morning to half-past ten at night, stopping only when at his meals. A cigar lasts him about forty minutes, now that he has reduced to an exact science the art of reducing the weed to ashes. So he smokes from fifteen to twenty cigars every day. Some time ago he was persuaded to stop the practice, and actually went a year and more without tobacco; but he found himself unable to carry along important work which he undertook, and it was not until he resumed smoking that he could do it. Since then his faith in his cigar has not wavered. Like other American smokers, Mr. Clemens is unceasing in his search for the really satisfactory cigar at a really satisfactory price, and, first and last, has gathered a good deal of experience in the pursuit. It is related that, having entertained a party of gentlemen one winter evening in Hartford, he gave to each, just before they left the house, one of a new sort of cigar that he was trying to believe was the object of his search. He made each guest light it before starting. The next morning he found all that he had given away lying on the snow beside the pathway across his lawn. Each smoker had been polite enough to smoke until he got out of the house, but every one on gaining his liberty had yielded to the instinct of self-preservation and tossed the cigar away, forgetting that it would be found there by daylight. The testimony of the next morning was overwhelming, and the verdict against the new brand was accepted.

At Elmira, Mr. Clemens works hard. He puts together there whatever may have been in his thoughts and recorded in his note-books during the rest of the year. It is his time of completing work begun, and of putting into definite shape what have been suggestions and possibilities. It is not his literary habit, however, to carry one line of work through from beginning to end before taking up the next. Instead of that, he has always a number of schemes and projects going along at the same time, and he follows first one and then another, according as his mood inclines him. Nor do his productions come before the public always as soon as they are completed. He has had one book finished now for five years, and another, his collected Library of Humor, has been practically ready for a year. But while the life at Elmira is in the main seclusive and systematically industrious, that at Hartford, to which he returns in September, is full of variety and entertainment. His time is then less restricted, and he gives himself freely to the enjoyment of social life. He entertains many friends, and his hospitable house, seldom without a guest, is one of the literary centres of the city. Mr. Howells is a frequent visitor, as Bayard Taylor used to be. Cable, Aldrich, Henry Irving, and many others of wide reputation, have been entertained there. The next house to Mr. Clemens's on the south is Charles Dudley Warner's home, and the next on the east is Mrs. Stowe's, so that the most famous three writers in Hartford live within stone's throw of each other.

At Hartford, Mr. Clemens's hours of occupation are less systematized, but he is no idler there. At some times he shuts himself in his working-room and declines to be interrupted on any account, though there are not wanting some among his expert billiard-playing friends to insist that this seclusion is merely to practice uninterruptedly while they are otherwise engaged. Certainly he is a skilful player. He keeps a pair of horses, and rides more or less in his carriage, but does not drive, or ride on horseback. He is, however, an adept upon the bicycle. He has made its conquest a study, and has taken, and also experienced, great pains with the work. On his bicycle he travels a great deal, and he is also an indefatigable pedestrian, taking long walks across country, frequently in the company of his friend the Rev. Joseph H. Twichell, at whose church (Congregational) he is a pew-holder and regular attendant. For years past he has been an industrious and extensive reader and student in the broad field of general culture. He has a large library and a real familiarity with it, extending beyond our own language into the literatures of Germany and France. He seems to have been fully conscious of the obligations which the successful opening of his literary career laid upon him, and to have lived up to its opportunities by a conscientious and continuous course of reading and study which supplements the large knowledge of human nature that the vicissitudes of his early life brought with them. His resources are not of the exhaustible sort. He is a member of (among other social organizations) the Monday Evening Club of Hartford, that was founded sixteen years ago by the Rev. Dr. Bushnell, Dr. Henry, and Dr. J. Hammond Trumbull, and others, with a membership limited to twenty. The club meets on alternate Monday evenings from October to May in the houses of the members. One person reads a paper and the others then discuss it; and Mr. Clemens's talks there, as well as his daily conversation among friends, amply demonstrate the spontaneity and naturalness of his irrepressible humor.

His inventions are not to be overlooked in any attempt to outline his life and its activities. 'Mark Twain's Scrap-Book' must be pretty well known by this time, for something like 100,000 copies of it have been sold yearly for eight years or more. As he wanted a scrap-book, and could not find what he wanted, he made one himself, which naturally proved to be just what other people wanted. Similarly, he invented a note book. It is his habit to record at the moment they occur to him such scenes and ideas as he wishes to preserve. All note-books that he could buy had the vicious habit of opening at the wrong place and distracting attention in that way. So, by a simple contrivance, he arranged one that always opens at the right place: that is, of course, at the page last written upon. Other simple inventions of Mark Twain's include: A vest, which enables the wearer to dispense with suspenders; a shirt, with collars and cuffs attached, which requires neither buttons nor studs; a perpetual-calendar watch-charm, which gives the day of the week and of the month; and a game whereby people may play historical dates and events upon a board, somewhat after the manner of cribbage, being a game whose office is twofold—to furnish the dates and events, and to impress them permanently upon the memory.

Mark Twain is now with George W. Cable, making a general tour of the country, each giving readings from his own works; and they are having crowded houses and most cordial receptions. It is not a new sort of occupation for Mark Twain. Back in the early days before his first book appeared, he delivered lectures in the Pacific States. His powers of elocution are remarkable, and he has long been considered by his friends one of the most satisfactory and enjoyable readers of their acquaintance. His parlor-reading of Shakespeare is described as a masterly performance. He has hitherto refused to undertake any general course of public readings, though very strong inducements have been offered to him to go to the distant English colonies, even as far as Australia. His present tour, which he began early in November, is to cover altogether a period of about five months.

To Mark Twain
(*On His Fiftieth Birthday*)

Oliver Wendell Holmes*

Ah Clemens, when I saw thee last,—
    We both of us were younger,—
How fondly mumbling o'er the past
    Is Memory's toothless hunger!

So fifty years have fled, they say,
    Since first you took to drinking,—
I mean in Nature's milky way—
    Of course no ill I'm thinking.

But while on life's uneven road
    Your track you've been pursuing,
What fountains from your wit have
    flowed—
    What drinks you have been brewing!

I know whence all your magic came,—
    Your secret I've discovered,—
The source that fed your inward flame—
    The dreams that round you hovered:

Before you learned to bite or munch
    Still kicking in your cradle,
The Muses mixed a bowl of punch
    And Hebe seized the ladle.

Dear babe, whose fiftieth year to-day
    Your ripe half-century rounded,
Your books the precious draught betray
    The laughing Nine compounded.

*Reprinted from *Critic*, 7 (November 28, 1885), 253, where it was dated "Boston, Nov. 23d, 1885."

So mixed the sweet, the sharp, the strong,
  Each finds its faults amended.
The virtues that to each belong
  In happier union blended.

And what the flavor can surpass
  Of sugar, spirit, lemons?
So while one health fills every glass
  Mark Twain for Baby Clemens!

An Interview with the Famous
Humorist/He Chats of Past and
Present/His Life as a Reporter

Anonymous*

I met Mark Twain the other day wandering around Washington and looking at pictures fifty years old as if they were new and inspecting with the interest of a rustic stranger the vivid bronze doors whose Columbian glories had bleared his eyeballs more than two decades ago. He strayed into the press gallery, threw back his gray overcoat, adjusted his gold spectacles on his nose and looked around.

"A good deal changed," he said, glancing at the life size photographs of Whitelaw Reid and younger editors which now decorate the walls, "and it seems a hundred years ago."

I asked him when he was there.

"I had a seat in the press gallery," he meditated, "let's see—in 1867—and now I suppose all the veterans are gone—all the newspaper fellows who were here when I was—Reid and Horace White and Ramsdell and Adams and Townsend."

"The ones you name happen all to be gone," I admitted, "some to the control of newspapers and some to the place where Dr. Potter says there are no newspapers, but some of the real veterans are still here. On those pegs in the corner some of the ancients still hang up their coats."

"Yes; some of these men I never knew in Washington; a few of them were here before my time. In fact, I was rather new and shy, and I did not mingle in the festivities of Newspaper Row. Probably most of the men you mentioned were perfectly unconscious of my existence. The *Morning Call* and Virginia City *Enterprise* did not make much of a commotion in the United States.

"I roomed in a house which also sheltered George Alfred Townsend, Ramsdell, George Adams, and Riley, of the San Francisco *Alta*. I represented the Virginia City (Nevada) *Enterprise*. Also, I was private secretary to Senator Stewart, but a capabler man did the work. A little later that winter William Swinton and I housed together. Swinton invented the idea—at least it was new to me—of manifolding correspondence, I mean of sending duplicates of a letter to various widely

*Reprinted from *New York Herald*, May 19, 1889, p. 19.

separated newspapers. We projected an extensive business; but for some reason or other we took it out in dreaming—never really tried it."

Here Mark walked into the gallery and looked down on the vacant Senatorial seats.

"I was here last," he went on, "in 1868. I had been on that lark to the Mediterranean and had written a few letters to the San Francisco *Alta* that had been copied past all calculation and to my utter astonishment, and a publisher wanted a book. I came back here to write it.

"Why, I was offered an office in that ancient time by the California Senators—Minister to China. Think of that! It wasn't a time when they hunted around for competent people. No, only one qualification was required—you must please Andy Johnson and the Senate. Nearly anybody could please one of them, but to please both—well, it took an angel to do that. However, I declined to try for the prize. I hadn't anything against the Chinese, and, besides, we couldn't spare any angels then."

"A pretty good place to write," I remarked, as we took seats.

"Some things," he said, "but an awfully bad place for a newspaper man to write a book, or at any rate for such a newspaper man as I was to write such a book as the publisher demanded. I tried it hard, but my chum was a story teller and both he and the stove smoked incessantly. And as we were located handy for the boys to run in, the room was always full of the boys, who leaned back in my chair, put their feet complacently on my manuscript and smoked till I could not breathe."

"Is that the way you wrote 'Innocents Abroad?'" I asked.

"No; that is the way I didn't write it. My publisher prodded me for copy which I couldn't produce, till at last I arose and kicked Washington behind me and ran off to San Francisco. There I got elbow room and quiet."

"It was apparently a wise move," I concurred, "but you could write here now, and this is exactly the place for a man like you. More intellectual society is attainable here than in any other city of the world. The only big mistake of your successful life, Clemens—for only his intimate friends address him as 'Mark'—is not coming to Washington to live. Why, all over the United States people of leisure and culture are—"

"Yes, I know, I know," broke in Clemens, "but don't tantalize me. Do you take a fiendish enjoyment in making me suffer? I know perfectly well what I am about, and I appreciate what I am losing. Washington is no doubt the boss town in the country for a man to live who wants to get all the pleasure he can in a given number of months. But I wasn't built that way. I don't want the earth at one gulp. All of us are always losing some pleasure that we might have if we could be everywhere at once.

"I lose Washington, for instance, for the privilege of saving my life. My doctor told me that if I wanted my three score and ten, I must go to bed early, keep out of social excitements and behave myself. You can't do that in Washington. Nobody does. Look at John Hay. Just fading away, I have no doubt, amid these scenes of mad revelry. My wife, you know, is practically an invalid too, so neither of us could keep up with the procession. No, the best place for us is quiet and beautiful Hartford, though there is a good deal of the society of Washington that I should delight in."

"I suppose you have been pirated a good deal," I said to Mr. Clemens. "I do not mean by illegal publication of your works, but by private individuals claiming to write your writings?"

"Oh, yes," he said, "considerably—some scores of cases, I suppose. One ambitious individual in the West still claims to have written the 'Jumping Frog of Calaveras County,' and another is sure that he produced that classic work known as 'Jim Wolfe and the Cats.' I suppose either would face me down with it; and their conduct has led me to conjecture that a man may possibly claim a piece of property so long and persistently that he at last comes honestly to believe it is his own. You know that poor fellow in New Jersey, so weak minded as to declare that he wrote 'Beautiful Snow,' and going down to the grave with tearful protests? And you know about Colonel Joyce and Ella Wheeler and 'laugh and the world laughs with you?'

"But I haven't been bothered that way so much as I have by personators. In a good many places men have appeared, represented that they were Mark Twain and have corroborated the claim by borrowing money and immediately disappearing. Such personators do not always borrow money. Sometimes they seem to be actuated by a sort of idiotic vanity.

"Why a fellow stopped at a hotel in an English city, registered as Mark Twain, struck up an acquaintance with the landlord and guests, recited for them and was about to accept a public dinner of welcome to the city, when some mere accident exposed him. Yet I myself had stopped for weeks at that same inn and was well known to the landlord and citizens. His effrontery was amazing."

"Did he resemble you?"

"I do not know. I hope and believe that he did not. Parties whom I have since been inclined to regard as my enemies had the indecency to say that he did.

"The same thing happened in Boston and several other cities. It was not pleasant to have bills coming in for money lent to me in Albany, Charleston, Mexico, Honolulu and other places, and my calm explanation that I was not there bringing sarcastic letters in reply with 'Oh, of course not! I didn't see you with my own eyes, did I?' &c, and I resolved that I would follow up the next swindler I heard of. I had not long to wait. A despatch came from Des Moines, Iowa:—

" 'Is Mark Twain at home?'

" 'Yes, I am here and have not been away,' I answered.

" 'Man personated you—got $250 from audience—shall I catch him?' came back, bearing the signature of a lawyer.

" 'Yes,' I telegraphed in reply; 'have sent you check for expenses.'

"He was a good while catching him—some weeks, perhaps months—and then he made me an elaborate report, giving the route of his labyrinthine and serpentine chase of the swindler, the money he had expended, and the information that he did not entirely and completely catch him, though he 'got near him several times.' I was out some hundreds of dollars.

"I was disgusted; and when I got another despatch—from New Orleans, I think it was—

" 'Man swindled audience with pretended lectures here last night, claiming to be you. What shall we do?' I telegraphed back unanimously, 'Let him go! Let him go!'

"I'd give $100, though, to see one of these doppel gangers who personate me before an audience, just to see what they look like."

Mark Twain goes down every winter to work for the passage of an international copyright law in conjunction with Edward Eggleston, Gilder and other authors. Senator Reagan, of Texas, a friend of Mark's, but an opponent of his pet measure, greeted him cordially last winter with "How are you, Mark? How are you? Right glad to see you! Glad to see you! Hope to see you here every session as long as you live!"

One of Mark Twain's favorite amusements, they say, is turning himself into an amateur guide and explaining to his friends the various objects of interest in the Capitol. He is particularly facetious over the pictures in the rotunda and the stone people in "Statuary" Hall. Arriving opposite the marble statue of Fulton, seated and intently examining the model of a steamboat in his hands, he indulges in a wide sweeping gesture and exlaims:—"This, ladies and gentlemen, is Pennsylvania's favorite son, Robert Fulton. Observe his easy and unconventional attitude. Notice his serene and contented expression, caught by the artist at the moment when he made up his mind to steal John Fitch's steamboat."

The humorist dresses a good deal more carefully than formerly. This is made necessary by his increasing amplitude, by his vast shock of gray hair, by his boisterous and ungovernable mustache and by his turbulent eyebrows that cover his gray eyes like a dissolute thatch. And when he talks he talks slowly and extracts each of his vowels with a corkscrew twist that would make even the announcement of a funeral sound like a joke.

The Art of Mark Twain

Andrew Lang*

The duty of self-examination is frequently urged upon us by moralists. No doubt we should self-examine our minds as well as our conduct now and then, especially when we have passed the age in which we are constantly examined by other people. When I attempt to conduct this delicious inquiry I am puzzled and alarmed at finding that I am losing Culture. I am backsliding, I have not final perseverance, unless indeed it is Culture that is backsliding and getting on the wrong lines. For I ought to be cultured: it is my own fault if I have not got Culture.

I have been educated till I nearly dropped; I have lived with the earliest Apostles of Culture, in the days when Chippendale was first a name to conjure with, and Japanese art came in like a raging lion, and Ronsard was the favourite poet, and Mr. William Morris was a poet too, and blue and green were the only wear, and the name of Paradise was Camelot. To be sure, I cannot say that I took all this quite seriously, but "we too have played" at it, and know all about it. Generally speaking, I have kept up with Culture. I can talk (if desired) about Sainte-Beuve, and Mérimée, and Félicien Rops; I could rhyme "Ballades," when they were "in," and knew what a *pantoom* was. I am acquainted with the scholia on the Venetus A. I have a pretty taste in Greek gems. I have got beyond the stage of thinking Mr. Cobden Sanderson a greater binder than Bauzonnet. With practice I believe I could do an epigram of Meleager's into a bad imitation of a sonnet by Joachim du Bellay, or a sonnet of Bellay's into a bad imitation of a Greek epigram. I could pass an examination in the works of M. Paul Bourget. And yet I have not Culture. My works are but a tinkling brass, because I have not Culture. For Culture has got into new regions where I cannot enter, and, what is perhaps worse, I find myself delighting in a great many things which are under the ban of Culture.

This is a dreadful position, which makes a man feel like one of those Liberal politicians who are always "sitting on the fence," and who follow their party, if follow it they do, with the reluctant acquiescence of the prophet's donkey. Not that I *do* follow it. I cannot rave with pleasure over

*Reprinted from *Illustrated London News*, 98 (February 14, 1891), 222.

Tolstoi, especially as he admits that "The Kreutzer Sonata" is not "only his fun" but a kind of Manifesto. I have tried Hartmann, and I prefer Plato. I don't like poems by young ladies in which the verses neither scan nor rhyme, and the constructions are all linguistically impossible. I am shaky about Blake, though I am stalwart about Mr. Rudyard Kipling.

This is not the worst of it. Culture has hardly a new idol but I long to hurl things at it. Culture can scarcely burn anything, but I am impelled to sacrifice to that same. I am coming to suspect that the majority of Culture's modern disciples are a mere crowd of very slimly educated people, who have no natural taste or impulse; who do not really know the best things in literature; who have a feverish desire to admire the newest thing, to follow the latest artistic fashion; who prate about "style" without the faintest acquaintance with the ancient examples of style, in Greek, French, or English; who talk about the classics and criticise the classical critics and poets, without being able to read a line of them in the original. Nothing of the natural man is left in these people; their intellectual equipment is made up of ignorant vanity, and eager desire of novelty, and a yearning to be in the fashion.

Take for example—and we have been a long time in coming to him—Mark Twain. If you praise him among persons of Culture, they cannot believe that you are serious. They call him a Barbarian. They won't hear of him, they hurry from the subject; they pass by on the other side of the way. Now I do not mean to assert that Mark Twain is "an impeccable artist," but he is just as far from being a mere coarse buffoon. Like other people, he has his limitations. Even Mr. Gladstone, for instance, does not shine as a Biblical critic, nor Mark Twain as a critic of Italian art nor as a guide of the Holy Land. I have abstained from reading his work on an American at the Court of King Arthur, because here Mark Twain is not, and cannot be, at the proper point of view. He has not the knowledge which would enable him to be a sound critic of the ideal of the Middle Ages. An Arthurian Knight in New York or in Washington would find as much to blame, and justly, as a Yankee at Camelot. Let it be admitted that Mark Twain often and often sins against good taste, that some of his waggeries are mechanical, that his books are full of passages which were only good enough for the corner of a newspaper. Even so, the man who does not "let a laugh out of him—like the Gruagach Gaire—at the story of the Old Ram, or of the Mexican Plug, or of the editing of the country newspaper, or of the Blue Jay, or at the lecture on the German language, can hardly have a laugh in him to let out. Chesterfield very gravely warns his son that it is wrong and vulgar to laugh; but the world has agreed to differ from Chesterfield. To "Homo Ridens" Mark Twain is a benefactor beyond most modern writers, and the Cultured, who do not laugh, are merely to be pitied. But his art is not only that of a maker of the scarce article—mirth. I have no hesitation in saying that Mark Twain is one among the greatest of contemporary makers of fiction. For some reason, which may perhaps be guessed, he has only twice chosen to exercise this art seriously, in *Tom Sawyer* and in *Hucklebury Finn*. The reason, probably, is that old life on the Mississippi is the only form of life in which Mark Twain finds himself so well versed that he can deal with it in seriousness. Again, perhaps his natural and cultivated tendency to extravagance and caricature is only to be checked by working on the profound and candid seriousness of boyhood. These are unlucky limitations, if they really exist, for they have confined him, as a novelist, to a pair of brief works, masterpieces which a fallacious appearance has confounded with boys' books and facetiae. Of the two, by an unheard-of stroke of luck, the second, the sequel, is by far the better. I can never forget nor be ungrateful for the exquisite pleasure with which I read *Hucklebury Finn* for the first time, years ago. I read it again last night, deserting *Kenilworth* for Huck. I never laid it down till I had finished it. I perused several passages more than once, and rose from it with a higher opinion of its merits than ever.

What is it that we want in a novel? We want a vivid and original picture of life; we want character naturally displayed in action, and if we get the excitement of adventure into the bargain, and that adventure possible and plausible, I so far differ from the newest school of criticism as to think that we have additional cause for gratitude. If, moreover, there is an unstrained sense of humour in the narrator, we have a masterpiece and *Hucklebury Finn* is nothing less. Once more, if the critics are right who think that art should so far imitate nature as to leave things at loose ends, as it were, not pursuing events to their conclusions, even here *Hucklebury Finn* should satisfy them. It is the story of the flight down the Mississippi of a white boy and a runaway slave. The stream takes them through the fringes of life on the riverside; they pass feuds and murders of men, and towns full of homicidal loafers, and are intermingled with the affairs of families, and meet friends whom they would wish to be friends always. But the current carries them on: they leave the murders unavenged, the lovers in full flight; the friends they lose forever; we do not know, any more than in reality we would know, "what became of them all." They do not return, as in novels, and narrate their later adventures.

As to the truth of the life described, the life in little innocent towns, the religion, the Southern lawlessness, the feuds, the lynchings, only persons who have known this changed world can say if it be truly painted, but it looks like the very truth, like an historical document. Already *Hucklebury Finn* is an historical novel, and more valuable, perhaps, to the historian than *Uncle Tom's Cabin*, for it is written without partisanship, and without "a purpose." The drawing of character seems to be admirable, unsurpassed in its kind. By putting the tale in the mouth of the chief actor, Huck, Mark Twain was enabled to give it a seriousness not common in his work, and to abstain from comment. Nothing can be more true and more humorous than the narrative of this outcast boy, with a heart naturally good, with a conscience torn between the teachings of his world about slavery and the promptings of his nature. In one point Mark Twain is Homeric, probably without knowing it. In the *Odyssey*, Odysseus frequently tells a false tale about himself, to account for his appearance and position when disguised on his own island. He shows extraordinary fertility and appropriateness of invention, wherein he is equalled by the feigned tales of Hucklebury Finn. The casual characters met on the way are masterly: the woman who detects Huck in a girl's dress; the fighting families of Shepherdson and Grangerford; the homicidal Colonel Sherborne, who cruelly shoots old Boggs, and superbly quells the mob of would-be lynchers; the various old aunts and uncles; the negro Jim; the two wandering impostors; the hateful father of Huck himself. Then Huck's compliment to Miss Mary Jane, whom he thought of afterwards "a many and a many million times," how excellent it is! "In my opinion she had more sand in her than any girl I ever see; in my opinion she was just full of sand. It sounds like flattery, but it ain't no flattery. And when it comes to beauty—and goodness too—she lays over them all." No novel has better touches of natural description; the starlit nights on the great river, the storms, the whole landscape, the sketches of little rotting towns, of the woods, of the cotton-fields, are simple, natural, and visible to the mind's eye. The story, to be sure, ends by lapsing into burlesque, when Tom Sawyer insists on freeing the slave whom he knows to be free already, in a manner accordant with "the best authorities." But even the burlesque is redeemed by Tom's real unconscious heroism. There are defects of taste, or passages that to us seem deficient in taste, but the book remains a nearly flawless gem of romance and of humour. The world appreciates it, no doubt, but "cultured critics" are probably unaware of its singular value. A two-shilling novel by Mark Twain, with an ugly picture on the cover, "has no show," as Huck might say, and the great American novel has escaped the eyes of those who watch to see this new planet swim into their ken. And will Mark Twain never write such another? One is enough for him to live by, and for our gratitude, but not enough for our desire.

Mark Twain

Henry C. Vedder*

On a certain street in Hartford, Conn., townsmen showing the local lions to the visitor from abroad will point with pride to a group of three comfortable, not to say handsome, houses as the homes of as many distinguished American writers. In one of these houses lives Charles Dudley Warner, in another, Harriet Beecher Stowe; the third, the finest of the three, is the winter home of the writer known the world over as Mark Twain. The winter home, I say, for this favorite of fortune has a summer home also, at Elmira, N. Y., where he has done most of his literary work of late years. Mr. Clemens is not like most American authors; his fertile season is the hot weather, when brainworkers in general are either taking a vacation or envying those who can take one. To a building detached from the house, and a room accessible to no one when he has once locked the door, he repairs every morning after breakfast, and remains there the better part of the day with his work. Those who think that books, especially the books of a "funny man," write themselves will do well not to express that opinion within reach of Mark Twain's arm—or pen. No American writer has won his fame by more honorable toil than Mr. Clemens. He has won wealth as well—but that, as Mr. Kipling says, is another story and shall be told later.

1.

It is not surprising that Mr. Warner and Mrs. Stowe should be neighbors in a staid Connecticut town—Mrs. Stowe was born in that State, and Mr. Warner is a New Englander. But that Mark Twain should have drifted to Hartford as a permanent residence is only less astonishing than Mr. Cable's emigration from New Orleans to Northampton, Mass. For Samuel Langhorne Clemens first saw the light in the village of Florida, State of Missouri. This was in 1835, at a time when Missouri was on the very frontier of civilization, and its exact limits had not yet been

*Reprinted from *New York Examiner*, April 6, 1893, p. [2]. With revisions, especially of the last three paragraphs, this essay became a chapter in Vedder's *American Writers of To-Day* (New York: Silver, Burdett, 1894).

defined. The condition of this western country at that time may be inferred from the fact that St. Louis was then a city of some twelve thousand people, while Chicago was not incorporated as a city until 1837, when it had rather more than four thousand inhabitants. It is not surprising, therefore, that all the education young Clemens received was what he could obtain in the village school of Hannibal. This was supplemented by his training in a printing-Office, which he entered at the age of thirteen. A bright boy in an old-fashioned printing-office is bound to pick up a very fair education of the practical kind. He is certain to learn spelling, punctuation, and the other minor moralities of literature, as these things are seldom learned by boys whose schooling may have been better, but who enter other callings. He would also pick up some knowledge of machinery; for in a country office the boy has to learn to work the press, and to repair it when it gets out of order, as it has a trick of doing often.

When the lad had acquired enough skill to call himself a journeyman printer he set out to see the world, and his native State thenceforth saw little of him. Those were the halcyon days of the "jour" printer. The world was all before him where to choose. He set out, with no kit of tools to carry, and with certainty of employment almost anywhere he might go, or of assistance from his fellows in the craft, thanks to a sort of freemasonry that prevailed everywhere among them. He might work his passage all around the continent and see life in all its phases, as no man of any other trade or profession could. We are told that Mr. Clemens worked at his trade by turns in St. Louis, Cincinnati, Philadelphia, and New York; and doubtless, if the whole truth were known, this would be a very imperfect catalogue of the places where he has stood at the case in his day.

By 1851 he had tired of wandering about in this way, and became enamoured of another calling not less adventurous. He "learned the river" and became a Mississippi pilot, continuing in this work for some ten years it would seem. At any rate, the next change in his life of which one can learn is his appointment in 1861 as private secretary to his brother, who had obtained an appointment as Secretary of the Territory of Nevada. Going to Nevada means, sooner or later, going into mining. It seems to have been sooner with Mr. Clemens, but he failed to "make his pile," though he did lay the foundations for sympathetic studies of life among the miners that he gave the world in "Roughing It." Perhaps it was because he "went broke" that he turned again to the printing-office, but this time he had a promotion; he was made city editor of the Virginia City "Enterprise." The rise from the composing-room to the editorial desk in those days, and in a far western town, was not so long a step. One conjectures that the city editor of the "Enterprise" "surprised by himself" the entire reportorial staff, and usually carried his office in his hat. What we are more interested to know than the number of assistants this city editor had is the fact that he began while in this service to write humorous contributions, and to sign them "Mark Twain,"—a reminiscence of his pilot days, when this was a frequent call from the man who was taking soundings from the deck of a Mississippi boat.

Mr. Clemens was now beginning his real work, but he had not yet "struck his gait," if we may borrow a phrase from the sporting world. In 1865, we find him in San Francisco, engaging in journalism and in mining operations. He spent six months of the following year in Hawaii, and on his return delivered lectures in California. These, together with other of his published writings, were gathered into a volume called "The Jumping Frog and Other Sketches" (New York, 1867). He was now fairly launched in a literary career, but his first great success was to come, though he had not long to wait for it. The publication of his account of a voyage through the Mediterranean, and travels in the adjoining countries, under the title of "The Innocents Abroad" (Hartford, 1869), made him famous at once; one hundred and twenty-five thousand copies were sold in three years, and probably not less than half a million copies have been sold by now, and yet the public is not tired of buying it. The fortunate author was now independent. After a brief connection with the "Buffalo Express," and the editing of a department in the "Galaxy," he settled for the rest of his life in Hartford,—not to be idle, but to work leisurely, with little or no temptation to spoil his writing by undue haste to get it to market. Since then he has published: "Roughing It" (Hartford, 1872), "The Adventures of Tom Sawyer" (Hartford, 1876), "A Tramp Abroad" (Hartford, 1880), "The Prince and the Pauper" (New York, 1882), "The Adventures of Huckleberry Finn" (New York, 1884), "A Yankee at King Arthur's Court" (New York, 1889), besides several other volumes of less note. He has also edited "A Library of Wit and Humor" (New York, 1888), the best collection of representative pieces by American humorists ever made. In the preface he characteristically remarks that, could he have had his way, the "Library" would have consisted wholly of extracts from his own works. The reader may season this with as many grains of salt as he chooses.

2.

The immediate and permanent popularity of *Innocents Abroad* is not wonderful; it is a book of even greater merit than the public gave it credit for possessing. It was read and enjoyed for its fun, and though nearly twenty-five years have passed it is still a funny book, whether one reads it now for the first or the forty-first time. But underneath the fun was an earnest purpose that the great mass of readers failed to see at the time, and even yet imperfectly appreciate. This purpose was to tell, not how an American ought to feel on seeing the sights of the Old World, but how he actually does feel if he is honest with himself. From time immemorial, books of travel had been written by Americans purporting to record their experiences, but really telling only what the writers thought they might, could, would, or should have experienced. These are the kind of travellers that are seen everywhere in Europe, Murray or Baedeker constantly in hand and carefully conned, lest they dilate with the wrong emotion—or, what is almost as bad, fail to dilate with the proper emotion at the right instant. For sham emotion, sham love of art, sham adventures, Mark Twain had no tolerance, and he gave these shams no quarter in his book. "Cervantes smiled Spain's chivalry away" is a fine phrase of Byron's, which, like most of Byron's fine phrases, is not true. What Cervantes did was to "smile away" the ridiculous romances of chivalry—chivalry had been long dead in his day—the impossible tales of knightly adventure, outdoing the deeds of the doughty Baron Munchausen, that were produced in shoals by the penny-a-liners of his time. Not since this feat of Cervantes has a wholesome burst of merriment cleared the air more effectually, or banished a greater humbug from literature than when *The Innocents Abroad* laughed away the sentimental, the romantic book of travels. Mark Twain, perhaps, erred somewhat on the other side. His bump of reverence must be admitted to be practically non-existent. He sees so clearly the humbug and pretence and superstition beneath things conventionally held to be sacred, that he sometimes fails to see that they are not all sham, and that there is really something sacred there. He was throughout the book too hard-headed, too realistic, too unimpressionable, too frankly Philistine, for entire truthfulness and good taste; but it was necessary to exaggerate something on this side in order to furnish an antidote to mawkish sentimentality. His lesson would have been less effective if it had not been now and then a trifle bitter to the taste. Since that time travellers have actually dared to tell the truth—or shall we say that they have been afraid to scribble lies so recklessly? Whichever way one looks at the matter, there is no doubt that American literature, so far as it has dealt with Europe and things European, has been more natural, wholesome, and self-respecting since the tour of this shrewd Innocent.

The same earnestness of purpose underlies much else that Mark Twain has written, especially *The Prince and the Pauper*, and *A Yankee at King Arthur's Court*. The careless reader no doubt sees nothing in the first of these books but a capital tale for boys. He cannot help seeing that, for it is a story of absorbing interest, accurate in its historical setting, and told in remarkably good English. In the latter book he will no doubt discover nothing more than rollicking humor and a burlesque of *Morte d'Arthur*. This is to see only what lies on the surface of these volumes, without comprehending their aim or sympathizing with the spirit. Not the old prophet of Chelsea himself was a more honest and inveterate hater of shams than Mark Twain. Much of the glamor and charm of chivalry is as unreal as the tinsel splendors of the stage—to study history is like going behind the scenes of a theatre, a disenchantment as thorough as it is speedy. *Morte d'Arthur* and Tennysons's *Idylls of the King* present to the unsophisticated a very beautiful, but a very shadowy and unsubstantial picture of Britain thirteen centuries ago. Even in these romances a glimpse of the real sordidness and squalor and poverty of the people may now and then be caught amid all the pomp and circumstance of chivalry. Nobody has had the pitiless courage heretofore to let the full blaze of the sun into these regions where the lime-light of fancy has had full sway, that we might see what the berouged heroes and heroines actually are.

But Mark Twain has one quality to which Carlyle never attained. Joined to his hatred of shams is a hearty and genuine love of liberty. His books could never have been written by one not born in the United States. His love of liberty is characteristic in its manifestation. In a Frenchman it would have found vent in essays on the text of *liberté, fraternité, equalité,* but eloquent writing about abstractions is not the way in which an American finds voice for his sentiments. Mark Twain's love of liberty is shown unostentatiously, incidentally as it were, in his sympathy for, and championship of, the down-trodden and oppressed. He says to us, "Here, you have been admiring the age of chivalry; this is what your King Arthur, your spotless Galahad, your valiant Launcelot made of the common people. Spending their lives in the righting of imaginary wrongs, they were perpetuating with all their energy a system of the most frightful cruelty and oppression. Cease admiring these heroes, and execrate them as they deserve." This, to be sure, is a one-sided view, but it is one that we need to take in endeavoring to comprehend the England of King Arthur. There is no danger that we shall overlook the romantic and picturesque view while Malory and Tennyson are read, but it is wholesome for us sometimes to feel the weight of misery that oppressed all beneath the privileged classes of England's days of chivalry.

3.

Except in the two books that may be called historic romances, Mark Twain has been a consistent realist. He was probably as innocent of intent to belong to the realistic school when he began writing as Molière's old gentleman had all his life been of the intent to talk prose. He was realistic because it came sort o' nateral to him, as a Yankee would say. His first books were the outcome of his personal experiences. These were many and varied, for few men have knocked about the world more and viewed life from so many points. Bret Harte has written of life on the Pacific coast with greater appreciation of its romantic and picturesque features, but one suspects with considerable less truthfulness in detail. The shady heroes and heroines of Bret Harte's tales are of a quality that suggests an amalgam of Byron and Smollett; they smack strongly of Bowery melodrama. Mark Twain's *Roughing It* is a wholesome book, and as accurate in its details as a photograph, but there is nothing romantic or thrilling about it.

It is in the Mississippi Valley, however, that our author finds himself most at home, not only because his knowledge of it is more comprehensive and minutely accurate, but because it is a more congenial field. Mark Twain understands California, admires it even, but he loves the great river and the folk who dwell alongside it. He is especially happy in his delineation of the boy of this region. If ever any writer understood boy nature in general, from A to izzard, the name of that writer is Mark Twain. He has explored all its depths and shallows, and in his characters of Tom Sawyer and Huckleberry Finn he has given us such a study of the American boy as will be sought in vain elsewhere. He has done more than this: he has given us a faithful picture, painfully realistic in details, of the ante-bellum social condition of the Mississippi Valley. The books, considered from any other point of view, are trash or worse. Their realism redeems them from what would otherwise be utter worthlessness, and gives them a certain value.

One ought also to mention the value of this writer's short stories. He has not done as much work in this line as one wishes he had, in view of the great merit of what he has written. Most of these stories are humorous in their fundamental conception, or have a vein of humor running through them, but they are not, for the most part, boisterously funny. They range in style from the avowedly funny tale of "The Jumping Frog of Calaveras" to the surface sobriety of "The £1,000,000 Bank Note." In the composition of the short story, Mark Twain is so evidently perfecting his art, as to warrant one in hazarding the prediction that much of his best work in future is likely to be done along this line.

4.

Even our English cousins—as a rule, not too lenient in their judgments of kin across the sea—admit that American humor has a distinct flavor. Not only so, they also admit that this flavor is delightful. To their tastes there is something wild and gamy about American humor, a "tang" that is both a new sensation and a continuous source of enjoyment. British commendation of American humor, however, is not always as discriminating as it is hearty. We must allow Englishmen the praise of having been prompt to appreciate the humor of Artemus Ward; but of late years they seem impervious to American humor, except of one type—that which depends for its effect on exaggeration. Exaggeration is, no doubt, one legitimate species of humor. The essence of humor lies in the perception of incongruity, and the effect of incongruity may be produced by exaggeration. This is the more effectively done if the style is "dry"; the writer must give no sign, until the very end (if even there), that he does not take himself seriously; the narrator must not by a tone of voice or change of facial expression betray any lack of exact veracity in his tale, or the effect is measurably lost. Mark Twain has frequently shown himself to be master of this style of humor. He can invent the most tremendous absurdities, and tell them with such an air of seriousness as must frequently deceive the unwary.

But this is not, as English readers mistakably imagine, the best type of American humor in general, or even the humor in which Mark Twain reaches his highest level. Exaggeration is comparatively cheap humor. Anybody can lie, and the kind of Mark Twain's humor most admired abroad is simply the lie of circumstance minus the attempt to deceive. It is morally innocuous, therefore, but it is bad art. No doubt it is frequently successful in provoking laughter, but the quality of humor is not to be gauged by the loudness of the hearers' guffaws. The most delightful fun is that which at most provokes no more than a quiet smile, but is susceptible of repeated enjoyment when the most hilarious joke has become a "chestnut." To borrow a metaphor from science, humor is the electricity of literature, but in its finest manifestation it is not static but dynamic. The permanent charm of humorous writing is generally in inverse ratio to its power to incite boisterous merriment when first read. The joker who gives a pain in the side soon induces "that tired feeling" that is fatal to continued interest. It is Mark Twain's misfortune at present to be appreciated abroad mainly for that which is ephemeral in his writings. His broad humanity, his gift of seeing far below the surface of life, his subtle comprehension of human nature, and his realistic method, are but dimly apprehended by those Britons who go off in convulsions of laughter the moment his name is mentioned. A false standard of what is truly "American" has been set up abroad, and only what conforms to that standard wins admiration. For that reason British readers have gone wild over Bret Harte and Joaquin Miller, while they neglected Bryant and Holmes, and for a time even Lowell, on the ground that the latter were "really more English than American, you know." Their own countrymen have a juster notion of the relative standing of American authors. In the case of Mark Twain they do not believe that he is rated too high by foreign critics and readers, but that his true merits are very imperfectly comprehended.

5.

Mr. Clemens has forever silenced those who affirm that a successful author, or at any rate a man of genius, must necessarily be a fool in business. No reader of his books needed to be assured that he is a man of much shrewdness, alert in observation, and understanding what he sees. These are qualities that make the successful man of affairs, and as a man of affairs he has been even more successful than as a writer. From the publication of his "Innocents Abroad" Mr. Clemens found himself in the fortunate position of an author sure of his audience. He had only to write and publishers would stand ready to bid against each other for his manuscript, and the public were equally eager for the opportunity to buy the book. Whether by good fortune or by design, the Innocents fell into the hands of a firm that sells books by subscription only. This is undoubtedly the most profitable method of publishing books for which there is a certain, a large, and an immediate sale. It did not take so shrewd a man long to discover that large as his profits were from the phenomenal sale of his books, the publisher reaped an even larger harvest of dollars. It took not much longer for Mr. Clemens to ask himself why he should not be both publisher and author, and take to himself both profits. With a man like him, to think is to plan, and to plan is to execute. The publishing house of Messrs. Charles L. Webster & Co. was the result of these cogitations. Mr. Clemens being the "Co.," and furnishing the capital to start the concern, while the laboring oar was held by a nephew. It is the popular belief that as a result of this venture, which has been wonderfully successful from the very beginning, Mr. Clemens has become a millionaire; certainly his fortune is a very handsome one for a man of letters to have amassed by his own unaided efforts, and without speculation. It is all been honestly earned by hard labor and wise business management.

It will be recalled that to the house belongs the honor of having paid the largest sum any author has received for a single work in the history of literature, in handing to Mrs. Grant something like $500,000 in all for the copyright and royalty on the sale of General Grant's *Memoirs*. No other firm in America, which is the same as saying in the world, could have handled such a work and made it pay such a profit to the author. This one incident in the history of the firm testifies to the energy of its management and the sagacity with which its methods have been directed. Besides publishing Mark Twain's writings—by subscription in the first place, but more lately in editions sold through the trade generally—the house is gradually lengthening its list of books and bids fair in no long time to take a high place among the publishers of the best current literature, as much by the number of publications bearing its imprint as by their high quality.

In private life Mr. Clemens is reputed to be one of the most genial and companionable of men. His friends say that he has never done himself justice as a humorist in his books. He produces his masterpieces of humor over a cigar with a few choice friends. Pity it is, if this be true, that there is not chiel amang them to take notes and prent 'em.

Mark Twain and His Recent Works

Frank R. Stockton*

Mark Twain's most notable characteristic is courage. Few other men—even if the other men could think of such things—would dare to say the things that Mark Twain says. To describe the travels of a man on a glacier, with particular reference to the fact that being pressed for time, he rode upon the middle of the glacier, which moves faster than the edges, is one of the bravest things in literature. It required courage to write "She," but She could not possibly exist, and glaciers do move.

Any one with a lively fancy may invent odd and even amusing characters and incidents, but the humorous situation of the highest order cannot be created; it must be evolved from a real situation. To do this requires not only skill but a bold spirit, for the humorist knows that an intelligent reader will probably see both situations, and if he compares unfavorably the evolved condition of affairs with the real one, the battle with that reader is lost. A pure creation of fancy does not presuppose courage; it gives little opportunity for comparative criticism.

Mark Twain is a high jumper, but he always jumps from the solid rock of fact and is not afraid of breaking his neck by falling back upon it. His funniest things are so funny because they are possible. An impossibility is a mill-stone about the neck of a joke. To load a frog with shot so that it cannot engage in a leaping-match is funny; but if one were to write of a whale inflated with balloon-gas so that it might shoot out of the water and skim through the air like a flying-fish, it would not be funny, it would be merely fantastic. In his humorous creations Mark Twain seldom plays upon words, he plays upon ideas; and as a pun would have no value were the words played upon treated without reference to their legitimate use, so he never forgets what a character is in the habit of doing when he makes him do something out of the common, and in his comical situations he uses the antithesis as if he were making a pun or an epigram.

It is the disposition of humorists to be prudent; they are careful about the rebounds of their missiles. It would be hard to find one who would not be afraid to ask if Adam were dead. Mark Twain's courage is shown not

*Reprinted from *Forum*, 15 (August, 1893), 673–79.

only in his combinations but in his descriptions. Take this account of the father of Huckleberry Finn—

> He was fifty and he looked it. His hair was long and tangled and greasy, and hung down, and you couldn't see his eyes shining through, like he was behind vines. It was all black, no gray; so was his long mixed up whiskers. There warn't no color in his face, where his face showed; it was white; not like another man's white, but a white to make a body sick, a white to make a body's flesh crawl—a tree-toad white, a fish belly white. As for his clothes—just rags, that was all. He had one ankle resting on t'other knee; the boot on that foot was busted, and two of his toes stuck through, and he worked them now and then. His hat was laying on the floor; an old black slouch, with the top caved in like a lid.

Another characteristic of Mark Twain is his use of pure and unadulterated fun. In this regard he differs from the older humorists. A great many of the things they wrote about are not funny in themselves; they are made so by the wonderful manner in which their witty authors have handled them. Mark Twain offers us the crude ore of fun. If he puts his private mark upon it, it will pass current; it does not require the mint stamp of the schools of humor. He is never afraid of not being laughed at. Consider, for instance, the passage in which the Yankee at the Court of King Arthur discovers St. Stylites at the top of his column—

> His stand was a pillar sixty feet high, with a broad platform on the top of it. He was now doing what he had been doing every day for twenty years up there—bowing his body ceaselessly and rapidly almost to his feet. It was his way of praying. I timed him with a stop watch, and he made 1244 revolutions in twenty-four minutes and forty-six seconds. It seemed a pity to have all this power going to waste. It was one of the most useful motions in mechanics, the pedal movement; so I made a note in my memorandum book, purposing some day to apply a system of elastic cords to him and run a sewing machine with it. I afterwards carried out that scheme, and got five years' good service out of him; in which time he turned out upwards of eighteen thousand first class tow-linen shirts, which was ten a day.

This is the pure ore of fun, just as it comes from the mine. It has not been coined or even cast into bars.

It must be remembered, however, that Mark Twain does not depend entirely upon the humor of his situations and conditions to make his points. His faculty and range of expression are wonderful, and it is his courage which gives to his expressions, as well as his inventions, their force and unique effect. His glittering phrases are as daring as they are bright, and they sparkle through all his books like stars in the sky. A humiliated person has the aspect of a "bladder that has been stepped on by a cow." A disguised king, practicing obeisances, looks about "as humble as the leaning tower of Pisa," and an orator is described "who loved to stand forth before a dazed world and pour forth flame and smoke, and lava, and pumice stone, into the skies, and work his subterranean thunders, and shake himself with earthquakes, and stench himself with sulphur fumes. If he consumed his own fields and vineyards, that was a pity, yes; but he would have his eruptions at any cost." The Yankee at King Arthur's court speaks thus of a damsel of the period—

> I was gradually coming to have a mysterious and shuddery reverence for this girl; for nowadays whenever she pulled out from the station and got her train fairly started on one of those horizonless trans-continental sentences of hers, it was borne in upon me, that I was standing in the awful presence of the Mother of the German Language.

Examples of the poignancy of expression with which Mark Twain spurs his readers into a proper appreciation of what he is telling them, are too abundant for further reference, but although he uses them so easily, he does not always find them necessary. Some of the funniest passages in his later works, as well as in those by which he made his reputation, contain not a flash of wit nor any unusual expressions. A combination is presented in the plainest and simplest way, and as the substances are poured together the humor effervesces, not in the author's story, but in the reader's mind.

We have an example of this in an article on ships in his last book. The author asserts that in these days Noah would not be allowed to sail from Bremen in the ark, without first being subjected to an official inspection. After discovering that Noah's ship is six hundred feet long and very large otherwise, the inspector asks him how many passengers he has, to which Noah answers, "Eight."

> "Sex?"
> "Half male, the other female."
> "Ages?"
> "From a hundred years up."
> "Up to where?"
> "Six hundred."
> "Crew?"
> "The same eight."
> "Have any of you ever been to sea?"
> "No, sir."
> "Where were you reared?"
> "On a farm,—all of us."
> "Who is Captain?"
> "I am."
> "You must get a Captain. Also a chambermaid. Also sick nurses for the old people. Who designed this vessel?"
> "I did, sir."
> "Is it your first attempt?"
> "Yes, sir."

"I partly suspected it. Cargo?"

"Animals."

"Wild or tame?"

"Mainly wild."

"Securely caged?"

"No, not caged."

"They must have iron cages. Who feeds and waters the menagerie?"

"We do."

"The old people?"

"Yes, sir."

"It is dangerous—for both. The animals must be cared for by a competent force. How many are there?"

"Big ones, seven thousand; big and little together, ninety-eight thousand."

"You must provide twelve hundred keepers."

"How many pumps have you?"

"None, sir."

"You must provide pumps."

"What is the nature of your steering apparatus?"

"We haven't any."

"Haven't you a rudder?"

"No, sir."

"How do you steer the vessel?"

"We don't."

"You must provide a rudder. How many anchors have you?"

"None."

"Provide twenty-five. Did I understand you to say this was your first attempt at ship-building?"

"My very first. I built this ark without having ever had the slightest training or experience or instruction in marine architecture."

"It is a remarkable work, sir. I consider it contains more features that are new—absolutely new and unhackneyed—than are found in any other vessel that swims the sea."

Sometimes a witty point in a remark is omitted in such a way that the effect is a great deal stronger than if it had been left in. In "A Petition to the Queen of England," Mark Twain objects to an income-tax which has been demanded of him as an author, and points out the fact that authors are not mentioned in the official schedule. Mr. Bright, a clerk of the Inland Revenue Office, had said to him, "You are taxed under Schedule D, section 14." Then, writes Mark Twain—

I turned to that place, and found these three things: "Trades, Offices, Gas Works." Of course, after a moment's reflection, hope came up again, and then certainty: Mr. Bright was in error and clear off the track; for authorship is not a trade, it is an inspiration; authorship does not keep an office, its habitation is all out under the sky, and everywhere that the winds are blowing and the sun is shining and the creatures of God are free. Now

then, since I have no trade and keep no office, I am not taxable under
Schedule D, section 14. Your Majesty sees that.

In this deft omission of a reference to gas-works the author draws out the
wit of his readers as a magnet draws needles from a cushion.

We who remember Mark Twain when his light first rose above the
horizon cannot help thinking of him as a humorist above everything else,
for it was as such he rose, and as such his radiance increased. We soon
came to know that he was also a philosopher and after a time that he was
a story-teller, but for all that and despite our added knowledge of him, we
still think first of his brightness, and often forget that his surface may be
inhabited or that he has an influence upon our tides.

His philosophy of course, came in with his humor and although the
fact was not always noticed, it often formed part of it. Later this
philosophic spirit grew and strengthened until it was able to stand alone,
and in some of his more recent writings it not only stands up very steadily
but it does some bold fighting. As illustrations of the workings of the
reasoning powers in his characters, we give two extracts from "Huckleberry Finn." In the first of these the boy deprecates the upbraiding of his
conscience in a case where he was not at all to blame—

> But that's always the way; it don't make no difference whether you do
> right or wrong, a person's conscience ain't got no sense, and just goes for
> him *anyway*. If I had a yaller dog that didn't know no more than a per-
> son's conscience does, I would pisen him. It takes up more room than all
> the rest of a person's insides and ain't no good, nohow.

In the following, Huckleberry is on a raft with Jim, a negro, who is trying
to escape from slavery, and they are approaching Cairo, the nearest point
of free soil—

> Jim said it made him all over trembly and feverish to be so close to
> freedom. Well, I can tell you, it made me all over trembly and feverish,
> too, to hear him, because I begun to get it through my head that he *was*
> most free—and who was to blame for it? Why *me*. I couldn't get that out
> of my conscience, no how, nor no way. It got to troubling me so I couldn't
> rest; I couldn't stay still in one place. It hadn't ever come home to me
> before, what this thing was that I was doing. But now it did; and it staid
> with me, and scorched me more and more. I tried to make out to myself
> that *I* warn't to blame, because I didn't run off Jim from his rightful
> owner; but it warn't no use, conscience up and says, every time, "But you
> knowed he was running for his freedom, and you could have paddled
> ashore and told somebody." That was so—I couldn't get around that,
> noway. That was where it pinched. Conscience says to me, "What had
> poor Miss Watson done to you, that you should see her nigger go off right
> under your eyes and never say a single word? What did that poor old
> woman do to you, that you could treat her so mean? Why, she tried to

learn you your book, she tried to learn you your manners, she tried to be good to you every way she knowed how. *That's* what she's done."

I got to feeling so mean and miserable I most wished I was dead. I fidgeted up and down the raft, abusing myself to myself, and Jim was fidgeting up and down past me. We neither of us could keep still. Every time he danced around and says "Dah's Cairo!" it went through me like a shot, and I thought if it *was* Cairo I reckoned I would die of miserableness.

Jim talked out loud all the time while I was talking to myself. He was saying how the first thing he would do when he got to a free state he would go to saving up money and never spend a single cent, and when he got enough he would buy his wife, which was owned on a farm close to where Miss Watson lived; and then they would both work to buy the two children, and if their master wouldn't sell them, they'd get an Ab'litionist to go and steal them.

It most froze me to hear such talk. He wouldn't ever dare to talk such talk in his life before. Just see what a difference it made in him the minute he judged he was about free. It was according to the old saying, "Give a nigger an inch and he'll take an ell." Thinks I, this is what comes of my not thinking. Here was a nigger which I had as good as helped to run away, coming right out flat-footed and saying he would steal his children—children that belonged to a man I didn't even know; a man that hadn't done me no harm. I was sorry to hear Jim say that, it was such a lowering of him. My conscience got to stirring me up hotter than ever.

In these passages the humor is merely sprinkled on the rest of the substance. It is like the fun of a circus-clown taking the money at the door; he may be a queer fellow, but he means business.

These extracts lead us insensibly from the consideration of Mark Twain as a funny man and as an expert in logical processes, to Mark Twain as a story-teller. In "The Prince and the Pauper," he took his stand as a writer of fiction with but little reference to his other and then better known qualifications. Of the success of this departure there can be no doubt, and there are critics of high order who consider "The Prince and the Pauper" our author's best work. But it must be remembered that in the average family the boys are as good as the girls; and if some of us marry the one and some of us the other, it is because of our own difference of sex.

It was quite natural that Mark Twain should become a story-teller. The man of broad sympathies, who is able, with interest to himself and others, to evolve the *may be* from the *is*, is sure to end by writing stories, no matter how he begins. He may do it in verse or he may do it in prose, but he will do it. He may set out on his career by describing his own travels, but this field will surely become too small for him, no matter how deep he may dig down into it, or how high he may build above it, and he will leap the wall into regions where he will make people who will travel wherever he chooses to send them, and do and say whatever he chooses to make them do and say. Thus came "Tom Sawyer" and "Huckleberry Finn," and thus came shorter stories, such as "The £1,000,000 Bank Note." In this we recognize, first of all, that unbounded courage which rises, as we have said, above all other characteristics of Mark Twain; what other author would have dared to put five million dollars into the hands of an intelligent tramp, and to tell him to go forth with it and seek adventures?

It is well known that the actor of comedy often casts longing glances toward the tragic mask, and when he has an opportunity to put it on, he often wears it so well that one cannot say he has no right to it. The same pen-point which will make a man laugh out in church, if gently pricked by it, will not only slay a bride at the altar, but will go entirely through her and kill her father who is giving her away. The figure with the tragic mask stalks through much of Mark Twain's work. In "The Prince and the Pauper" he darkens the page like a semi-weekly eclipse; while in the feud of the Shepherdsons and the Grangerfords in "Huckleberry Finn," he throws himself with such earnestness into his tragic action that his comic mask drops unnoticed from his hand and might be lost forever, were it not caught on one of the six arms of the picture of the young woman about to jump from the bridge.

Long live that comic mask! With such a forest of points for it to catch upon, there will be no danger of its ever being lost, and while Mark Twain lives he will not cease to be the man of the double stroke—the Bismarck of humorists.

The Famous Story-Teller Discusses Characters/Says That No Author Creates, but Merely Copies

[Lute Pease]*

"Mark Twain" and his manager, Major Pond, left Portland yesterday morning for the Sound, where he will join Mrs. Clemens and his daughter at Tacoma. After lecturing there, and at Olympia, Seattle, Victoria and Vancouver, B.C., he will sail from Vancouver, August 16, with the whole party, for Honolulu.

As was contemplated, Mr. Clemens' tour around the world will take at least a year, and very likely longer. He will be in the hands of his Australian agent some nine months, lecturing in the leading cities of Australia, New Zealand, India and South Africa, after which he will visit the British Isles, where he will doubtless remain a considerable time.

At the Portland, yesterday morning, Mark Twain stood surrounded by a medley of handbags waiting for a carriage to the train. A blue nautical cap confined a part of his big mane of hair, but it bulged out at the sides and behind, a grizzly wilderness. With that bushy growth tumbling over his big head, the bushy mustache and the bushy brows streaming to the right and left, a face rugged as if chiseled by nature's hand from a block of granite, Mark Twain is certainly about as striking and picturesque a character as ever looked out of the pages of any of his own books. And, when to his anything but commonplace appearance is added the originality of his manner, its absolute carelessness, its lazy, cynical good humor, he becomes one of the most interesting men in the world to meet, even if one had never heard of him.

Dozens of people came up to reach over the array of handbags and shake hands with Mark Twain. Most of them claimed to have met him before, and his face wore a rather puzzled look sometimes as he was reminded of various places and occasions where he had met them in days gone by. That genial, courteous gentleman, Major J. B. Pond, was busy with introductions and other matters, but the carriage didn't come, so Mark and the major bundled into the 'bus, handbags in hand, and were off.

"Portland seems to be a pretty nice town," drawled the author of "Tom Sawyer," as the bus rolled down Sixth street, "and this is a pretty

*Reprinted from *Portland Oregonian*, August 11, 1895, p. 10. Twain was especially pleased with this interview.

nice, smooth street. Now Portland ought to lay itself out a little and macadamize all its streets just like this. Then it ought to own all the bicycles and rent 'em out and so pay for the streets. Pretty good scheme, eh? I suppose people would complain about the monopoly, but then we have the monopolies always with us. Now, in European cities, you know, the government runs a whole lot of things, and, it strikes me, runs 'em pretty well. Here many folks seem to be alarmed about governmental monopolies. But I don't see why. Here cities give away for nothing franchises for car lines, electric plants and things like that. Their generosity is often astonishing. The American people take the yoke of private monopoly with philosophical indifference, and I don't see why they should mind a little government monopoly."

"What about that book of travels you are going to write on this trip, Mr. Clemens? Will it be something like the 'Innocents Abroad', or the others?"

"Well, it won't describe the same places by any means. It will be a lazy man's book. If any one picks it up expecting to find full data, historical, topographical, and so forth, he will be disappointed. A lazy man, you know, don't rush around with his note book as soon as he lands on a foreign shore. He simply drifts about, and if anything gets in his way of sufficient interest to make an impression on him, it goes into his book. General Sherman told me that when he made his trip abroad, he found just about what he needed in my old books to guide him to what interested him most. He said it was too much bother to wade through the conventional guide books, which mentioned everything, so he dropped them by the wayside. That's just what makes traveling tiresome, I think—that ever-present anxiety to take in everything, whether you can enjoy it and digest it or not—that fear that you won't get your money's worth if you leave anything mentioned in the guide book behind. What's the use of making a business of traveling when you are out for pleasure? While I am not going to write a guide book, yet if it can help people to enjoy the same journey, why, I shall think it something of a success."

Mr. Clemens, during this time, had sauntered through the depot, and on into the smoking compartment of the Olympia car, where he settled himself comfortably in a corner.

"There must be some reason," said he, "why a fine town like Portland has not long since built a new depot. What is the reason?"

It was explained to him that the completion of the new station had been delayed through two of the roads interested in its construction having gone into receiverships.

"Well, I haven't had an opportunity to see much of Portland, because, through the diabolical machinations of Major Pond over there, I am compelled to leave it after but a glimpse. I may never see Portland again, but I liked that glimpse."

Some one asked him about the story that was published in one of the San Francisco papers not long since, about an old-time Mission-street bartender named Tom Sawyer. This individual had asserted that he had met Mark Twain in 'Frisco many years ago with a jolly party and that all went out together and got still jollier, and that Mark had slapped Sawyer on the back with the remark: "I am writing a book about just such a boy as you must have been, and I'm going to name him after you."

"That story lacks a good deal in the way of facts," said Mr. Clemens. "One doesn't choose a name that way. I have always found it rather difficult to choose just the name that suited my ear. 'Tom Sawyer' and 'Huckleberry Finn' were both real characters, but 'Tom Sawyer' was not the real name of the former, nor the name of any person I ever knew, so far as I can remember, but the name was an ordinary one—just the sort that seemed to fit the boy, some way, by its sound, and so I used it. No, one doesn't name his characters haphazard. Finn was the real name of the other boy, but I tacked on the 'Huckleberry.' You see, there was something about the name 'Finn' that suited, and 'Huck Finn' was all that was needed to somehow describe another kind of boy than 'Tom Sawyer', a boy of lower extraction or degree. Now, 'Arthur Van de Vanter Montague' would have sounded ridiculous, applied to characters like either 'Tom Sawyer' or 'Huck Finn.' "

"Both those books will always be a well of joy to innumerable boys, Mr. Clemens."

"Well," said Twain with a smile. "I rather enjoyed writing them. The characters were no creation of my own. I simply sketched them from life. I knew both those boys so well that it was easy to write what they did and said. I've a sort of fondness for 'em anyway.

"I don't believe an author, good, bad or indifferent, ever lived, who created a character. It was always drawn from his recollection of someone he had known. Sometimes, like a composite photograph, an author's presentation of a character may possibly be from the blending of more than two or more real characters in his recollection. But, even when he is making no attempt to draw his character from life, when he is striving to create something different, even then, however ideal his drawing, he is yet unconsciously drawing from memory. It is like a star so far away that the eye cannot discover it through the most powerful telescope, yet if a camera is placed in proper position under that telescope and left for a few hours, a photograph of the star will be the result. So, it's the same way with the mind; a character one has known some time in life may have become so deeply buried within the recollection that the lens of the first effort will not bring it to view. But by continued application the author will find when he is done, that he has etched a likeness of some one he has known before.

"In attempting to represent some character which he cannot recall, which he draws from what he thinks is his imagination, an author may often fall into the error of copying in part a character already drawn by another, a character which impressed itself upon his memory from some book. So he has but made a picture of a picture with all his pains. We mortals can't create, we can only copy. Some copies are good and some are bad."

Just then the train started and Mark Twain said good-bye to Portland. A lot of people are sorry he did not remain to lecture another night.

Mark Twain to Pay All/On His Way Around the World Now to Raise the Money

[Samuel E. Moffett]*

Sam L. Clemens (Mark Twain), who is about leaving for Australia, in an interview concerning the purpose of his long trip said:

"I am idle until lecture-time. Write, and I will dictate and sign. My run across the continent, covering the first 4,000 miles of this lecturing tour around the world, has revealed to me so many friends of whose existence I was unconscious before, and so much kindly and generous sympathy with me in my financial mishaps, that I feel that it will not be obtrusive self-assertion, but an act of simple justice to that loyal friendship, as well as to my own reputation, to make a public statement of the purpose which I have held from the beginning, and which is now in the process of execution.

"It has been reported that I sacrificed for the benefit of creditors the property of the publishing firm whose financial backer I was, and that I am now lecturing for my own benefit. This is an error. I intend the lectures as well as the property for the creditors.

"The law recognizes no mortgage on a man's brain, and the merchant who has given up all he has may take advantage of the rules of insolvency and start again for himself. But I am not a business man, and honor is a harder master than the law. It cannot compromise for less than one hundred cents on the dollar, and its debts never outlaw.

"I had a two-thirds interest in the publishing firm, whose capital I furnished, and if the firm had prospered I should have expected to collect two-thirds of the profits. As it is I expect to pay all the debts. My partner has no resources, and I don't look for assistance from him. By far the largest single creditor of this firm is my wife, whose contributions in cash from her private means have nearly equaled the claims of all others combined. In satisfaction of this great claim she has taken nothing, except to avail herself of the opportunity of retaining control of the copyrights of my books, which, for many easily understood reasons—of which financial ones are the least—we do not desire to see in the hands of strangers.

*Reprinted from *San Francisco Examiner*, August 17, 1895, p. 2; reprinted widely at the time. This statement was regularly cited during the next fifteen years. Correspondence establishes Moffett, Twain's nephew, as at least a coauthor of this text.

"On the contrary, she has helped and intends to help me to satisfy the obligations due to the rest.

"The present situation is that the wreckage of the firm, together with what money I can scrape together, with my wife's aid, will enable me to pay the other creditors about 50 per cent of their claims. It is my intention to ask them to accept that as a legal discharge and trust to my honor to pay the other 50 per cent as fast as I can earn it. From my reception thus far on my lecturing tour I am confident that if I live I can pay off the last debt within four years, after which, at the age of sixty-four, I can make a fresh and unencumbered start in life.

"I do not enjoy the hard travel and broken rest inseparable from lecturing, and if it had not been for the imperious moral necessity of paying these debts, which I never contracted but which were accumulated on the faith of my name by those who had a presumptive right to use it, I should never have taken to the road at my time of life. I could have supported myself comfortably by writing, but writing is too slow for the demands that I have to meet; therefore I have begun to lecture my way around the world. I am going to Australia, India and South Africa, and next year I hope to make a tour of the great cities of the United States.

"In my preliminary run through the smaller cities on the northern route I have found a reception the cordiality of which has touched my heart and made me feel how small a thing money is in comparison with friendship.

"I meant, when I began, to give my creditors all the benefit of this, but I begin to feel that I am gaining something from it too, and that my dividends, if not available for banking purposes, may be even more satisfactory than theirs.

                                        MARK TWAIN."

Mark Twain in Sydney/
A Further Interview

Anonymous*

Mark Twain landed in Sydney to-day. He is spare and undersized, and there is nothing about him to fill the eye. Physically he is disappointing. Intellectually he is like many another humourist; he seems cast in a somewhat sombre mould.

"Life," he said looking from beneath his fair shaggy eyebrows, "is not at all a humorous thing. I have never found it a joke, and I am serious if nothing else. Man as a normal creature is serious now and then. One of us, say a scribbler like myself, pen in hand, may get a moment of enlightenment. A sudden thought may slip in, and then comes humour. That, however, is a contribution which the gods have sent his way, and which really is not of man. It comes from some place, the key of which he does not possess to open it at his will. Yes, life is serious, and man is the most serious part of it.

"Now you have heard," he continued, "that I am the laziest man in the United States, yet I tell you, and I believe, it is perfectly demonstrable that there is no such being as a perfectly lazy man. Just consider that every man has a gift either large or small. It may be to play billiards or to imitate Paderewski. Whatever that gift is man takes a native delight in exploiting it, and it is a most difficult thing to prevent him from exercising that gift. There are hundreds of interests that the human race possesses. In the case of any particular man ninety-nine out of a hundred of these interests may not appeal to him, so that so far as they are concerned he is the laziest of beings. He is too lazy to do this, too lazy to do that, but when you arrive at his gift he is not lazy. It is difficult then to keep him from working night and day. So I frankly admit that in regard to many human things, I am, if you like to use the term, phenomenally lazy, lazy in every way that you can possibly imagine, until it comes to writing a book. Then there is no more industrious man in the world than myself. Let me alone and I will work with my pen until I drop from fatigue. Then the only trouble my family have with me is digging me out of my chair when my day's work is done. To the extent I describe, then, I am lazy or industrious

*Reprinted from *Melbourne* (Australia) *Argus*, September 17, 1895, p. 5.

112

just as you please. Understand, I don't philosophise. I leave that for newspapers to do. I simply state a fact."

Having thus swept away what evidently was looked on somewhat as a personal aspersion Mark Twain discursively alluded to one of his most memorable experiences.

"I was only in London for a day," he remarked, "but that day lives with me for ever. There is only one London. It is unique. I went there to meet my old friend, Mr. Stanley, and he was good enough to bring some 75 or a 100 of his friends to greet me. There was not one of the men present who had not earned his claim to personal distinction. As I chatted with them the thought was always present, 'This is not the only gathering of the kind in London. There are many more roofs here covering the world's great to-night.' That thought has lived with me, and I want to be told where to-day is there another city which can produce such a spectacle without effort. The wealth and intellect of the world is centralised there. It is wonderful, and what cannot be said of the nation which has evolved such a city! That day's visit certainly was one of the most memorable experiences.

"Then, if you ask what man has impressed me most, I hardly know what to say. Still I think above all men I would put General Grant. His was a grand figure and his was a noble nature. It was so simple and so beautiful. Standing face to face with him you looked at a man with a mighty record, and yet it was not the knowledge of that fact, but the man's latent power that was so impressive with him. It was just as with the Rev. Thomas Starr King, of San Francisco, who was so renowned a preacher in that city thirty years ago. It was the perseverance of that man that distinguished him above others. So it was with General Grant. Of course, General Grant had great contemporaries. There were Sheridan and Stonewall Jackson, the latter with his deep religious fervour—just such another as Gordon, and the former with his profanity. Oh, my! he could swear. Still, I suppose, after all, that was merely a matter of environment. If he had the same training and the same surroundings as General Jackson I suppose he would have been much the same.

"Do I mind saying what I think about Bret Harte?" said Mark Twain in reply to an inquiry. "No. But mind if I speak strongly it is merely a personal opinion. I detest him, because I think his work is 'shoddy.' His forte is pathos, but there should be no pathos which does not come out of a man's heart. He has no heart, except his name, and I consider he has produced nothing that is genuine. He is artificial. That opinion, however, must be taken with some allowance, for, as I say, I do not care for the man."

Mark Twain uttered this sentence with an emphasis that left no doubt as to his earnestness, and then went on to say,

"I have no objection to my views being known. It is purely a personal criticism. I dare say, when I go to London, I shall meet him, but what of that? I am most moderate in my dislikes. There are only three or four persons in the world to whom I have had any antipathy, and the Almighty has removed most of them. It does seem wonderful that I should not have been allowed to get at them before they died. On the other hand, I have devoured what Rudyard Kipling has written. He is wonderful, and, strange to say, I met him before he was known to fame. One day when I was stopping at a country place for the summer I got a card, on which was written that the bearer had come from Allahabad or some such place, fourteen thousand miles away, to see me. Now, this I took to be a tremendous compliment, and then when he was admitted he said he had only travelled from New York. Well, that was 275 miles, so I forgave him his story. His card fell into the hands of my daughter, who, impressed with what he had written on it, and the compliment paid me, kept it 12 months. Later, Kipling's name was in everyone's mouth, but I had not the slightest idea that he was the man who had rung in the 14,000 mile fiction on me till I read the account of his tour in the London *World*. Then I realised that he was identical with my visitor of 12 months' before, and sent my daughter to look up the card, which she had fortunately kept. We have met frequently since then, and he is a most interesting personage. We in the United States, of course, look up to Nathaniel Hawthorne as possessing that something which marks genius and makes man live for ever. It is always remarkable to me that he should have written such incisive English at a time when that was not the prevailing style of authors, and it is still more remarkable when you travel on the Continent to find that the one book which has been translated as the best type of American literature is *Helen's Babies*."

Mark Twain on the Platform

Unfortunately, perhaps, for himself, but decidedly fortunately for the people who have the pleasure of listening to him, Mark Twain has been dragged out of his American study by pecuniary losses to the footlights of the lecture-platform and the admiring gaze of his multitudinous readers. It is quite twenty years since the author of "Huck Finn" spoke across the footlights, and even at that distant date his lectures were very few in number, so that the people who have seen or heard the humorist in public prior to his present lecturing-tour must be very limited indeed. Perhaps it is a good thing that Mark Twain has been compelled to take to lecturing for a time, as it will enable him to visit countries previously unknown to him, and, as he has already promised, result in "Tramp Abroad," Vol. II., being published. In fact, Mark Twain has so arranged his tour that he will not revisit any of the countries which form-ed such excellent scope for witty observation in his well-known book. Mark Twain placed himself unreservedly under the care of that well-known Colonial lecture-agent, Mr. R. S. Smythe, who has negotiated so many big "stars" through the Colonies. Crossing from San Francisco, the humorist opened his tour in Sydney in the middle of September. His tour, which will last a year, extends over all the Australian Colonies, New Zealand, Mauritius, Ceylon and South Africa. He had an offer of 2000£. for ten lectures in London, but for the present had to refuse it. He will finish his Colonial tour, and get the resultant book off his hands before thinking of a trip to England.

As a lecturer—or rather, story-teller, for the author objects to be called a lecturer—Mark Twain is, and has proved himself to be, in his opening Australian "At Homes," a decided success. Like Charles Dickens, he relies entirely on his old books for the pabulum of his discourses, but, unlike the author of "Pickwick," he does not read long extracts from these books. He takes some of his best stories—"The Jumping Frog," "Huck Finn," the difficulties of the German language, *par exemple*—and re-tells them, with many subtle additions of humour and some fresh observa-

---

*Reprinted from *Sketch* [London], 12 (November 27, 1895), 245; reprinted at the time in *Critic*, NS 25 (April 25, 1896), 286.

115

tions, in the most irresistibly amusing manner. He is in no sense a disappointment as a humorist. He starts his audience laughing in the very first sentence he utters, and for two hours keeps them in a continual roar. The only serious moments occur when, with the unutterable pathos of which the true humorist alone is capable, he interpolates a few pathetic touches which almost make the tears mingle with the smiles. Every story he tells serves the purpose of illustrating a moral, and, although, for the most part, he talks in low, slow, conversational tones, at times he rises to real bursts of eloquence—not the polished, grandiloquent eloquence of the average American speaker, but the eloquence conveyed in simple words and phrases, and prompted by some deep and sincerely felt sentiment. The author has the power of seeming to jest at his serious side, just as in his books; but there is no mistaking the seriousness with which, for example, he is moved by the remembrance of the iniquities perpetrated on liberty in the old slavery days amid which Huck Finn and Jim the slave lived. He makes the most unexpected anecdotes point the most unexpected morals, but it is the recital of the old, familiar stories without any moral attaching to them which pleases most, coming as they do warm from the brain of the man who invented them.

Mark Twain steals unobtrusively on to the platform, dressed in the regulation evening-clothes, with the trouser-pockets cut high up, into which he occasionally dives both hands. He bows with a quiet dignity to the roaring cheers which greet him at every "At Home." Then, with natural, unaffected gesture, and with scarcely any prelude, he gets under weigh with his first story. He is a picturesque figure on the stage. His long, shaggy, white hair surmounts a face full of intellectual fire. The eyes, arched with bushy brows, and which seem to be closed most of the time while he is speaking, flash out now and then from their deep sockets with a genial, kindly, pathetic look, and the face is deeply drawn with the furrows accumulated during an existence of sixty years. He talks in short sentences, with a peculiar smack of the lips at the end of each. His language is just that of his books, full of the quaintest Americanisms, and showing an utter disregard for the polished diction of most lecturers. "It was not" is always " 'twarn't" with Mark Twain, and "mighty fine" and "my kingdom" and "they done it" and "catched," and various other purely transatlantic words and phrases, crop up profusely during his talk. He speaks slowly, lazily, and wearily, as of a man dropping off to sleep, rarely raising his voice above a conversational tone; but it has that characteristic nasal sound which penetrates to the back of the largest building. His figure is rather slight, not above middle height, and the whole man suggests an utter lack of physical energy. As a matter of fact, Mark Twain detests exercise, and the attention must be very strong to induce him to go very far out of doors. Rolf Boldrewood called on him in Melbourne, and had the greatest difficulty in the world to persuade him to take a drive. With the exception of an occasional curious trot, as when recounting his buck-jumping experiences, Mark Twain stands perfectly still in one place during the whole of the time he is talking to the audience. He rarely moves his arms, unless it is to adjust his spectacles or to show by action how a certain thing was done. His characteristic attitude is to stand quite still, with the right arm across the abdomen and the left resting on it and supporting his chin. In this way he talks on for nearly two hours; and, while the audience is laughing uproariously, he never by any chance relapses into a smile. To have read Mark Twain is a delight, but to have seen and heard him is a joy not readily to be forgotten. The humorist is accompanied on his tour by his wife and charming second daughter.

Mark Twain as an Historical Novelist

William Peterfield Trent*

Some years since, I amused myself during a railway journey between Providence and New York by watching a man in front of me read *The Adventures of Tom Sawyer* steadily for an hour without once cracking a smile or giving a chuckle. Even a slow reader must in that time have got to the inimitable scene in which Tom gets his chums to whitewash the fence and pay him for the privilege of being allowed to do it, so I felt warranted in concluding that the saturnine stranger in front of me was a prodigy who had never known the pleasure of a hearty laugh and never been a boy. Perhaps, however, he had previously read Professor Charles F. Richardson's pathetic advice to Mark Twain and our other humorists to "make hay while the sun shines," and had concluded, as a good American Philistine, that, the vogue of these humorists being but temporary, it would be highly improper for a devotee of eternity to concern himself with their works save for the laudable purpose of drawing from them the salutary lessons with regard to idleness and want of sobriety and decorous dulness. He had evidently never read Professor Brander Matthews's appreciative essay on "Mark Twain's Best Story," or he would have learned that our greatest humorist had already laid up perennial if not eternal treasure in the very book he was then reading so sedately and in its admirable sequel.

Whether Mark Twain himself has taken Professor Richardson's advice seriously to heart and determined to win a permanent place in literature by coming out in the high but to him new role of historical novelist, is a point on which I have no definite information; but I suspect that he was thinking more of his favourite heroine, Joan of Arc, than he was of himself when he began the story that we have all been reading of late in the pages of *Harper's Magazine*. Self-consciousness is not a characteristic of Mr. Clemens's art, and, like other great writers, he probably knows deep down in his soul that he will best secure the suffrages of posterity by writing simply and truly about that which he is fullest of and best understands. He also knows probably that the portion of the reading public which treats him as a mere humorist is sadly mistaken, and that he

*Reprinted from *Bookman* [New York], 3 (May, 1896), 207–10.

118

has already done work in fiction that the world will not willingly let die. It is most likely, therefore, that his new role of historical novelist has been assumed by the veteran writer for no self-seeking purpose, but simply because he has been caught in the eddies of that enthusiasm for the Maid of Orleans which has been sweeping of late over the literary world.

In attributing a new role to Mr. Clemens I have spoken advisedly, for although he has twice before essayed fiction of a historical cast, it is only with the *Personal Recollections of Joan of Arc* that he has challenged criticism as a historical novelist, properly speaking. That juvenile classic, which has charmed many an older reader, *The Prince and the Pauper*, depends for its interest rather upon Mr. Clemens's thorough knowledge of a boy's heart and his power to bring out the pathos inherent in a situation mainly based on the world-old contrast implied in the title of the story than upon the historical environment in which the characters of that story work out their respective destinies. But in a true historical novel the interest depends as much upon the fact that its characters move and live and have their being in an epoch removed from the present as upon the fact that they act, and feel, and think along lines that are universally true for the human race in all times and in all lands. Tested by this criterion, that other of Mr. Clemens's books to which he has given a historical setting, *A Yankee at King Arthur's Court*, falls still farther short of being a historical novel. It is really the work of a humorist, not of a novelist—of a humorist who seeks to gain his effects mainly by the use of violent contrasts, which are as likely to stir up feelings of repugnance in a reader as to move him to hearty and genuine laughter. The satiric purpose, too, of the book removes it still farther from the category of historical fiction, although for some readers, perhaps, this may give it its chief value.

But in the *Personal Recollections of Joan of Arc* we have a deliberate contribution to a class of fiction which, after suffering an eclipse for the space of a generation, has been of late steadily gaining in popular favour. Beginning in *Harper's Magazine* for April, 1895, it has run a course of thirteen months, shrouded in as much mystery as editorial wit could devise and the author's stylistic idiosyncrasies could keep up. Almost immediately critics and general readers alike began to suspect that no one save Mark Twain could be hiding his features behind a mask supposed to represent the countenance of the Sieur Louis de Conte, page and secretary to the martial maid, and this suspicion changed to certainty when they read the elaborate descriptions of the Paladin's powers of lying and of the Sieur Louis's attempt at a poem to the fair Catherine Boucher. But editor and supposititious translator kept their peace, while the artists furnished their excellent illustrations and the public read and enjoyed. Now, however, that the story is finished, the critic's time has arrived, although for any detailed examination one should await the appearance of the unmutilated book.

I do not purpose any elaborate criticism here, but only to start a few questions which must sooner or later be answered. Has Mark Twain at last made Professor Richardson's advice about making hay as superfluous in the eyes of the public at large as it is now in the eyes of Professor Matthews and of all who properly appreciate *Tom Sawyer* and *Huckleberry Finn?* Has he succeeded in writing a great book or even a thoroughly satisfactory historical novel? Has he atoned in part for the wanton injuries done to the noblest woman that ever lived by the English of her time and for the injustice done her memory in dramas which are properly credited to the greatest poet of England and the world? Has he taken his stand by De Quincey's side as an inspired champion of a still more inspired heroine? These are the important questions that criticism will have to answer with regard to Mr. Clemens and his book, and with all due humility and regret I am compelled to make the confession that it is my opinion that the final answer of criticism will be a reluctant but decided "No." Not that a sympathetic reader or critic of the future will think for an instant that Mr. Clemens has not conceived his heroine's greatness in a worthy manner, that he has not told her story in a simple and moving style, that he has not at times set before us in vivid colours scenes of imperishable interest and importance. He has done all this, but it seems to me that he has failed, as many another writer has done ere now, to fuse properly the historic and the purely imaginary or fictive elements of his narrative. He has given us a large piece of mosaic work; first we have a slab of history, then a slab of fiction, and so on, with the history predominating over the fiction. It is true that the historical events that fill so many pages are told with an insight, a verve, a humour that professed historians might well envy; but the fusing process has not taken place, and the history and the fiction are separate, though in juxtaposition. Such was not the method of him who was at once the first and the greatest of historical novelists—that Sir Walter who, whatever certain modern critics may say, grows greater with the years both as a writer and as a man.

There are, I fear, other defects in the *Personal Recollections* that will not escape the attention of the critic, but that require only the slightest notice here. Mr. Clemens has essayed the difficult task of making Joan his chief character, and I rather think that his admiration for her has prevented him from making her really human and alive. It is true that he often presents her to us in her homely peasant's dress and ways, and he not infrequently strikes a note of genuine pathos; but too often he has to content himself with that most disappointing form of description, to wit, exclamatory comment. Yet if Joan does not truly live, hardly any other character can be said to breathe, unless it be Sieur de Conte himself, who is certainly full of high-minded appreciation of his noble mistress, but expresses it in a manner that makes one wonder how he got as far east as Domremy, if, as we are told, the Normans were the Yankees of France. De Conte may not have been a Norman, but his speech bewrayeth him to a "Yankee at the Court of Charles VII." Perhaps, however, I am too sweeping in denying life to the characters who follow the Maid's fortunes. The Paladin, although he is simply a variation of a well-worn type of boaster, does live when he is entrusted with Joan's standard, and when he dies defending it, and La Hire lives both when he curses, which is frequently, and when he prays, which is emphatically seldom.

It would be an ungracious task to indulge in verbal criticism or to endeavour to show that one often detects a lack of imagination in descriptive passages that especially require it. It is not every reader who will object to the close of a paragraph describing Joan's approach to the throne of the disguised Charles, which is couched in the following style: "They were not expecting this beautiful and honourable tribute to our little country maid." The lack of *timbre* in the adjectives here employed, the lack of imagination seen in the description of Joan in armour rising aloft like "a silver statue," which occurs more than once; the lack of taste, if not of humour, shown in the story of the mad bull's breaking up the funeral procession; the lack of a sense of proportion displayed in the lengthy treatment of the trial, will have little meaning to the reader who reads for amusement simply, but will probably show the critic where one of the chief defects of Mr. Clemens's work lies. It lies, it seems to me, in the fact that Mr. Clemens is not primarily a man of letters. But fortunately for American literature and for the permanent fame of a man whom no one can know without loving and honouring, the creator of Tom Sawyer is something far more than a mere man of letters, even a great one; he is something far more than a mere humorist, even a thoroughly genial and whole-souled one—he is a great writer. Like Balzac himself he can afford to let critics have their say about his style, in the consciousness that he has understood and expressed the workings of the human heart.

Mark Twain—His Work

Brander Matthews*

There are many advantages in the growing practice of signing a literary criticism with the name of the writer; and not the least of them is that it permits the writer to praise heartily and abundantly those whom he truly admires, taking on himself all responsibility for his eulogy. I don't know whether or not *The Book Buyer* would allow me to say anonymously all that it might be quite willing to have me say over my own signature. The wielder of the editorial *we* cannot but take into account average public opinion; it is that indeed he has chiefly to reckon with. But an individual writer, isolated by his own signature, may be a chartered libertine, having full license to say what he pleases. Now, it has long pleased me to think and to say that the average public opinion does not yet rate at its full value the work of the admirable story-teller who is known to all of us as Mark Twain.

The public having once made up its mind about any man's work, does not relish any attempt to force it to unmake this opinion and to remake it. Like other juries, it does not like to be ordered to reconsider its verdict as contrary to the facts of the case. It is always very sluggish in beginning the necessary readjustment, and not only sluggish, but somewhat grudging. Very naturally it cannot help seeing the later works of a popular writer from the point of view it had to take to enjoy his earlier writings. Now, as it happens, the earlier writings of Mark Twain gave little or no promise of the high qualities to be found in certain of his later works. Many of the sketches included in the "Jumping Frog" and most of the account of the "Innocents Abroad" were little more than "comic copy." They were very good "comic copy" indeed, but none the less did they reveal the conventions, the formulas, and the limitations of "comic copy."

The Mark Twain these two books disclosed was a shrewd and keen-eyed observer, having broad fun, abundant humor, and exuberant fantasy, and so deficient in reverence for the equator that he treated the ordinary degrees of longitude and latitude without any respect whatever. Properly enough, he was classified promptly as a professional humorist—

*Reprinted from *Book Buyer*, NS 13 (January, 1897), 977–79.

as a writer whose sole duty it was to make us laugh, and to whom therefore we need never give a second thought after the smile had faded from our faces. In any attempt to take stock of our native literature, Mark Twain was set down as a mere rival of the other pseudonymous fun-makers, John Phoenix, Artemus Ward, and Josh Billings. Even in 1886 Charles F. Richardson, in his solid tomes on "American Literature," solemnly warned Mark Twain and his fellows that, "clever as they are, they must make hay while the sun shines," since "twenty years hence, unless they chance to enshrine their wit in some higher literary achievement, their unknown successors will be the privileged comedians of the republic." And yet when this complacent judgment was delivered, Colonel Sellers had already found "Millions in it!" Tom Sawyer had already reluctantly let the contract for whitewashing his aunt's fence, and Huck Finn had already been a witness of the Sheperdson-Grangerford feud. Even in 1886 it might have been possible to perceive that the narrator of the adventures of Colonel Sellers, of Tom Sawyer, and of Huckleberry Finn was to be ranked with the creators of Ichabod Crane and of Hosea Bigelow, rather than with the mere fun-makers of the comic papers. Half of Professor Richardson's twenty years have now come and gone; and Mark Twain has since given us "Puddenhead Wilson," with its sombre figure of Roxy, sold down the river by her own son. He has chosen also to tell reverently and indeed almost devoutly the wonderful story of Joan of Arc. And yet there are not a few readers of his books careless and thoughtless enough to think of him even now as only "the privileged comedian of the republic."

The first of our humorists he is still, fortunately for us, with all the qualities we found in his earlier books, but now riper and richer. The "Jumping Frog" and the "Innocents Abroad" did not call forth more laughter than was evoked by later books like "Life on the Mississippi," "Roughing It," the "Stolen White Elephant," and "A Tramp Abroad." And these later books were in every way better than the earlier books of the same kind: they revealed less effort, a broader outlook on life, a deeper insight into human character; they showed that Mark Twain had learnt how to suggest the pathos that must underlie true humor; they were better written also—indeed, for his purpose, no American author to-day has at his command a style more nervous, more varied, more flexible, or more direct than Mark Twain's. The tale of the Blue Jay (in "A Tramp Abroad") is as well told as it is full of humor sustained by unstated pathos; and the account of Mark Twain's own training as a cub-pilot (in the earlier chapters of "Life on the Mississippi") is as vigorous in narrative as it is valuable as a record of a vanished phase of American life.

For these volumes of mingled realism and humor I have a relish as hearty as any reader's; but I must confess that my fondness is less for some other and more fantastic volumes—for "A Connecticut Yankee at King Arthur's Court," for one, and for "The Prince and the Pauper." In neither book can Mark Twain give his finer qualities full scope. My liking is still less for "Tom Sawyer Abroad," in which the admixture of the realistic trio of Tom and Huck and Jim in purely fantastic adventures seems to me unfortunate. And noble and dignified as is the "Joan of Arc," I do not think that it shows us Mark Twain at his best; although it has many a passage that only he could have written, it is perhaps the least characteristic of his works. Yet it may well be that the certain measure of success he has achieved in handling a subject so lofty and so serious, will help to open the eyes of the public to see the solid merits of his other stories, in which his humor has fuller play and in which his natural gifts are more abundantly displayed.

In "Tom Sawyer," in "Huckleberry Finn," and in "Puddenhead Wilson" Mark Twain is something more than "the privileged comedian of the republic"; he is something very different from this,—something far more important. He is like Cervantes in that he makes us laugh first and think afterwards. Mr. Ormsby, in an essay which accompanies his translation of "Don Quixote," points out that for a full century after its publication that greatest of novels was enjoyed chiefly as a tale of humorous misadventures, and that three generations had laughed over it before anybody suspected that it was more than a merely funny book. It is perhaps rather with the picaroon romances of Spain that "Huckleberry Finn" is to be compared than with the masterpiece of Cervantes; but I do not think it will be a century or take three generations before we Americans generally discover how great a book "Huckleberry Finn" really is, how keen its vision of character, how close its observation of life, how sound its philosophy, and how it records for us once and for all certain phases of Southwestern society which it is very important for us to perceive and to understand. The influence of slavery, the prevalence of feuds, the conditions and the circumstances that make lynching possible—all these things are set before us clearly and without comment. It is for us to draw our own moral, each for himself, as we do when we see Shakespeare acted.

"Huckleberry Finn," in its art, for one thing, and also in its broader range, is superior to "Tom Sawyer" and to "Puddenhead Wilson," fine as both these are in their several ways. In no book in our language, to my mind, has the boy, simply as a boy, been better realized than in "Tom Sawyer." In some ways "Puddenhead Wilson" is the most dramatic of Mark Twain's longer stories, and also the most ingenious; like "Tom Sawyer" and "Huckleberry Finn," it has the full flavor of the Mississippi Valley, in which its author spent his own boyhood, and from contact with the soil of which he always rises reinvigorated. It is by these three stories, and especially by "Huckleberry Finn," that Mark Twain is likely longest to live in our literature.

It remains for me to say now only that this new library edition of Mark Twain's works is in every way worthy. Six volumes have now appeared—seven, if the *Joan of Arc* be included, which the others match in height at least. They are all seemly tomes, clear in print, broad of page, simple in binding. The *Connecticut Yankee*, the *Prince and the Pauper*, *Life on the Mississippi*, and *Huckleberry Finn*, each fills a volume by itself. In the volume with *Tom Sawyer Abroad* we have "Tom Sawyer, Detective," and also the selection of sketches hitherto published under the name of the first of them, the "Stolen White Elephant"; and, in like manner, the second half of the volume the *American Claimant* contains a score or so of essays and tales.

Mark Twain Smiling through His Tears, but in Sore Straits

Anonymous*

"Of course, I am dying."

And Mark Twain smiled grimly.

"But I do not know that I am doing it any faster than anybody else. As for dying in poverty, I had just as soon die in poverty here in London as anywhere. But it would be a little more difficult, because I have got quite a number of friends, any one of whom I believe would be good for a month's provision, and that would drag out the agony a fairly long time."

I could not help thinking there was something forced in the careless tone. Was it possible that the reverses of fortune of the author of so many works bubbling over with wit and humor and philosophy and high spirits were as serious as has been recently stated? It is true that Mr. Clemens denied the report first published—namely, that he was dying in a state of extreme poverty—and certainly he looked in fairly good health when I saw him a couple of days ago in his house at Chelsea, and yet there was a difference in his physiognomy.

It was more lined and much thinner than when I saw him last. His hair is as bushy as ever and is now almost snowy white, and there was a species of hopeless resignation in his bearing that was in painful contrast to his one time easy going carelessness; and in spite of his disclaimer, in spite of his assertion that he was perfectly well, I was convinced that if his physical health were of the best he was, nevertheless, so disturbed by mental worries that the report of his failing condition was practically well founded.

"No, I assure you," he added, "I am as well as ever I was. You see, you must not attach too much importance to my wife's remark that I was not in a condition to receive visitors. That simply meant that I was in bed. Now most women think that if a man does not get up before twelve o'clock there must be something wrong with him, and as I never do get up before then, my wife thinks I am not in good health. As a matter of fact, when you were announced I told her to have you shown up to my room, but you can never persuade a tidy woman to show a stranger into an untidy bedroom, and so that did not work.

*Reprinted from New York Herald, June 13, 1897, Sec. 4, p. 1.

"I said to her, 'Show him up. Send some cigars up. I am comfortable enough.'

" 'Yes,' she said, 'but what about him?'

" 'Oh,' I said, 'if you want him to be as comfortable as I am make him up a bed in the other corner of the room.' That did not work either, so I thought the best thing to do was to get up and come to see you."

Chatting in this way I introduced as delicately as possible the subject of the reports published recently in the American press, to which he gave the answer that opens this interview.

As a matter of fact, however, I heard from other sources that since the death of his daughter, some months ago, Mr. Clemens has been trying to hide his grief, trying to live down his bereavement in complete isolation. Until a few days ago, in fact, very few people were in the secret of his whereabouts, and had it not been that a cousin of his here in London fell ill Mark Twain's name would not probably have been brought up in connection with any such statement as that he was dying and in complete poverty, for, although his losses with the Webster publishing firm have been so serious as to engulf the whole of his fortune, he is, perhaps, the last man in the whole world to let any one know of his financial difficulties so long as he has strength to hold his pen or so long as his fertile brain can evolve thoughts.

His cousin fell ill, and, the names being the same, the two men were confused. The financial losses sustained by Mr. Clemens were well known, and the elements for the report that he was dying in poverty are there all ready to hand.

From the same source I learned that, in spite of Mr. Clemens' sturdy disclaimer, he is overwhelmed with financial embarrassments, but there was only his air, which seemed dreadfully like that of a man trying to keep his head above water and not succeeding too well, to support his assertion.

"Poverty," he said, "is relative. I have been in poverty so often that it does not worry me very much. A more serious matter is the money owing to other people, not by any fault of mine, and yet owing to them by me. But I do not trouble about the rumors that go about in regard to me. Why should I? The rumor will die itself if you will only give it three days. Start any rumor, and if the public can go with its curiosity unsatisfied for three days something else will spring up which will make the public forget all about the first one. Therefore, when people talk about my dying, or as really happened a few days ago about my being dead, I do not take the slightest notice. I know perfectly well that the public will forget all about it if I let it alone. I keep on ploughing away and working and working and hoping and hoping, but the idea of being in poverty does not either trouble me or frighten me."

"What are you working upon just now?"

"On my journey round the world. Everybody has done his little circumnavigation act, and I thought it about time I did mine, so I have been getting it ready for the press since I have been here, and therefore, for the matter of that, the book is just my impressions of the world at large. I go into no details. I never do, for that matter. Details are not my strong point, unless I choose for my own pleasure to go into them seriously. Besides, I am under no contract to supply details to the reader. All that I undertake to do is to interest him. If I instruct him that is his fate. He is that much ahead."

"I had thought of calling it 'Another Innocent Abroad,' but following advice, as the lawyers say, I have decided to call it 'The Surviving Innocent Abroad.'

"Now, my wife said, 'But that is not true, because there's so-and-so in Cleveland, and that and the other in Philadelphia.' But, I said to her, 'I will fix that.' So I am going to put a little explanatory note to that title pointing out that although there are still in existence some eight or ten of the pilgrims who went on the Quaker City expedition some twenty-eight years ago, I am the only surviving one that has remained innocent.

"In fact, that title 'The Innocents Abroad,' could only be strictly applied to two even at the time it was written, and the other is dead."

"When do you expect the survivor to appear?"

"Oh, about Christmas," said Mark Twain. "Christmas is a good time to bring out a book. Everybody is thinking about Christmas presents, and the pious are praying that Divine Providence may give them some clew as to what to give for a present, and the book, if it comes just at the right time, is about as good a thing as one could desire. It must come just at the right time though. In other words, the opportunity to secure the present must happen just at the moment when the impulse to give one is felt."

"It is a strange thing," he went on to say, "how much more charity there would be in this world if opportunity only coincided with impulse. It is years ago since a lecturer and missionary came to Hartford. He had a vast amount of experience among the city poor—among the worthy poor, I mean, for there are many more poor than there are worthy. And one night I went off to hear about the misery and distress he had seen. I remember I had four one hundred dollar bills in my pocket, with some small change, just enough for the sake of appearance when the plate came round.

"Well, he began to tell us about suffering in the city slums, and about a husband, with his dogged courage, striving and fighting to make both ends meet, and about the little wife, with her brave smile, choking down the lump that rose in her throat, and about the children crying for bread. And as he went on I felt my enthusiasm for his cause rising higher and higher, and I said to myself, 'I'll give one of those bills when that plate comes round.' But he continued, and told about how work failed, and the husband came home with a white, despairing face, and the little wife looked up at him still cheerily smiling, while her heart was breaking, and how the children pined and wasted away for lack of nourishment. Oh, it was terrible! It was heartrending! And it so played on my feelings that I thought, 'I cannot bear this any more. I must help them. I'll spare two of those bills!'

"And then he told how sickness came and how the brave wife at last lay dead and the husband sat by her side with his heart broken and his brain reeling, holding her dead hand in his while sheriffs took the bed upon which she had laid. And the children were huddled in a corner, crying softly and affrighted, and my feelings were wrought up to such a pitch that I said to myself, 'For God's sake, send that plate round, so that I can pour my sympathy into it. I'll give those four bills, and if I can get a piece of paper, I'll write a check for something more. I can very well spare a little money for a cause like that.'

"But the lecturer went on talking and talking, and as he talked my enthusiasm calmed and calmed, and the red flush of my sympathy became paler and paler. And when he had been talking about half an hour I had saved one of those bills, and when he had talked five minutes more two of those bills were mine again, and when he had been talking an hour I had won all four back, and, by gosh, when he finally did send that plate round I borrowed ten cents out of it to pay my carfare home."

There was such a sympathetic sound, however, in Mark Twain's voice that I wonder how much he really did put in the plate, for one of the most striking characteristics of the man is his profound affection for humanity, a characteristic that comes out in many and many an unexpected place in his writings, welling up from unsuspected depths of kindliness in his nature.

As, for example, speaking about his stay in Paris and his visit to the French law courts, he said, "The basis of French legal procedure is humor, and, like the best humor, it is made up of tragedy. What, for instance, can be more ludicrous from the point of view of justice and more tragic from the point of view of humanity, than the examination of a prisoner in France. Think of it. A man is accused of a crime, and his judge appears to bend all his energies not upon discovering the truth, but upon proving him guilty.

"He usurps in certain ways the functions of the Almighty. In fact, if all those tricks to entrap man into convicting himself were adopted at the last Judgment even reverence would not prevent you saying that it was a low down trick on the part of the Great Judge. It appears to me all right that a lawyer should be paid to prosecute and should do his duty loyally to convict you if you are guilty. It is equally right that the lawyer should be paid to defend you. But that a judge should interfere and, in fact, should do anything except take into consideration the evidence and weigh probabilities in obscure points is monstrous."

"I once thought of writing about French law, for it is a most engrossing subject. Many a time I ask myself what was the good of tearing down the Bastille if they saved the machinery it contained. They simply took the abuses somewhere else and destroyed a piece of valuable property, which was a foolish waste.

"The material system of punishment, too, seems to me utterly wrong. Imagine a sentence passed on the man Acciarito, who attempted to stab the King of Italy! Think of it! Seven years' complete, absolute, solitary confinement! Why, no crimes that man can do merit such punishment."

"I often think of a man of whom I had heard nothing before. He told me he had studied drawing under so-and-so, anatomy under this celebrated artist and coloring under that great man. I said, 'Yes, that is all right. You have learned the details of your art, but did you ever paint a picture?' When he said 'No' I said, 'Well, you are not an artist until you have done so.'

"Similarly we make a lawyer study Blackstone and statute law and common law, and we try him before a jury and see what his skill as an orator is, but we never ask him the crucial questions, Have you ever committed a crime? Have you ever undergone a term of imprisonment? Because until that has been done a man is not fit to sit in judgment upon his fellow creatures.

"It is such a little thing that stands between all of us and crime at one time or another of our lives.

"As I said about charity, if the impulse to kill and the opportunity to kill came always at the same instant, how many of us would escape hanging. We have all of us at one time or another felt like killing something, and we have all of us at one time or another had the opportunity to kill something; but, luckily for us, impulse and opportunity did not coincide. If a man is rich and he does want to kill something he can take his gun and go out and shoot. He lets off steam in that way, and the sore place gives over hurting. I used to have a rage and let it expend itself in the letter box."

"If any one had done something to me that annoyed me or put me out, I would sit down and write a letter to him, and I would pour out all my thoughts and all the bitterness and anger and contempt and indignation and invective in my heart, and when I had cleaned myself out thoroughly I would put that letter in the box, and my wife would see that it did not go.

"She used to say when she saw me sitting down:—

"What are you going to do?"

"I am going to answer this letter. I would——"

"But you know you won't send it."

"I know that, but, by George, I am going to write it."

And Mark Twain laughed as though he enjoyed the matter very much, adding, "I have been sorry many a time that those letters were not kept, because when a man is in a thoroughgoing temper, he finds things to say worth preserving."

The Real "Mark Twain"

Carlyle Smythe*

When in the course of his talking tour round the world Mark Twain visited the famous Towers of Silence, one of our party desired to "snapshot" the scene, but permission was peremptorily refused. Curious to discover why what had readily been accorded to others should be so sternly denied to us, I asked a Parsi friend, who happened to be there, what he imagined to be the reason. Without hesitation he replied, "They are afraid Mark Twain wants the picture for the purpose of making fun of the Towers." Such is, to use Professor Brander Matthews' phrase, "the penalty of humour." Once a man has stood upon his head the public decline to believe that he can assume any other attitude; and the good Parsis very fairly represented the average person who has decreed that merrymaking is Mark Twain's only serious business. Further, it is tacitly accepted as certain that he whose mind is so spontaneously framed to mirth must surely find life all cakes and ale. True enough, the clown is always welcome in the ring, but are there not moments when he longs to rid himself of his cap and bells, and prays to be, for an interval, as other men are, suffered to play a serious part in life? Undoubtedly; and here is the little rift in the felicity of the mirth-maker, and no writer has been more heavily penalised in this respect than the author of "A Tramp Abroad." People will at once reply, "But no man could possibly look so serious as Mark Twain unless he was a born humorist." Nevertheless there is a serious Mark Twain of whom the world knows little or nothing. Some readers, of course, must have recognised that beneath the foaming fun and fancy, which often breaks into boisterous burlesque, there are deeps of earnest and suggestive thought; and that in his later works, such as "A Connecticut Yankee at the Court of King Arthur," and "Pudd'nhead Wilson," there are abundant proofs that the writer has quite as firm a grasp of some of the profoundest problems of the day as many of the specialists have. But those who share these views form a very narrow circle of his admirers.

I shall not be guilty of any indiscretion in saying that Mr. Clemens not infrequently feels the role of humorist intolerably irksome, and fur-

*Reprinted from *Pall Mall Magazine*, 16 (September, 1898), 29–36.

ther, that he would prefer to be remembered by his more serious works than by his purely humorous. Probably if a plebiscite of his admirers were taken, a huge majority of votes would be cast in favour of "Huck Finn" as Mark Twain's masterpiece. That also is my own opinion. In any case "The Prince and the Pauper" and "Joan of Arc" would not stand high on the poll, yet they are the favourites of their author. This marked and peculiar preference has always appeared to me a positive indication of the basic seriousness of Mr. Clemens's temperament. Indeed, very often the suspicion is provoked among those who know him intimately that his antic disposition is largely assumed, and that fundamentally the author of "The Innocents Abroad" is a sedate savant who has been seduced from the paths of high seriousness by a fatal sense of the ridiculous. His tastes certainly seem to support this view. He is no musician, although a fervid lover of music; but beyond a strong and natural affection for the simple negro melodies of his native land, his taste runs to Wagner. He once told me that he would walk twenty miles to hear *Tannhaüser*. Unlike all the other good Americans, Mr. Clemens has no desire to go to Paris when he dies, for his predilection among nations, the Great Republic of course excluded, is for Germany. This is not merely because of the opportunities for lifelong study which the eccentricities and genders of the German language offer, but because the sober industry and fine intelligence of the people accord with the fundamental disposition of his own mind and character. The frivolity of the French is as abhorrent to his nature as is their lubricity; and probably, if you pressed Mark Twain, he would admit that an article of his creed is that the Court language of Hades is French. It is common among English people to assume that the author of "A Connecticut Yankee at the Court of King Arthur" is somewhat cantankerously disposed towards England. Such is far from being the case, for although he laughs at many of the crusted anachronisms in our Constitution, as one nurtured in an American atmosphere needs must, Mark Twain at heart is a sincere admirer of the English and a profound lover of England. If the Democrats ever come into office again they might do much worse than send S. L. Clemens to St. James's. I do not think a better index of his real feeling for England can be afforded than an incident in our Indian tour.

The famed and fantastic pile of buildings in Lucknow, known as the Chattr Manzal or Umbrella Palace, built for his harem by the lascivious and opulent Nazir-ud-din, is now devoted to the kindly uses of the United Service Club, whose members entertained the Tramp Abroad after his first reading in the Mohammed Bagh. Responding to the toast of his health, Mark Twain, who is incurably American in thought and principle, deplored the strained relations then existing between England and America in consequence of Mr. Cleveland's letter to Congress, but he ridiculed the idea of the two peoples going to war. The Americans did not hate England; on the contrary, many Americans were moved by sentiments of the deepest friendship, founded, as one had avowed in Congress, on a pride of common ancestry. Mr. Clemens went on to say that he personally had never realised the intensity of this sentiment so clearly as during his sojourn in Lucknow. "When I visited," he concluded, "the battered and ivy-mantled ruins of the Residency, and was able there on the very spot to conjure up in my mind a picture of the heroic deeds and glorious deaths those decaying walls had witnessed, I could not but be proud that I too was of the same race as those heroes, that the blood of the ancestors of those men ran also in my veins." It may be interesting to recall in this connection that an ancestor of the author of "A Connecticut Yankee at the Court of King Arthur" was one of the judges of Charles I. Heredity may explain much in that volume that is unpalatable to English taste.

Mr. Clemens's literary preferences, although curiously eccentric, are entirely serious. He has a gluttonous appetite for books, but his taste is the despair of his family and friends. If he ever had a palate for poetry it has become atrophied, as was the case with Darwin; and now the one poet whose works afford him any pleasure is Browning, whom he reads aloud with a rare understanding of the spirit of the verse. Roughly speaking, I may say that he reads anything in prose that is clean and healthy, yet he has never been able to find a line in Thackeray which interested him. Addison and Goldsmith are thrown away upon him; and Meredith, perhaps not unnaturally, provokes him to laughter. I asked Mr. Clemens one day how he explained this indifference to the acknowledged master-craftsmen in his own trade. The explanation candidly given was, "I have no really literary taste, and never had." Yet this is an explanation whose chief vice is that it fails to explain; for he is a thorough admirer of Stevenson, and reads Mr. Kipling as much for style as for subject, while I have heard him quote both Shakespeare and Tennyson purely out of a delight for the melody of the words, because, as he says, the phrase "tastes good in the mouth." My own judgment is that this occasional relish for a poetic phrase is the survival of a taste that has decayed through disuse, or become depraved through the reading of newspapers, to which he is addicted almost as much as to smoking bad cigars. The latter are a byword among his friends. One day, in search of a smoke, he entered a "cigar divan" in Chelsea, where he was living at the time. The tobacconist, recognising him, said, "I'm afraid, Mr. Twain, you could not smoke my cigars." "I'd like," drawled Mr. Twain, "to see the cigar I couldn't smoke." Similarly I should like to see the newspaper he could not read. This devotion to newspapers is, I believe, the explanation why commonly he fails so hopelessly to appreciate the masters in literature; why he could not finish "The Newcomes" without showing signs of distress, why when Professor Brander Matthews recommended him "Barry Lyndon" as a monumental work, and Mr. Howells entreated him to read "Esmond," he could find no scene to interest him in either.

It would be quite wrong to conclude from this failure that Mark

Twain is indifferent to the value of serious craftsmanship in letters. Personally, he is a most laborious architect in the building of phrases, as those only know who have seen him "on the job," or glanced through his notebooks, a page from one of which, by the way, may be seen in his latest volume, "Following the Equator." The rare exception is to pitch upon a line that has not been revised; and this scrupulousness seems to grow with each succeeding book. "The Innocents Abroad" was written in two months, at the rate of about five thousand words a day. "Following the Equator," which is about the same length, occupied eight months, apart from the time spent in travel and taking notes. During the inception of a work, Mr. Clemens lives a life of ascetic seclusion, scorning all exercise and recreation. He goes into his study at about nine in the morning, and will not leave his manuscript till towards seven in the evening. During the interval, the only nourishment he allows himself is tobacco, which, roughly speaking, he smokes all day. The constitution which tolerates this abuse is the puzzle of physicians, for although the pulse and temperature are commonly suspiciously abnormal, Mr. Clemens enjoys tolerably robust health. The book finished and despatched to the publisher, its author proceeds to forget it as speedily as possible, and ordinarily succeeds. Lockhart relates how, when "The Bride of Lammermoor" was placed for the first time, in its complete shape, in Scott's hands, its author did not recollect one single incident, character, or conversation; and again, Thackeray states that when once looking over some back numbers of "Pendennis," he came upon "a passage which I had utterly forgotten as if I had never written it." But Sir Walter dictated "The Bride" at a time when he was in great physical pain, and the composition of "Pen" was interrupted by a severe illness. Mr. Clemens forgets the incidents and passages in his books with provoking and inexplicable regularity. An instance of this he records in his latest volume. It was at his first reading in Melbourne, when the boys in the gallery shouted out, as soon as he appeared on the stage, "Is he dead, Mark?" The author failed to place the incident referred to until some hours after. Again in the same city a lady asked him to include in his programme the story of the yellow dog. For the life of him he could not recall the faintest outline of that story, and it was only after mentioning the request to his wife that he was reminded of the incident in "Pudd'nhead Wilson," the latest book he had published.

The labour squandered by Mr. Clemens upon the construction of his sentences is largely its own reward; and his experiences testify to the fallibility of criticism in even amusing measure. Upon no work has he lavished more care than upon "Joan of Arc," which is the result of seven years' labour. As the narrative purports to be from the pen of Le Sieur de Conte, page and secretary to Joan, a simple-minded, uncultured country squire, Mr. Clemens's object was to throw off his usual style, and affect one of simple, straightforward, unadorned English. The divergence of opinions, even among leading critics, upon his literary style has been so hopelessly irreconcilable that it is not surprising that during twenty-five years no book has been sent, with Mr. Clemens's permission, "for review." Upon Mark Twain's style there must necessarily be different opinions. Moreover, his performances are unequal. He is as a prose writer probably at his worst in "The Innocents Abroad"; at his best in "The Prince and the Pauper" and "Huck Finn." Nor is he insensible of his failings in this respect. One evening, at a dinner party in Lahore, a gentleman remarked, "Oh, Mr. Clemens, I was glancing through 'The Innocents Abroad' the other day, and was surprised to discover a glaring error in grammar." "If you only found one," replied Mr. Clemens, "you were fortunate. The last time I looked at it, to refresh my memory of a passage, I discovered scores." But there is one feature in Mark Twain's written page that merits notice: he has never found it needful to step outside the covers of an English dictionary to express his thoughts. He has never been guilty of that parade of erudition which finds expression in the use of stereotyped foreign quotations that, far from improving the sentence into which they are imported, debase it as a specimen of good English. In this respect his style and diction, although possibly, as Mr. Lang avers, purely American, are not unworthy of imitation by many who, as Mr. Lang himself, variegate their pure English with hackneyed quotations.

Matthew Arnold, after spending an evening with Mark Twain at Hartford, and after a good deal of intentionally serious talk on the latter's part, said to a common friend with whom he was walking home, "Is Mark Twain never serious?" Again I remember the editor of a leading Cape paper asking Mr. Clemens whether there were not certain passages in his works which clearly were not intended to be funny. The great critic and the journalist were alike possessed with the same suspicion that in all Mark Twain says or writes the humorous intention is ever present. They resembled the Parsi, and a lady who was taken to Mr. Clemens's first reading in Port Elizabeth. From the moment he uttered his opening sentence she began to laugh, and continued to laugh so loud and so often that she grew a nuisance, and became finally so intolerable that she had to be taken out. It then transpired that she was quite blind. Having been taught that Mark Twain was the funniest man in the world, and probably having some of his richest passages read to her, she persisted in finding in every sentence laughing matter. Despite Matthew Arnold's disappointment, the general conversation of Mr. Clemens is far oftener of a serious turn than not, and his preference in selecting a programme for public reading is for the quieter passages of his works. But precisely as a leading English paper regretted he should waste his time upon "Joan of Arc," so the general public regret the inclusion of the serious items in his lecture programme. If Mark Twain has any antipathy against appearing on the lecture platform, it is because of the need to eliminate from his reading the serious items, and because of a belief that it is an undignified work to stand up before a lot of people who, having no respect for the senatorial dignity of his years, insist merely that he shall crack jokes to them for an hour or so. In his disposition there is a strongly developed serious strain, and he resents bitterly its enforced suppression.

Mr. Clemens, of course, admits that the public have a sort of prescriptive right to expect only mirth from him—for years he has encouraged them in that mistake—and that consequently when anybody buys a book or attends a lecture by Mark Twain, the primary expectation is to be amused. Accordingly, to sell a serious work, without warning as to its character, is almost gaining money under false pretences. Now, if Mr. Clemens suffers from any serious ailment, it is an enlargement of the conscience. It is this which forced him to disregard the advice of his friends at the time of his financial failure four years ago, when, instead of assigning his estate like any business man, he dedicated his days to the full payment of his creditors. Every penny of this debt he has just discharged, and at sixty-four he begins life again. Similarly, when "Joan of Arc" was first published, he insisted that the anonymity of the author should be strictly preserved. Such a decision, it is needless to add, involved a considerable financial sacrifice; but it seemed the right course to pursue in justice to his readers—smaller terms, but an easier conscience. Manifestly, however, that method is impracticable in the case of a series of lectures. It is this conscientiousness which sharply distinguishes Mark Twain from what I may call the order-in-the-slot species of authors, whose standing invitation to publishers is "put an order in the letter-box and the figure will write." Mr. Clemens will not accept an order from publisher or newspaper, because he will not forfeit the right of burning his manuscript if it falls below his usual standard in the opinion of himself and his chief literary adviser, whom I shall not name, but merely say that Mr. Clemens has been guided by the same critic throughout his literary life. Of no writer could it be more justly said, "he gave the people of his best, the worst he kept." The Australian journals contended one against the other in making him alluring offers to write a description of the "Melbourne Cup," and American journals cabled to Johannesburg, practically speaking, blank cheques for an interview with the Reform prisoners at Pretoria. But he was firm in his adhesion to what is assuredly a good and useful rule. Only once, I believe, was he tempted, and the contract was a nightmare during performance and a disappointment after.

Any sketch of the real Mark Twain would be unfinished without some reference to his great love of children. The creator of those delightful child-heroes, Huck Finn and Tom Sawyer, could not but be a devout lover of the young. His susceptibility to children may, perhaps, be best illustrated by the fact, which I have often noted, that his best platform successes are on those occasions when he is able to catch sight, among his audience, of some intelligent and appreciative child-listener, to whom he could, quite regardless of the adults, deliver his lecture. When this has happened the whole audience were assured of a high time, for the discovery of this favoured mite seemed to inspire the speaker to his best efforts, and he would enjoy himself to the top of his bent in making this chosen child happy. Often afterwards he would regret that he could not see the child, and make her acquaintance, just as if he were under some obligation to her. Upon one occasion—it was at Lucknow—there was a delightful little girl well up towards the front, who was conspicuous for her naive and evident enjoyment: to her the whole lecture, with its whimsical recipe for the moral regeneration of the world by sin-vaccination, was mainly delivered. Just before the banquet at the Chattr Manzal a guest was telling Mr. Clemens of the little creature's delight, and of a difference of opinion between her and her parents as to the precise number of possible sins. As it happened, the child was right; whereupon Mr. Clemens insisted there and then, before the banquet, upon being allowed to write a short note to his unknown little friend, giving her his signed declaration that her statement was correct—that there were only 354 sins, and all the experts in the penitentiaries of the world had not been able to invent any more. This trait, this exceeding love of children, is a very just index to the whole character of Mark Twain, who in very many respects has the heart and disposition of a little child.

There is, of course, much autobiography in his published writings, but in one of his latest there is an unconscious piece of self-portraiture, where the author says of a character, "he was always so good and kind, and moony, and absent-minded, and lovable." That is the real Mark Twain, who, in his love of the young and the basic seriousness of his character, closely resembles the author of "Alice in Wonderland." If, like Lewis Carroll, he had entered orders, he would have made an excellent parson; even now, if he would discard his fatal pseudonym when doing serious work, as did the late Mr. Dodgson, and sign himself, for instance, "Samuel Connecticut," his appearance and disposition would not belie the pious fraud. His considerateness for others is of almost episcopal dimensions. What, for example, could be a better proof of consideration for the convenience and feelings of others than Mr. Clemens's assumption of a pseudonym! "I chose my pseudonym" he explained to me, "because to nine hundred and ninety-nine persons out of a thousand it had no meaning, and also because it was short. I was a reporter in the Legislature at the time, and I wished to save the legislators time. It was much shorter to say in their debates—for I was certain to be the occasion of some questions of privilege—'Mark Twain,' than 'the unprincipled and lying Parliamentary reporter of the *Territorial Advertiser*.' "

In this rough outline of the real Mark Twain, the man who has probably contributed more than any of his contemporaries to the literature of innocent merriment, I have insisted mainly upon an apparent paradox, that the author of "The Innocents Abroad" is at bottom a grave and reverend senior. I have pleaded for this both because it is a fact, and because sufficient attention has not been paid to it. Modern English literature is so amply supplied with men who try to be funny, that there is a novelty and refreshment in meeting with an unchallenged humorist who strives to be serious. The position, however, appears so anomalous that readers doggedly persist in disbelieving in its possibility. More surprise could not be expressed at the reported breach of a fundamental law of nature than is occasioned when a regular reader of Mark Twain meets the author in his natural and serious mood, or chances upon "Joan of Arc." The flat disappointment finds expression in some such phrase as, "Well, I never! It isn't a bit like Mark Twain." The pity of this all is that some of Mr. Clemens's best literary work is thus neglected and unappreciated. Yet, strange as it may seem, there do exist people who read and relish, humorous and serious alike, all that Mark Twain has produced. In proof of this statement I offer the following anecdote. A lady one day entered the leading bookstore of Hartford, Connecticut, and inquired for Taine's "English Literature." The shopkeeper replied that he had never written such a book. "But are you quite sure?" queried the lady. "Absolutely certain," riposted the bookman; "for I've read every line he has published, from 'The Jumping Frog' upwards."

Mark Twain in London/
He Talks of His Visit and
His Doomsday Book

Anonymous*

Mark Twain has just arrived in London, and he gave me an audience yesterday, as the Emperor Francis Joseph gave him one before he left Vienna. "Mr. Clemens," said Mr. Chatto, his publisher, and I fumbled for the German oration which I had prepared. Alas! I had forgotten it at home, and all I could do was to explain that.

"No matter," remarked the American humorist, with easy gravity, "we'll do without it."

He sat down on one chair, I taking another; then he pulled out a cigar and got it alight. By the time it was blowing freely he was on his feet again, and walking up and down the room. While he walked he talked.

"Well, now," I had asked him, "what brings you to London—why have we such luck?"

He seemed to like it put that way; anyhow, I thought I caught a twinkle in his eye. It was banished almost before it had arrived, and I argued with myself, "Why, he is serious enough for a Scotch humorist."

He was, for he went on, "You see, my American publishers are about to issue an edition de luxe of my books in twenty-two volumes. I have come to London to arrange for the issue of a similar edition through my publishers here, Messrs. Chatto. The volumes will include all my writings, which I have revised for the purpose. The publishers are trying to make the books nice—as fine books as they can. The two editions will be limited to a thousand copies each—limited, mark ye!

"Yes," he soliloquised, "I fancy it's the limitation to a thousand copies that is the chief charm and value of an edition de luxe. I don't expect to read this edition de luxe myself, although you needn't tell that to anybody else. Frankly, you know, I don't suppose that anybody ever reads an edition de luxe. No one puts bric-à-brac to any very practical purpose. There's some human instinct which makes a man treasure what he is not to make any use of, because everybody does not possess it."

Next, he gave me an instance in proof, taken from his own experience with Sir Walter Scott.

*Reprinted from *London Chronicle*, June 3, 1899, p. 3; at the time reprinted in *New York Tribune*, June 10, 1899, p. 8.

"What trouble didn't I go to when I was in Edinburgh in order to get hold of an original Waverley Edition? Naturally, I had to pay a fancy price for it, which is a detail. The point is that it stands in our bookshelves to this day untouched. We have handier volumes of Scott, and read them and admire the others. Part with that edition? Not at all; it's a possession, an asset."

Here was a chance to introduce the subject of those wonderful memoirs which Mark Twain is preparing for the readers of a hundred years hence. I did so, by way of a sly question as to what were his literary plans. He took the inquiry as cheerfully as could have been expected, seeing that it referred to a doomsday book. Nay, he chatted on it freely, merely interrupting himself when he had to rout out another cigar.

"No," were his words, "I'm not expecting to write any more for publication. You naturally ask why. I have been writing diligently for thirty years, and I had arranged to stop some time ago. However, I was so situated that I was obliged to keep that pot-boiling pen going. The man is entitled to a holiday for the rest of his life who has written for twenty-five years, or been a soldier that long, or made himself useful or ornamental in any capacity for such a period. My holiday will consist in writing two books, simply for the private pleasure of writing. One of them will not be published at all: the other is written for the remote posterity of a hundred years hence."

Curiosity was strong in me to exclaim, "Won't you give us some of the contents now?" Mark Twain must have seen this, since he went on to say what the book, which is to be published, will not be.

"Although the 'Chronicle' thinks I'm going to write harsh things about people, that is an error. I said originally there would be no malice, and that is the truth. I want to set down the facts about people, and in some cases the facts may not be pleasant. But they will at least be void of malice. The 'Chronicle' pronounces the idea not to be original. I did not contend that it was. I knew it was not. There has not been an original idea in the world from Adam's time until our own.

"What I mean," he resumed, "is that no man produces an idea out of his own head. The idea first comes from the outside; you cannot grow an idea. Why, Adam could not invent the idea of modesty. He went naked until he learned from the outside that to be naked was immodest. I'm not attaching any large importance to this, for I have a sense of modesty, although Adam hadn't. I got it from Adam; I did not invent it."

We fell upon a historical precedent of Talleyrand, vouched for by Mark Twain. He left, didn't he, a book to be published when he should be dead fifty years.

"Ah," observed Mark Twain, "that was a political and historical work. The value of the book which I propose is of another sort; it presents merely portraits of folks with whom I have come in contact—humble folks and otherwise. That, precisely, may not have been done before, but, as I have remarked, I don't claim any originality. It has been intended a thousand times."

He added, what I must not forget, that he has arranged for the preservation of the manuscript. It was all I could do to refrain from asking the name of his literary agent.

"Part of the manuscript," he assured me, "is already written, and I shall so arrange matters that it will be to somebody's interest to publish the lot when the time comes. I know how to manage that, too."

So far, I had managed not to ask Mark Twain, "What is the real story of that German speech of yours which was to be delivered to the Emperor Francis Joseph, but which you forgot?" It was useless to bottle the question down any longer.

"Necessarily," he almost rebuked me, "anybody prepares for an audience with an emperor, because it is essentially formal. You prepare yourself to say the right thing in the best words. I made that preparation, and there were only eighteen words in the sentence. That was very short for a German sentence, which generally covers a good deal of ground. Mine was a compressed sentence."

"You had rehearsed it all beforehand—gone over the field, so to speak?"

"Wouldn't you? But, you see, the Emperor at once began to talk in an entirely informal way, and I didn't remember, until some little period after, that I had a speech in stock. We were indulging in a pleasant talk; no ceremony about it. Then I recollected, and I blurted out to the Emperor that I had memorised a very good speech, but that it had gone clean out of my head. 'Oh,' he said, agreeably, 'it isn't necessary.' Strangely enough, I can't recall the seventeen words yet, though a minute ago I fancied I had them."

My suggestion was that perhaps they would recur to him before he had finished his doomsday book. Meanwhile, I got him to give me what I may call a brief appreciation of the Austrian Emperor.

"Yes, indeed," it ran, "he struck me as a very fine fellow altogether. Necessarily, he must have a great deal of good, plain, attractive human nature in him, or he could not have unbent in the easy manner which I have described. You and I could not unbend if we were emperors. You agree. We should feel the stiffness of the position. Francis Joseph is just a natural man, although an emperor."

"You were impressed with him both as a man and as an emperor?"

"Why, certainly; I was greatly impressed by him. I liked him very much. I had seen him on several occasions when he was performing public functions. I had not met him before. His face is always the face of a pleasant man, with a kindly good nature. He is a man as well as an emperor—an emperor and a man."

"Humor—has he humor?"

"He has a sense of humor. One is incomplete without that. The

Emperor of Austria has a sense of humor easily discernible by the sparkle in his eyes. For the rest, throughout the Austro-Hungarian Empire this is recognised—that in these times it is the Emperor's personality, and the confidence all ranks have in him, that preserves the real political serenity in what has the outside appearance of being the opposite."

After the Emperor, Vienna and the Viennese, and Mark Twain testified handsomely of both. He had chatted of the Emperor in words as ready as they were hearty. He tackled the Emperor's capital with an equal flow of expression.

"You cannot live a couple of years in Vienna," he said, "without becoming pretty thoroughly saturated with the fascination of both the people and the city. The disposition of the citizen of Vienna is commonly described by the German word 'gemüthlich.' This is not quite translatable into English, but perhaps our nearest word to it is 'genial.' One soon becomes contented in Vienna, and is never quite willing to go away again."

Finally, I asked Mark Twain, as one who had viewed it from a distance, what he thought of the great coming together of England and America? He straightened himself up, feeling the whole Anglo-Saxon man, lit a fresh cigar, and delivered verdict.

"It has always," his words were, "been a dream of mine, this closer relationship between England and America. I hardly expected to live to see that dream realised, but it has gone far enough towards realisation to furnish me with contentment. As far as the English people are concerned, I knew that this friendly feeling was already blossoming four years ago—when I was in Australia."

"During your tour round the world, of course?"

"Yes. Mr. Cleveland had just issued that proclamation which threatened for a moment to embroil the two countries. But the people in Australasia and in India were as friendly and as hospitable to me as if there were not a suggestion of gunpowder in the air. Neither in social gatherings nor in the lecture hall did anyone say anything which could remind me that friction existed between England and America."

"You might have been at home?"

"Practically. The Australian and Indian papers never spoke of this episode with anything like bitterness, but were always moderate in tone, rational, kindly. Therefore, as I say, this English feeling is not a new birth, but is already four years old as evidenced in my personal experiences. Dear me! I could find more than one incident to suggest that it dates much farther back. It was a commander of a British warship at Havana, I should say as much as thirty years ago, who saved an American vessel's crew from being shot down, without trial, by the Spanish Government of Cuba on an uninvestigated charge of coming there with filibustering intentions."

"Then the American feeling?"

"I have spoken of the English attitude. The attitude of native-born Americans has been of this friendly sort towards England as long back as I can well remember. If there has been a feeling of any other sort I chanced upon it so rarely that it made no impression on me."

Mark Twain stood for a few moments silent, thinking. Next, he addressed me in words deeply felt, quietly uttered, which I shall make the final ones here.

"I am glad," they were, "that the present feeling between the two countries received an added and powerful impulse from a literary source, the handicraft of the pen, my guild—the English-speaking world's outburst of sympathy when the life of Rudyard Kipling was threatened."

Mark Twain

Henry Harland*

What is the explanation of Mark Twain's great, continued, and very peculiar popularity? I say peculiar, because Mark Twain is not merely, like Mr. Hall Caine and Miss Marie Corelli, popular with the masses; he is popular also with the remnant; his works are enjoyed and esteemed by people of taste and cultivation—and that, in spite of faults, of vices, which, one would imagine antecedently, must render any work, to people of taste and cultivation, utterly abhorrent.

Let us be cruel (that we may be kind in due season), and give to a few of Mark Twain's more conspicuous and constant vices their common names. In re-reading *The Innocents Abroad*, for instance, I think one cannot help being struck by the vulgarity that mars the book, and by the illiteracy, by the ignorance and the inaccuracy, by the narrowness, the provincialism, above all by the perpetual, the colossal irreverence. And yet, one reads *The Innocents Abroad* with pleasure, even perhaps with some degree of profit; it is still, for all its vices, and much as they offend one, it is still a book one likes. Why? What is the explanation?

I'm afraid we shall never discover the explanation, unless we begin by considering the vices somewhat closely. It will only be by recognising and eliminating them, that we shall obtain, in the end, the residue of saving virtues. And we may eliminate at the outset, if you will, we may condone as venial, Mark Twain's illiteracy, ignorance, and inaccuracy. When he alludes to the grave-digger's discourse over the skull of Yorick, when he mentions that the signal for the fighting on St. Bartholomew's Day was rung from the towers of Notre Dame, when he translates "Genova la Superba" "Genoa the Superb"—it is easy to lift an eyebrow, shrug a shoulder, smile, and pass on. Even when he tells us that the "pax hominibus bonae voluntatis," which he saw blazoned in gold on the walls of St. John Lateran, "is not good scripture," we can commend him, in charity, to the intercession of St. Jerome. But Mark Twain's vulgarity, his narrowness, his provincialism, his irreverence, are made of sterner stuff. They are in the very texture of his work, not merely on its surface—they are of its spirit, they inform it, they determine its savor; and they are all

*Reprinted from *London Daily Chronicle*, December 11, 1899, p. 3.

bound and mixed up together, they are inseparable; it is impossible to discuss one without connoting the others. They are different manifestations, as it were, of the same constitutional defect: a total inability, namely, to respect what he cannot understand; an instant conviction that what he cannot see does not exist, and that those who profess to see it are hypocrites—that what he does not believe is inevitably false, and that those who profess to believe it are either hypocrites or fools. As if a color-blind man were to condemn as fools or hypocrites those who profess to see blue in the Union Jack, or to admire the splendors of a sunset.

It is this constitutional defect, I fancy, which accounts for Mark Twain's most egregious solecisms, for his most unlovely blasphemies. It is this which leads him to the perpetration of his numberless cheap and dreary jests about the "Old Masters." It is this which so deprives him of any sense of proportion as to enable him to write seriously of Raphael, Michael Angelo, and Canova in the same breath; to explain that the exterior of St. Peter's is "not one-twentieth part as beautiful as the Capital at Washington"; to suggest that it is the supreme mission of art to "copy nature with faultless accuracy"; to prefer the marble millinery which has occasioned most of us a shudder in the Campo Santo at Genoa to the "damaged and dingy statuary" of the Louvre; to declare that "wherever you find a Raphael, a Rubens, a Michael Angelo, or a Da Vinci, you find artists copying them, and the copies are always the handsomer. Maybe the originals were handsome when they were new, but they are not now."

It is this terrible inability to respect what he cannot understand, this fatal readiness to despise those whose opinions he does not share, which makes it possible for Mark Twain to crack his ghastly jokes about death, his dreadful jokes at the expense of things that to the majority of civilized mankind are sacrosanct, his jokes at the expense of the saints, and the pictures and relics of the saints—nay, at the expense of more sacred relics still, at the expense of the Crown of Thorns and the True Cross. "They say St. Mark had a tame lion, and used to travel with him—and everywhere that St. Mark went the lion was sure to go." "When we see a party looking tranquilly up to heaven, unconscious that his body is shot through with arrows, we know that that is St. Sebastian." "I think we have seen as much as a keg of these nails." What nails? Nails from the True Cross, if you can believe me. It is always, I suppose, the same inability to respect what he cannot understand which makes it possible for Mark Twain to write facetiously of his travels in Palestine, and to crack a final joke about the True Cross in the presence of the Holy Sepulchre.

All this is surely very shocking; to some of us it must be very repulsive. Why is it, then, that in spite of all this we can still read Mark Twain with pleasure, perhaps with profit, still esteem him, and acknowledge his good right to the popularity, even with the remnant, which he has won? Why must we still reckon *The Innocents Abroad* among the books we like?

Well, certainly not, at any rate, certainly not because of its humor. The humor of the book, one is surprised to find on re-reading it after a lapse of years, is by no means its most salient feature nor its brightest merit—is indeed, for the most part, extremely thin, flat, and inexpensive. Sometimes, in our weaker moments, it may excite a pale flicker of a smile; never a laugh; never, never—*au grand jamais*—that deep internal glow which is our response to humor in its finer flower. But if it is not the humor of the book, what is it?

I wonder whether it isn't in some measure—no, in great measure—the downright barbarism of the book? The big, bluff, rough, honest barbarism of the book and of its writer? What Mark Twain cannot see, he cannot see at all; he cannot believe in it, he cannot allow for it; you and I are hypocrites (or fools) for professing to see it. But what he can see, he sees with the unwearied eyes of the barbarian, of one to whom the old world is new—of a shrewd, clear-headed barbarian, outspoken, fearless, sincere, who knows how to present his impressions lucidly, vividly. And it is necessarily interesting to get a clear-headed barbarian's impression of our old world, interesting and fascinating. He will gibe at our gods, mock at our sacred mysteries, profane our shrines, march booted and bare-headed upon our holy ground, he will outrage our sensibilities, trample upon our conventions, assault our prejudices and our fond illusions; but never mind. He cannot see what we can see, and we cannot hope to make him see it; but he will see much that we have not seen, and we (because the larger contains the less) shall be able, when he points it out, to see it with him. Fancy travelling through Europe with a keen-witted English-speaking pilgrim from the moon—visiting Paris and the Louvre with him, Rome and the Vatican, Naples, Constantinople, Athens, Como, and the Hellespont, and listening to his commentaries upon these familiar sights. Would it be instructive, suggestive, amusing, exhilarating? Well, Mark Twain, this pilgrim from the Mississippi valley, brings to Europe eyes very nearly as fresh as the moonman's. It is instructive, suggestive, amusing, exhilarating to travel with him. He speaks his own quaint manner of English with fluency and energy and picturesque eloquence; and he is good-humored and wholesome; and his heart is in the right place.

Of course, *The Innocents Abroad* is not the best of Mark Twain's books. *Roughing It*, I think, is a better book; I am sure *Tom Sawyer* and *Huckleberry Finn* are better books. But the qualities and the defects of *The Innocents Abroad* are the qualities and the defects of Mark Twain's temperament, and they are present in varying proportions in all his books: vulgarity, narrowness, irreverence, freshness of vision, honesty, good-humor, wholesomeness. Mr. Brander Matthews, in a "Biographical Criticism" accompanying these volumes, says that Mark Twain "must be classed with Molière and Cervantes." But then Mr. Brander Matthews, in the same article, brackets the late Mr. J. R. Lowell also with Molière and

Cervantes, and that somehow shakes one's faith in Mr. Matthews' judgment. Time will show.

The present "édition de luxe" of Mark Twain's works is handsomely printed upon good imitation hand-made paper, and ornamented by some of the worst wash-drawings (by a Mr. Peter Newell) that it has ever been my lot to see. "Theatre" is spelled "theater," "centre" "center," and "traveller" is allowed but a single "l."

Mark Twain to Spend Winter
Here/Author Returns
an Anti-Imperialist

Anonymous*

"Mark Twain," sometimes known as Samuel Clemens, on the *Minnehaha*, returned home last night after an absence in the outside world of five years, and landed on his native shores with a smile of good-natured fun on his lips that even the terrible experience he has passed through could not dim. The great humorist has triumphed over his own misfortunes, as well as those of others, a thing which is said to be impossible even for philosophers.

"I have had lots of fun," remarked Mr. Clemens, as he came down the gangplank. "I have enjoyed myself, except for a twinge of dyspepsia now and then, in every country and under every sky. Fun has no nationality. It has the freedom of the world. But I think I had most fun in Vienna, with the poor old Reichsrath. I was there for a year and a half, and had plenty of time to take it in. It was one of the biggest jokes I have ever seen, and I enjoyed it immensely.

"Now, I have lied so much, in a genial, good-natured way, of course, that people won't believe me when I speak the truth. I may add that I have stopped speaking the truth. It is no longer appreciated—in me.

"I have found that when I speak the truth, I am not believed, and that I have never told a lie so big but that some one had sublime confidence in my veracity. I have, therefore, been forced by fate to adopt fiction as a medium of truth. Most liars lie for the love of the lie; I lie for the love of truth. I disseminate my true views by means of a series of apparently humorous and mendacious stories."

"Mr. Clemens, have you had time to give any thought to the grave question of imperialism?" I asked.

"It is most too grave a question for one of my temperament, but I have taken a try at it. I have thought of it, and it has got the best of me.

"I left these shores, at Vancouver, a red-hot imperialist. I wanted the American eagle to go screaming into the Pacific. It seemed tiresome and tame for it to content itself with the Rockies. Why not spread its wings

*Reprinted from *New York Evening Telegram*, October 16, 1900, p. ?, as a shorter version of the text in *New York Herald*, October 16, 1900, p. 4. Clipping in Mark Twain Papers of Bancroft Library.

over the Philippines, I asked myself? And I thought it would be a real good thing to do.

"But I have thought some more, since then, and I have read carefully the treaty of Paris, and I have seen that we do not intend to free, but to subjugate the people of the Philippines. We have gone there to conquer, not to redeem.

"We have also pledged the power of this country to maintain and protect the abominable system established in the Philippines by the Friars.

"It should, it seems to me, be our pleasure and duty to make those people free, and let them deal with their own domestic question in their own way. And so I am an anti-imperialist. I am opposed to having the eagle put its talons on any other land.

"But I want to say that I cannot conscientiously support Mr. Bryan. I am not so much of an anti-imperialist as that. I have been told that I cannot vote in this election, but if I could I should not vote for Mr. Bryan. As to what I would do I cannot say, as I am a mugwump, and a mugwump won't vote until he has had plenty of time to look the thing over."

"Have you any books about ready for publication?"

"No; but I have several on the way. I wrote myself out in the line of anecdotes and humorous sketches in my last book. I ran short even in that and could barely find enough material to fill it.

"I am now falling back upon fiction; but, as I have said, my fiction is different from the fiction of others. No matter what I write in that line people will think that I am hiding some truth behind the stalking horse of a story."

"Will you have an American story?"

"You see, I write the story and then fill in the place, like blanks in a railway form. The places don't count so much. The story is the thing.

"I shall very probably write a story with the scene laid in this country, or I shall place the scene of one of my present uncompleted stories here. This can be done rather handily, after the whole story is written.

"But I am not going to publish another book for at least a year."

Mr. Clemens says that he has made his plans for at least a year.

"I shall spend the winter in New York, making my home at the Earlington Hotel. I shall spend the time very quietly, doing nothing but reading and writing a little on my books, and doing some little work for the magazines.

"I do not expect to see much of the bright side of the city; that is, I shall not go out much to the theatres and other places of amusement. I expect to keep close and devote my time to reading, smoking and as little work as possible.

"In the spring I shall return to Hartford, Conn., where Mrs. Clemens, my daughters and myself will settle down for some home life, after nine years of wandering up and down on the earth.

"No. I shall not lecture. I have abandoned the lecture tour that I had almost arranged."

Mr. Clemens is looking as young as he did nine years ago, when he left this country on his first extended tour abroad. His face has as few wrinkles, and there does not seem to be one in that kindly countenance that has not been traced and graven by good nature, fun and laughter. His hair and mustache are a shade whiter, and his form is a little more bowed, but he seems to be in better health than he was in 1891.

He left America in 1891, and went to the baths of Aix les Bains; then, in a few months, to Berlin, where he lectured. In 1892 he lived on the Riviera, then retreated again to the German baths, and in 1893 went to Florence, Italy, where he lived for several months, and while there completed "Joan of Arc" and "Pudd'nhead Wilson."

After this he spent two years in France, where he says he wrestled, like Jacob, day and night, but in vain, with the intricacies of the French grammar. He gave it up.

In 1895, he returned for a short time to this country. Then he started on another tour, which embraced Asia, Africa and Australasia.

An American Humorist

James L. Ford*

I myself was the original discoverer of Mark Twain, at least so far as our school was concerned, and the other day, as I sat talking to the ruddy-faced and grizzled man of sixty-five, my memory went back just one-third of a century, and I saw myself once more seated with my companions around the big stove in the upper hall of the old schoolhouse rubbing with witch-hazel extract the shins and elbows that had been bruised in the playground and reading aloud in turn from the "Jumping Frog."

We were too young then to understand a great many things that some of us know now. I know that I had no idea that the author of the little book of sketches that had fallen into our hands was in the legitimate line of succession to the leadership of American humor—a line that may be said to have begun with Lieutenant Derby and ended with Bill Nye. I do not mean to say that Mark Twain was deposed from the leadership, he simply rose to higher things, and now, wisely enough, is devoting his later years to books which, like "Joan of Arc," and "Huckleberry Finn," are far more likely to outlive the twentieth century than are "The Innocents Abroad" or "The Gilded Age."

We were too young, we boarding-school youngsters, who gathered nightly about the big stove to anoint our shins with witch-hazel and our minds with pure, healthful and vigorating humor—to this very day the peculiar smell of that ointment never fails to recall to my mind the story of the bad little boy who did not come to grief—we were too young to know anything about the history of American humor or the technique of the professional humorist. But we had pretty clear ideas as to what was funny, and on the night that I came into the upper hall with the "Jumping Frog" in my hand, we had an adjourned session after the teacher had made his rounds, and, until far into the night we sat listening to those wonderful stories and muffling and choking down our laughter for fear it would be heard two floors below. That night we voted that the new humorist was pretty nearly as funny as Dickens and considerably funnier than Artemus Ward.

I have learned a great deal since then about humorous literature, the

*Reprinted from Collier's Weekly, 26 (November 3, 1900), 11.

way in which it is prepared and the men who have achieved fortunes and reputation in some cases, delirium tremens and poverty in others, by their skill in its preparation, and now, after a lapse of a third of a century, I see no reason why the verdict rendered by half a dozen boys on that winter's night should be reversed.

The story of the life of Samuel L. Clemens has been told and retold a thousand times. But it is a story which cannot be told too often to the rising generation of America, nor is there any writer in the land, no matter of what sex, age or previous condition of seriousness, who can fail to profit by a close study of a literary career which had its beginning in our own native soil, and whose constant upward tendency from that day until the present has scarcely a parallel in the craft of letters of to-day.

It is impossible to discuss his work without comparing it in a way with that of his contemporaries and taking into account the rather peculiar literary age in which he has lived and achieved his reputation. One of the peculiarities of this age is that it has produced very few writers whose work has improved and mellowed and ripened as the years went by. The subject is not a pleasant one for consideration, nor do I care to mention by name the many who have entered the field with a book or a story of remarkable brilliancy and promise, and then gone doddering slowly down the broad path that leads to weak babblings and afterward complete silence. We have only to mention the name of any American writer of the past quarter of a century and then ask ourselves, whether it is his first or his last book by which he is recalled to memory. That will tell the story, and I am afraid that in nine cases out of ten the story is not one of sound healthful literary growth.

I do not think that any one will deny that Mark Twain's name will be linked in our literary history with that of his later and more serious work—the finer fruit of ripened thought, experience and travel—rather than with the first outcroppings, rich as they were, of that native humor that was so keen and homely and racy of the soil. But a few days ago, as I listened to his talk about his journey around the world and thought of the great and honorable task for which that journey had been undertaken, it seemed to me that the great humorist had not yet passed his prime; and as he spoke vaguely and in uncertain notes about the work which he has laid out for his future years, the idea impressed itself upon me that the great book of his life is yet to be written, and that, should his life be spared, it still remains for him to give to the world the work by which he will be remembered throughout all time.

It is scarcely necessary to speak of the enormous debt of honor that impelled Mr. Clemens to undertake the most extended tour of the age at a time of life when most writers are thinking only of rest from their labor. It is a pity, however, that the complete story of that remarkable journey—of the strange and distant lands visited, of the enormous audiences that assembled everywhere to see this representative American writer, of the rapidity with which the debt was wiped out—cannot be told in full as a valuable lesson to the rising generation. There is one fact in connection with it, however, that must have impressed itself upon those who have either heard Mr. Clemens talk about it or read the printed interviews on the day following his arrival, and that is his keen sense of the dignity of humor.

I wish that every actor, as well as every humorist, could be made to study the way in which this distinctive American, on his return to his native land, rises to the dignity of the occasion and discusses the countries that he has visited and the remarkable personages whom he has met with a seriousness that the subject demands. Nothing is easier for a comedian than to "clown" a part for the purpose of "getting a laugh." But there is only one way in which a comedian can win enduring popularity and renown, and that is by knowing when to resist the temptation to be funny. It is a pitiably small achievement to make the unthinking laugh. The comedian can do it by falling down on the stage and making a face, and the travelled humorist can always prod guffaws out of fools of a certain class by calling the Queen of England "Mrs. Guelph," and alluding to the Emperor of Germany as "Bill."

In this school of literary humor, the counterpart of that to which the comic stage policeman, with his red whiskers and stuffed club, belongs, the average oyster opener can be taught to excel in a few easy lessons. But it is only a great humorist with the proper respect for his profession who can be serious and respectful and dignified when he knows that a great part of his audience is hoping and expecting that he will be funny at the expense of what he has seen and learned in foreign lands.

"After having travelled and seen and studied as much as I have during the past five years, and especially after having been received with such great consideration wherever I have been," said Mr. Clemens thoughtfully, "it would ill become me at the moment of my return to speak lightly or in a merely humorous vein of my journey." And that remark is thoroughly characteristic of the man.

He was lecturing in Australasia at the time of President Cleveland's Venezuela letter, but not even the feeling engendered by that document could interfere with the cordiality of his reception or the success of his entertainments. At Pretoria he saw President Kruger and also paid a visit to the Jameson Raiders, who were there in prison and whom he endeavored to cheer by telling them of the various great works, such as "Don Quixote" and "Pilgrim's Progress," which never would have been written had not their authors been put in jail. But somehow, according to Mr. Clemens, his words did not seem to have a very cheering effect on that fortunate prison. The pleasantest city that he found in Europe was Vienna, where he remained from July, 1897, to May, 1899. There he made one or two speeches that have since become world-famous, and met a great many of the principal citizens, including among others the Emperor of Austria.

His present plans are not yet decided upon, but it is probable that he will spend the winter in New York, where he has hosts of friends and where he is certain to become a notable figure in the social and literary life of the town. In the spring he may return to his old home in Hartford, there to devote himself to the literary work that he has in hand.

Paradoxical as it may seem, it is the subordination of the humorous element to the serious side of his character that has made Mark Twain's work perhaps the greatest of its kind in this country. It is because of this serious vein of thought that he is bound to outlive men who have been mere fun-makers or jugglers of words.

I shall never forget that it was he who first taught me the important lesson that bad little boys do not always come to grief in the end, and particularly cheering that lesson was to me at the time that I learned it. Some of the good little boys who read the "Jumping Frog" at the same time that I did, have not acquitted themselves as well as their teachers predicted that they would, and personal modesty prevents any reference to what has since happened to some of the others. It was that same quality of truth and seriousness that gave a real value to "The Innocents Abroad," which, apart from its delightful humor, is one of the very best books of European travel that I have ever read.

The author of that book—the Clemens of a third of a century ago—was a man well schooled in the life of the Mississippi River and the crude civilization of Western mining towns. He was a man who absorbed knowledge naturally and easily, as, fortunately for him, his pores had not been clogged by a four years' course of classical education. He had been thinking for a long while before he began to write, and when he took up his pen he set about his work with a seriousness of purpose that was akin to the seriousness of his face, and that solemn manner of delivery which we expect in our humorists, and which at the present day is a puzzle to a good part of the British public.

Artemus Ward was the first man who ever dared to say funny things in London with a serious cast of countenance, and it is largely due to his influence, and in later years to that of Mark Twain, that our national humor has obtained the extraordinary hold that it now has on the English reading public of the world.

The Mark Twain of to-day is the Mississippi pilot of "Jumping Frog" fame, mellowed by forty years of the sort of education that only contact with the very best side of the world can give. He has the same drawl, the same bushy hair, the same serious face, clear eyes and ruddy skin. His education has been of the kind that sinks deep and leaves externals almost unchanged. Few men of his day have enjoyed better opportunities than he for seeing life under many and varied conditions, and knowing the distinguished men and women of his own and other countries. What he found to do during the ten months that he spent in England, or the twenty that he passed in Vienna, he did not tell me; but that the world will be the gainer for his work and study during that period of time, I have no manner of doubt.

The marvel to me is that a man can remain so many years abroad and return so little changed as to externals, and with not a perceptible trace of foreign manner or accent. I suppose it is because his personality—which is strongly American—permeates him through and through, and is not a mere outward veneer to be removed when the fashion changes.

[Paying Off His Debts]

James B. Pond*

After an absence of five years Mark Twain returned last month to his home from "a tour around the world to pay his debts." In a tribute in the New York *Times*, Major Pond discusses the humorist and his remarkable five years' trip as follows: On the fifteenth of July, 1895, he began his tour in Cleveland. The great Music Hall there gave him a send-off with an audience of over 3,000 people who packed the building, on a mid-July night, with the mercury in the nineties. He had been very ill, subject to many annoyances from being dragged from a sick bed to appear in supplementary proceedings in New York the day before starting, and suffering from a huge carbuncle that had kept him confined to his home for seven weeks. In my announcement of the tour across the continent "Mark" suggested to me that traveling around the world was nothing as everybody did that, but what he was traveling for was unusual; everybody didn't do that. From Cleveland he went by the steamers *Northland* and *Northwest* to Duluth, Minn., and St. Paul and Winnipeg, and over the Great Northern route to Puget Sound, Vancouver, and Victoria, B. C., where he sailed on the 21st day of August by steamship *Warrimoo* for Australia, having delivered twenty-four lectures in twenty-two cities. It was not until he reached Great Falls, Mon., half way across the continent, that Mark was able to leave his hotel, except as he was driven to and from the lecture hall or took a short walk, but a greater exhibition of courage and determination I never witnessed than in these struggles from day to day to carry through the work he had planned for ridding himself of the bondage of debt. At Seattle he was interviewed by his nephew, Mr. Samuel Moffett of the San Francisco *Examiner*, when he gave himself four years to make money enough to pay his debts. Two years from that time he wrote me from Lucerne, Switzerland, that he was now satisfied that those debts would be paid off a year earlier than the prophecy and without any further help from the platform, and that he was now a cheerful man; that he had managed to pull through the lecture campaign, although from the first night in Cleveland to the last one in Cape Town it has been pretty hard work; that he believed that in Cape Town he stood

*Reprinted from *Current Literature*, 29 (December, 1900), 709-10.

on a platform for the last time. Later I wrote, offering him $10,000 if he would deliver ten lectures on his return home this autumn. He replied that no terms I could offer would remove his prejudice against the platform. He had lectured once in Vienna and once in Budapest for fun, not for money; that he liked to talk for nothing about twice a year; but talking for money was work and "that takes the pleasure out of it." I consider Mark Twain one of the greatest geniuses of our time. I think I know him better than he is known to most men—wide as his circle of acquaintance is, big as his reputation is. He is as great a man as he is a genius, too. Tenderness and sensitiveness are his two strongest traits. He has one of the best hearts that ever beat. One must know him well fully to discern all of his best traits. I sometimes think that he fights shy of having it generally suspected that he is kind and tender-hearted, but many of his friends do know it. He possesses some of the frontier traits—a fierce spirit of retaliation and the absolute confidence that life-long "partners" in the Western sense develop. Injure him and he is merciless, especially if you betray his confidence. Gen. Grant and "Mark Twain" were the greatest of friends. C. L. Webster & Co. (Mark Twain) published Gen. Grant's Memoirs. Yet how like and unlike are the careers of the soldier and the citizen! Grant, poor, a tanner, a small farmer, selling cordwood for a living, with fewer prospects for rising than any ex-West Pointer in the army; then the greatest military reputation of any age; twice President of the United States, the most honored guest of peoples and rulers who ever made the circuit of the earth. "Mark Twain," a printer's apprentice in a small Missouri River town, then a "tramping jour" printer, a Missouri River roustabout, guarding freight piles all night on the levee for pocket money; a river pilot, a rebel guerrilla, a reporter in a Nevada mining town, then suddenly the most famous author of the age, a man of society, the most aristocratic clubs of America and all around the civilized globe flung open to him; adopted with all the honors into one of the most exclusive societies on this continent; the favored companion of the most cultivated spirits of the age, welcomed abroad in all Courts almost as a crowned head. "Peace hath its victories," etc. There is indeed another parallel between Grant and "Twain." Grant found himself impoverished two years before his death, when was left to him the most heroic part of his life work, to write his memoirs (while he knew he was dying), for which, through his publishers, C. L. Webster & Co., (Twain) his family received nearly $500,000. That firm failed in 1894, leaving liabilities to the amount of $80,000 over and above all it owned, for "Mark" to pay, and which he has earned with his voice and pen in a tour around the world, paying every creditor in full, in one year less time than he calculated when he started in Cleveland on July 15, 1895. Yes, there is a parallel between the two great heroes, more like than unlike. It is an enviable homecoming this most popular writer in the English language is having.

A Little Man and a Great Subject

Anonymous*

Prof. Harry Thurston Peck has seen fit to give to the American public his opinion of Mark Twain. "The Bookman," which is edited by Mr. Peck, owes its popularity partly to the fact that it is the best periodical of its kind in this country—which is not saying very much—and partly to the really interesting collection of literary gossip and news which it contains. But it is not, under Mr. Peck's guidance, destined to become the great enlightening literary influence of the American people, although the confidence with which that gentleman exploits his personal opinions seems to indicate something of the kind. For instance, Mr. Peck attacks Mark Twain in this wise:

> Putting aside all prejudice and looking at his work in a purely achromatic way, a critical and truthful judgment upon Mark Twain can be summed up in a very exiguous space.

Twice within two months Mr. Peck has claimed that peculiar and perfect balance of judgment, that pellucid clearness of vision, and that unflinching frankness which are popularly supposed to belong only to the authors of the Bible. He has assured his readers that he, and only he, is quite unprejudiced, candid, and reasonable. The other opinion for which he has recently claimed this infallibility of judgment was that expressed on the hazing question, when he declared his belief that the fourth class men at West Point were "yaps," and needed the refining and salutary influence of systematic prize-fighting, lawbreaking, and clandestine persecution in order to make them gentlemen. He has also claimed infallibility on questions of correct English, correct breeding, and campaign problems, and if he keeps on it is possible that he will be issuing papal bulls instead of the other kind.

After explaining his intention to tell a misguided and groping public the real truth about Mark Twain, he proceeds:

*Reprinted from *Washington* (D.C.) *Times*, January 31, 1901, p. 4. The essay by Peck, "As to Mark Twain," *Bookman* [New York], 12 (January, 1901), 441–42, is reprinted in Frederick Anderson, ed., *Mark Twain: The Critical Heritage* (London: Routledge & Kegan Paul, 1971), pp. 231–34.

158

Mark Twain is first and last and all the time, so far as he is anything, a humorist and nothing more. He wrote *The Jumping Frog* and *Innocents Abroad* and *Roughing It,* and these are all the real books that he ever wrote. He set forth the typically American characters of Colonel Sellers and Tom Sawyer and Huckleberry Finn, and these are all the real characters that he ever drew.

How Mr. Peck reconciles his statement of the reality of the characters mentioned with his other statement about the unreality of the books in which they figure, and how a real book can exist without any real characters, he does not explain. There are some things which the reader has to find out by the light of nature.

After some more remarks about the folly of people who take Mark Twain seriously, and assertions that his later books cannot be read at all, the critic concludes: "A hundred years from now it is very likely that 'The Jumping Frog' alone will be remembered."

The opinion of an educated flea on the subject of a solar eclipse might be interesting from a scientific point of view, but not valuable. So with Mr. Peck's opinion of the fame of Mark Twain. Like the brain whence it issued, it is worth something for dissecting purposes. In the beginning, there is a peculiarly bourgeois flavor about the assumption that "nothing but a humorist" is a crushing phrase. It belongs to the deadly serious era of the country academy, when the valedictorian of the class arises, with the world on his shoulders, and begs his fellow-students to be serious, because life is not a joke. The humor of Mark Twain is the quality in which he is greatest, and also most American. It has been given to this country to take great things lightly, to hide deep feeling with a jest, to cloak pathos with humor, and indignation with satire. The soldier goes to his death with a grim jest on his lips, the captain of industry, weighted with a burden of responsibility, struggling with obstacles all but insurmountable, will not admit even to his friend that the strain is killing him, but makes a mock of his toil. There is a gigantic irony in the darkest dangers of the Republic, and if our serious moods are cloaked with laughter, there is a sob in the laughter, and an undertone of sadness in all our fun. That is the American spirit, and of that spirit Mark Twain, biggest, best and most human of our writerfolk, is the living embodiment. The half-fledged American may take life with the solemnity of a promenading penguin—the men who really bear the burden of the day seek refuge in a gayety of spirit which is not thoughtlessness, but true courage. This saving quality of humor is our antidote for cynicism, pessimism, and the solemn Philistinism of Mr. Peck's essay on "The Little Touches." The average American, after reading that essay, will believe that Mr. Peck is fully competent to do the worrying for the whole country, and therefore a handy person to have in the house.

If Mark Twain were "nothing but a humorist," it would not hinder his being the greatest author we have. But those who have read his "Life on the Mississippi" know that he can also, on occasion, be a poet and though his ethical arguments are usually veiled with satire, there is invariably a clearness, a sanity, and a just balance about his view of moral problems which produce somewhat the effect of an unusual quantity of ozone in the air, or a bright, sunshiny morning after a week of rain. He never takes a small or biased view of a thing. The bombast of sham chivalry and the absurdities of mock religion, the crudities of half-formed civilization and the rottenness of ancient abuses, are not spared by him; and yet, through it all, there is a whimsical, tender affection for poor, old, abused, warped, troubled humanity. The sin he hates, but never the sinner, and that is where he differs from smaller people who are apt to hate the sinner, but not the sin. In the wholesomeness, breeziness, and largeness of his views, even more than in his command of language or his insight into character, Mark Twain is great. He does not need the conventionalities of literature to make his ideas impressive; he can find the problems of the universe in a flat-boat, and make you see them there. He can put a whole philosophical system into the mouth of Huckleberry Finn, and its force will be just as apparent through the slang of the Mississippi Valley as it would in the scientific language of Kant—if not more so. There is no pose, no artificiality about Mark Twain; and that is one reason why, in a convention-ridden world, he has not produced the effect that smaller men, masquerading in large suits of armor, often do. When he encounters the conventions, the conventions fall, with the suddenness experienced by Sir Launcelot when lassoed by The Boss in that incomparable idyl of fun, "The Connecticut Yankee at King Arthur's Court." One cannot, however, expect Mr. Harry Thurston Peck to appreciate the picturesqueness of such a combat. It would be out of character. He could no more do it than Mark Twain himself could have gone before the world as Prof. Sammy Langhorne Clemens. As Mr. Peck once remarked, there is everything in a name.

Mark Twain on McKinley

[Rollo Ogden]*

We have already expressed our gratitude for the great service which Mr. Twain has rendered his countrymen, since returning to America, by administering to them large doses of wholesome truth in the form of satire. At first, his very victims shook with laughter. It was only Mark's admirable fooling, you know. But when his shafts began to pierce even the thick hide of our complacent Imperialists, they lost interest in the great American humorist. They had laughed gleefully, and slapped each other on the back, when he impaled Tammany on the lance of his irony; but the moment he began to let the sawdust out of their Imperial doll, they wondered at his poor taste, and feared his wit was growing dull. Anyhow, it was only after-dinner nonsense of his, which he himself would soon be ashamed of.

But Mr. Clemens returns to the attack in greater force than ever in the February *North American.* His satirical weapons never were keener, or played about the heads of Imperialists with a more merciless swish. In one long burst of sarcasm he exposes the weariful hypocrisy of the American policy in the Philippines, and covers it with ridicule mountain-high. Mark Twain was never a respecter of persons, and in this grim satire of his he flies straight at the highest. It is President McKinley whom he finds to have been playing "the European game, the Chamberlain game," when "the Philippine temptation" proved too strong—not only playing it, but playing it badly. Of the President's noble utterance about "criminal aggression," Mark says cruelly: "The memory of that fine saying will be outlived by the remembrance of no act of his but one—that he forgot it within the twelvemonth, and its honorable gospel along with it." Another dart of the satirist's, levelled at the same devoted head, is Mr. Twain's description of "the Trinity of our national gods," each with "the emblem of his service"—Washington, the sword of the Liberator; Lincoln, the Slave's Broken Chains; "The Master," the Chains Repaired. This is flat *lèse*-McKinley, in our humble opinion.

For theme and title of his delicious though biting satire, Mr. Clemens chose "The Person Sitting in Darkness." He rightly divined that benighted

*Reprinted from *Nation*, 72 (February 7, 1901), 104–05.

161

heathen, for whose good and goods we are making such great exertions, must be puzzled at our strange mixture of greed and godliness. Our satirist's aim is to explain the mystery. This he does by a long recital of "the historical facts" (Mark Twain being the inimitable historian), winding up with a summary which we cannot refrain from quoting. He kindly expounds the facts to the Sitter in Darkness:

> They look doubtful, but in reality they are not. There have been lies; yes, but they were told in a good cause. We have been treacherous; but that was only in order that real good might come out of apparent evil. True, we have crushed a deceived and confiding people; we have turned against the weak and the friendless who trusted us; we have stamped out a just and intelligent and well-ordered republic; we have stabbed an ally in the back and slapped the face of a guest; we have bought a Shadow from an enemy that hadn't it to sell; we have robbed a trusting friend of his land and his liberty; we have invited our clean young men to shoulder a discredited musket and do bandit's work under a flag which bandits have been accustomed to fear, not to follow; we have debauched America's honor and blackened her face before the world; but each detail was for the best. We know this. The Head of every State and Sovereignty in Christendom and ninety per cent of every legislative body in Christendom, including our Congress and our fifty State Legislatures, are members not only of the Church, but also of the Blessings-of-Civilization Trust. This world-girdling accumulation of trained morals, high principles, and justice, cannot do an unright thing, an unfair thing, an ungenerous thing, an unclean thing. It knows what it is about. Give yourself no uneasiness; it is all right.

It is a sure instinct which leads Mr. Clemens to barb his arrows with satire like this. In no other way can you so effectively assail a certain kind of sanctimonious and official humbug. Argument it sheds like rain. Appeals on moral grounds it answers with fresh rolling of the eyes heavenward. But a sarcastic flaying, like Mark Twain's, with a vigorous rubbing of salt on the raw, is the only way to reach a consciousness so deeply cased in fat. "Mr. Dooley" was the earliest to see this, and we hear amusing tales of the wondering amaze produced in the White House intellect by some of his irreverent jests. But Mark Twain easily steps to the front, and shows the youngsters that the *vieux sabreur* is still master of them all. Like another Aretino, it will soon be said of him that no monarch (or President) will dare commit a *sottise* or crime without first taking measures to avert his terrible satire.

The courage which Mr. Clemens has displayed is as great as his skill of pen. Other satirists have wreaked themselves upon the dead. It was in the 'Dialogues des Morts' that Cortes and Montezuma were set to discussing the morals of conquest *ad majorem Dei gloriam*, and also *ad majorem hominis pecuniam*. But Mr. Twain has boldly struck the shield of the living. His joking is no joke for its objects. Not counting the risk to his personal popularity, he has let us see the flame of his honest anger burning against shams and cheating in the highest matters of national policy. He is a man to be reckoned with in this business. The ordinary epithets cannot be flung at him. Mark Twain is no bilious, white-livered, wall-eyed hermit of a timid and foreign-aping Little American. He is "entirely American," as Mr. Howells has just affirmed, the strong native product of our great West. He is also a man who looks at this question in world-perspective. He has stood before kings. He is not dazzled by rhetoric about the American Empire. Growth of our soil and travelled observer of other nations, Mark Twain comes home to tell our flaunting Imperialists that he sees through their hypocrisies. Tell us what you think of him, champions of Imperialism! Let the blear-eyed professors and the dyspeptic editors off for one day, and give us your honest opinion of this typical and whole-hearted American, who stepped from the pilot-house of a Mississippi steamboat into first a national and then a European fame, and now fearlessly sides with the Filipinos against their American oppressors.

Mark Twain: More Than Humorist

R. E. Phillips*

The art of humorous story-telling is, according to Mark Twain, a distinctly American creation. "The basis of this art," he says, "is to string incongruities and absurdities together in a wandering and sometimes purposeless way and seem innocently unaware that they are absurdities." It is, it seems to me, with some such definition as this in mind that we have accustomed ourselves to refer to him as the "great American humorist." From the popular point of view he has defined his own work to a nicety. For nearly half a century we have accepted and approved the label. He is the great American humorist. But he is more than that. And so clearly is this the case that were the contrary true more than a good half of his work, at the least estimate, could never have been written.

It is a curious fact that for all time and almost without exception the world's greatest humorists have been among its keenest thinkers and observers. It was so with Cervantes and his "Don Quixote," with Ben Jonson and the "Silent Woman," with Addison and "Sir Roger de Coverley," and it is so with Mark Twain. Moreover, the public has never admitted this serious basis of all the best humor without a struggle. It took more than a hundred years after the publication of "Don Quixote" for the world to see in it anything more than a tale of comic misadventures. Doubtless this spirit, summed up in two words in the old saw "once a humorist always a humorist," accounts in some measure for the present popular *précis* of Mark Twain. Yet, in the main, as already noted, with the exception of stories like the "Jumping Frog," and the like, which are purely humorous both in manner and conception, by far the largest part of Mark Twain's work is serious. One is bound to recall, for instance, that "Life on the Mississippi," "Roughing It," and parts of "Tom Sawyer," and "Huckleberry Finn," are primarily records of actual experience; and that works like the "Innocents," and "Tramp Abroad," "Following the Equator," etc., depend at least for their point of view upon this same underlying motive. It would be well, therefore, if one is to consider Mark Twain for the moment as something more than humorist to have in mind some clear idea of the main incidents in his early experience which has

*Reprinted from *Book Buyer*, 22 (April, 1901), 196–201.

164

just been referred to as the underlying motive—the first cause, as it were—of a large part of his work.

The first few years of his life, then, Mark Twain spent in the little "out-at-the-elbows, slave-holding" town of Hannibal, Missouri. There his family had moved from the town of Florida, also in Missouri, where, in 1835, Mark Twain was born. Previous to this the family had lived first in Lexington, Kentucky, and just before moving to Missouri, in Jameston, Tennessee. During the residence in Tennessee his father took up a large tract of land—some 80,000 acres—in the hope of providing for himself and family by the expected rise in land values. But in this he was disappointed, and the incident is only noted here because years later it furnished the idea for the "Gilded Age," which in 1873 the author wrote in collaboration with Charles Dudley Warner.

In 1847 his father died and Mark Twain was left with very little property, to shift for himself. He was then only twelve years old. He left school at once and went into a printing office with his brother. In 1853 began his "wander years." He came to New York, supporting himself by odd jobs of type-setting, and the like, and until 1857 lived the free life of a wanderer, first in New York, then in St. Louis, Muscatine, and finally in Keokuk, Iowa. In 1857 he met Horace Bixby and learned from him the difficulties of steamboat piloting along the Mississippi. Of this period he says: "I am to this day profiting by that experience; for in that brief, sharp schooling, I got personally and familiarly acquainted with about all the different types of human nature that are to be found in fiction, biography or history. The fact is daily borne in upon me that the average shore employment requires as much as forty years to equip a man with the same sort of education."

For nearly three years he served as cub-pilot on the Mississippi. With the advent of the Civil War his occupation was at once wiped out and he enlisted with the Confederates in the army. But he did not stay there long. He recently explained his sudden leave-taking by claiming that his plan of closing the rebellion by surrounding Grant and driving him into the ocean was not favorably received by his superior officers. At any rate, he soon left the army and is next heard from in Nevada as private secretary to his brother, who held a government position there. A year of fortune-hunting followed in the silver mines of the Humboldt and Esmeralda regions. His experiences here are told in "Roughing It." Soon after, he became editor of the *Virginia City Territorial Enterprise*, and later, legislative correspondent at Carson City, where he first assumed the writing name of "Mark Twain"—the Mississippi leadsman's call for two fathoms. Mr. Howells has recently said that Mark Twain writes English as if it were a "primitive and not a derivative language;" and this is in large measure due to the influence of his Western newspaper training of that period.

But something more than the ability to write English as if it were a "primitive language" came from that vigorous school of Western and

Southwestern training. And first of all the short series of autobiographical sketches just mentioned. Here the stories are what they pretend to be—records of experience. They present a series of definite pictures of actual life. In "Roughing It," for example, the author has given us the first and the only effectively true account we have of that "free, disorderly, grotesque society of men—swarming hosts of stalwart men"—in whom was bound up the story of the rise, growth and culmination of the silver-mining fever in Nevada. The result is in some degree humorous, because such a society had its broadly humorous side. The episodes of Scotty Briggs in his interview with the clergyman about Buck Fanshaw's funeral, and that of Brigham Young who in his desire to make a small present to his favorite wife, to the value only of twenty-five dollars, is finally obliged to invest in several hundred at the same price in order to keep peace in the family, are examples of the best humor in the book. The first is the more effective because it grows out of the subject and so, while just as amusing as the other, adds to the understanding and appreciation of the picture as a whole. The latter is a return to the old method of incongruity of which the early sketches offer the best instances. But such episodes are rare. Fully half of the book is serious. One effective incident like that of the wife and the miners in whose eyes a woman in camp was a "rare and blessed spectacle," stands for more than the combined effect of all the purely humorous incidents in the book.

Similarly in "Life on the Mississippi." Here again the real, actual and living predominates; the purely humorous or whimsical is secondary. The story goes that the author after the publication of the "Innocents"—his first considerable success—was besieged by publishers on all sides with the cry for more "copy." He had no more "copy" to offer. He felt that he was written out. He confided his predicament to a friend and happened at the same time to relate some of his experiences as a cub-pilot along the Mississippi. The result was that the value of the material was at once recognized, and the author was urged to tell his experiences exactly as they had occurred, in book form. This he has done in "Life on the Mississippi." The philosophy, point of view and ideas of the book are those of the river-men. It is a history of the motives, generosity, brutality, humor, even, of the life of that time along the Great River. All this is well told. Bits of description—such, for instance, as the race of the two steam-boats down the river ending in the unexpected explosion and conflagration—are particularly vivid. As an example of humor, the contest between the "Child of Calamity" and the "Corpse-maker of Arkansaw" is one of the best. It may, indeed, be taken as typical of all or of nearly all the humorous episodes in the book. The humor is on the order of the "Scotty Briggs" rather than the "Brigham Young" type. That is, it is in general based on the study and observation of character; and the characters whose whimsical traits are woven into incidents and episodes are more or less intimately connected with the idea of the narrative as a whole.

Here, from a purely humorous point of view, is a step in advance. But as yet the study and development of character results only in episode. In its further development it lies at the basis of the author's best humor, and of his success, in so far as he may be called successful, as a writer of romance. Meanwhile, the "Gilded Age" better, perhaps, than any other of the author's works, illustrates this imperfect method of introducing the study of character as a subsidiary interest, rather than as the main underlying idea. Here it is not enough to say that in the character of Colonel Sellers we have the best there is in the "Gilded Age"; nor that in the contrast between his irrepressible buoyance—his "millions in it"—and the actual failure of all his plans and ambitions we have the author's first development of the humorous and pathetic side by side in a single character; nor, finally, that the character is a masterpiece of observation, and the first man in the author's fiction. For while this is undoubtedly true it only emphasizes the main point that after all the character of the Colonel represents only an incidental part, and so fails to make the book as a whole effective.

The contrary is true, on the other hand, of what may be considered, with the possible exception of the "Prince and Pauper," and the "Connecticut Yankee at the Court of King Arthur," the best Mark Twain has done in the way of fiction. In "Tom Sawyer" and "Huck Finn," for example, the characters of the two boys stand for everything. The main effect here is undeniably that of humor, and it is so primarily because "Tom" and "Huck" are humorous characters. They are real boys. One of them is Mark Twain. Naturally, the life of a boy in the Southwest, forty and more years ago, was different in many respects from what it is today. Then there was more freedom, more chance for adventure. But boys' logic and motives change but little. The desire to "show off" is as strong to-day as it ever was with Tom Sawyer; and the efficacy of the "sore toe" in getting a fence whitewashed is as sure. The only difficulty now a days is that we no longer have any fences to whitewash. Conditions have changed. The motive must be applied in a different way. But it still remains, and because this is so, and because this universal motive has been understood and applied in these two works, the humor of "Huck Finn" and "Tom Sawyer" is as effective now as it was then, and undoubtedly always will be—a fact which could not have been the case had these two characters been developed merely as a secondary or subsidiary interest.

In both these books, however, there is something other than humor and the delineation of humorous character. In the character of Huck Finn, the outcast and son of the village drunkard, is summed up in some sort the entire spirit of justice and equality—democracy in its broadest sense—of the Southwest of half a century ago. He is more than the

Lazarillo of the picaresque novel; more, even than Hugo's Gavroche, the immortal ragamuffin of fiction. For they were only gamins, the outcasts of the lowest round of society. Huck Finn is the equal not only of all the characters in the book, but of all readers. In spite of his birth, he is human; he has our sympathy; we must own him brother. It is the consummate art of the author that has brought this result to bear. But it is the broad spirit of equality, the result of actual experience and long familiarity with the ideas and ideals of that early Southwestern life that, in the first instance, made the conception of such a character possible.

As a writer of romance, however, Mark Twain can never be wholly successful because he cares so little—practically not at all—for effective construction. Even in the two works just referred to there is no climax. The stories might be continued indefinitely. They end only with the end of the book. The most effective bit of construction in all its works is seen in the short story of the "Man that Corrupted Hadleyburg." Here the construction is well-nigh perfect. In idea, too, and in conception and development of character within short story limits, the "Hadleyburg" story is a masterpiece. It is conceived and worked out in the manner of Cervantes. And as a good-humored satire on the whims and foibles of one phase of our social life it stands, it seems to me, of all Mark Twain's writings, easily first.

But it is rather to the qualities that underlie his merits as a writer of romance and a humorist than to these merits in themselves that we wish here to call special attention. Mark Twain has so long been a cosmopolitan that we are in danger of forgetting, in speaking of him only as a humorist, how thoroughly American he is—especially in his point of view. Or, better still, how thoroughly Western he is. He has never been educated up—or down—to many of the false standards of Eastern and European culture. He still holds to the old ideas. Moreover, he is a Westerner of that time when the West had not yet come to borrow its ideas and so-called culture from its Eastern neighbors. He represents the West as it was forty years ago. His point of view is primitive, elemental, uneducated, perhaps, if reckoned by Eastern "book-learning" standards of education. But he knows *men.* And his work has the sovereign merit of being honest, unaffected, vigorous and above everything, fearless. Of this point of view the best illustration is to be found, perhaps, in his first success—the "Innocents Abroad." Here from the beginning we have the hard sense of the West set against the established customs and "culture" of the East. Mark Twain was the first man to look upon the catacombs as a joke. Turner's "Slave Ship," floundering about in that "fierce conflagration of reds and yellows" reminded him of a "tortoise-shell cat having a fit in a platter of tomatoes." And as for the "Old Masters," he considered the modern copies in all respects superior to the originals. Twelve years later, in the "Tramp Abroad," his judgment is somewhat modified. But, after all, his satire in both instances is directed not against one phase or another of art but against those who persist in seeing in art what from his point of view is not there. Both the "Innocents," and the "Tramp Abroad" are protests against affectation. In asking about the mummy "Is it dead?" he directs his flings not so much at the mummy as at those who pretend to admire mummies because it is fashionable to do so, although they are really incapable of any such aesthetic enjoyment. The humorous description of Bassano's "Hair Trunk" as the world's artistic masterpiece proves, moreover, that his point of view is still essentially American and Western however much it may have been modified by twelve years of "cultivation;" and in its humorous application to the obvious absurdities of many phases of European life, of which the protest against the blind worship of "art" is only one example, lies the main interest and significance both of the "Innocents" and of the "Tramp Abroad." Their method is the method of "Don Quixote"—the application of the philosophy of common sense to social foibles.

But from this point of view—which we are wont to call "thoroughly Western"—there is a much more significant result than this first protest against insincerity and affectation. And here we come to what seems to me the keynote of the character of Mark Twain as a serious writer. I refer to his sense of absolute fairness and justice, already noted in passing as one of the underlying motives in "Huck Finn." In one of his early sketches called the "Bloody Massacre," Mark Twain satirizes quite mercilessly his own efforts toward becoming the champion of justice and right; and here he deplores the fact that in this sketch the public only read as far as the "bloody" part, and passed over the underlying idea. That is the trouble today. The public forgets, or what is worse, will not admit that there is anything in Mark Twain beyond mere humor. They prefer to be amused. They read the "bloody" part and skip the rest. But the fibre is none the less there. In "Joan of Arc" the character of the "Maid" is based wholly upon the author's conception of what is just and right. It is his evident sympathy with her not as a romantic character in history, but as a human being forced to the highest sacrifice injustice can bring, that counts for most in the effectiveness of the book of which the "Maid" is the central figure. Similarly, in the "Prince and Pauper." Here the idea of justice is universalized. The old problem of class distinction, democracy based upon merit and equality, is written into a story for children. In a slightly different sense the same is true of the "Connecticut Yankee at the Court of King Arthur"; although here, of course, the more serious opinions are woven about a central motive which is purely whimsical. The chapter on "Sixth Century Political Economy," and repeated references throughout the book to the respect he has for any kind of "unearned supremacy," show in what direction these opinions tend. Moreover, this animating spirit of justice may be observed as the basis of a large part of his writing in which humor even as a secondary motive does not exist. In the essay on the "Defence of Shelley," the author criticizes Professor Dowden for upholding an unjust view of the poet's relations with Mary Godwin, for no other reason than that the blame for the separation should have been Shelley's and not his wife's. Again, with Mark Twain, to an unusual degree, the book is the man. The recent fortunate outcome of the relations between the author and his former publishers is only a concrete example of his spirit of justice applied to every-day life and conditions. Even in the recent humorous incident of the cab—humorous chiefly because the wrong motive has been attached to the unusual proceeding of a man constituting himself, of his own accord, a "social" policeman—we have only a practical demonstration of the ideas already developed in the story called "Traveling with a Reformer."

In the last article Mark Twain has published—advice to the "Person Sitting in Darkness"—his conception of justice and his ideas as an humanitarian are for the first time applied to world politics and questions of international importance. The conclusions reached in this article will doubtless appeal to all those who are opposed to the attitude of the present administration toward the "savages" of the East. As a whole, however, it may be said that the article is rather a clever caricature upon the conditions, as they are supposed to exist, than a valid argument that wrong is being done by our present Eastern policy. But on one question raised in the article there can be no ground for dispute. It is evident that the "Person Sitting in Darkness" has as much right to live and live without the interference of others for mere pecuniary gain as the most enlightened among us. And this, after all, is the broadly humanitarian view here taken by the author. In this respect Mark Twain is in exact opposition to the attitude of "jingoism" of which, for instance, Mr. Kipling is so consistent an exponent. Upon Mr. Kipling it has been charged that he is more responsible, perhaps, than any other one man in England for the "most diabolical development of the foul art of war." Moreover, he urges taking up the white man's burden only where England stands to win and so to derive thereby added glory and commercial or pecuniary advantage. This is not to say that he has created the situations which have led to the troubles either in Africa or in the East. But, in treating of these situations as they exist, he has been the first to cry as Dick Heldar did: "Give 'em hell! Oh, give 'em hell!"

Now Mark Twain in his way is just as patriotic as Kipling, but he is quieter about it. He goes at it in a different way. He is less of a "jingo." With Mark Twain the key-note is justice—not war and conquest for gain. He stands up for American standards because he believes that these standards are just. But he does not go so far as to say that we as Americans—or at least those set in high places over us—are infallible. The advice to the "Person" proves this most abundantly. And yet he is not opposed to war as such when in its results it means progress and advancement of modern methods and civilization. "The great bulk of the savages," he says in one place, "must go." The white man needs their lands, but he objects to the manner of their taking-off. For instance, speaking of the reduction of population in South Africa by Mr. Rhodes' "slow-misery and-lingering-death" system he says, "Rhodesia is a happy name for that land of piracy and pillage and puts the right stain upon it." In general, however, the influence of Mark Twain is for peace rather than for war and conquest and always—first, last and all the while—for justice, absolute democracy and humanity. This stands for more than humor, and more than success as a novelist. And it is largely through the recognition of the fact that underlying a great part of his work runs the undercurrent of seriousness of which justice, contempt for affectation and love of humanity are among the chief characteristics, that we shall eventually come to the best appreciation of Mark Twain as the "great American humorist."

Mrs. Astor Injures Mark Twain's Feelings

Anonymous*

"The men who have amassed their millions in all sorts of ways have not had advantages in their youth; they have never had the college education without which no man can be a gentleman."—Mrs. Astor, in an interview before she sailed.

"Do you mean to say that Mrs. Astor says that?" asked Samuel L. Clemens (Mark Twain) when he was seen at his home in Riverdale yesterday afternoon.

"Why that's a direct personal insult. Mrs. Astor and I will have a falling out over that, I'm afraid. To be told to my face, and in cold type at that, that I am no gentleman! And all because I wasn't fortunate enough to have a rich father to send me to college. It's too bad, too bad.

"It's enough to take the heart out of a man and make him scorn the world. But, then, there is one ray of hope. If it was not for that I would be tempted to leave this rude world.

"Perhaps Mrs. Astor, when she uses the word gentleman, doesn't have the same meaning in view that we other rude people have.

"She probably means a leader of cotillions; a spic-and-span dandy, who knows enough to observe the ordinary rules of politeness when he is on parade, and who has a valet at home to tell him what clothes are proper to wear.

"No, no; I can't believe that she could be so cruel and cold-blooded as to rob me of the only hope that is left me, that I am a gentleman. She must have meant something else than 'gentleman' as we use it.

"A gentleman, a kindly, courteous, unselfish man, who thinks first not of himself, but of his fellow man, that is what a gentleman is; not one of these society 'chappies' who in reality is one of the most selfish men on earth.

"Why, Mrs. Astor can't mean that Andrew Carnegie is no gentleman. He may be too pushing, or too shy, and stand around silently, in corners, not knowing what to say or what to do. But what does that show?

*Reprinted from *New York American and Journal*, March 10, 1902, p. 3. William Randolph Hearst's *San Francisco Examiner* ran essentially the same story, and his *New York Evening Journal* ran a shorter version. Twain convincingly insisted that this story was a fabrication.

It only means that he is not an adept at hypocrisy. It does not detract from the true worth or the kindly, courteous nature of the man.

"Abraham Lincoln didn't have a college education, yet he was known for his kindly, courtly ways, and his absolute unselfishness. He was always ready and willing to sacrifice his money and his time, as well as his own convenience, to help a woman or child. He may have been rough and coarse in his talk and actions, and perhaps wouldn't have graced Mrs. Astor's drawing-room, but he was a true gentleman for all of that.

"Oh! you can pick out any number of them you want. Take the men of prominence in the United States to-day and pick out the true gentlemen. I'll venture that nine out of ten of them never had a high school education, let alone a college education.

"Why, the finest gentleman I ever knew was an old California miner who could hardly write his own name. He was a forty-niner, and he and his partner had struck it rich in the early days. The old man had neither chick nor child and he had worked hard all his life, and when he did get his money he hardly knew what to do with it.

"He didn't try to jump into society, or to push his way with the 'big fellows' there. He continued to live with the people he had associated with all his life, and many an act of kindness was done, many a wandering son and father saved, many a sorrowing woman's burdened lightened and her life brightened by an unknown donor whose identity was only known to a few.

"It was different with his partner. He had a wife and two daughters with social aspirations, and after a whole lot of pushing and hauling and shoving they landed in society. The expense was too much of a drain on the husband's purse, and he speculated, with the inevitable outcome. He lost his entire fortune and shot himself. Then it was the true gentlemanliness of the old man showed itself. The widow and her daughters had no one to turn to but him, and he didn't disappoint them. He saved their home for them when everything else went under the hammer, and he maintained them in it in all the regal style to which they were accustomed, although he still lived in his old lodgings. He lived long enough to see both of the girls well married and the mother comfortably settled for life. Then he died in a charity hospital in San Francisco. He had spent every penny he owned on the family of his partner.

"That is what a gentleman is. A college education necessary? It's all rubbish."

Degree for Mark Twain

Anonymous*

The graduating exercises of the State University of Missouri took place to-day. The programme included several special attractions. The feature was the conferring of honorary degrees of LL. D. on a number of distinguished personages, including Mark Twain, the humorist; James Wilson, Secretary of Agriculture; Ethan Allen Hitchcock, Secretary of the Interior; B. T. Galloway, Chief of the Bureau of Plant Industry, and Robert S. Brookings of St. Louis.

Mark Twain was the centre of attraction. Since his arrival from Hannibal yesterday he has been given a continual round of banquets, dinners, and similar entertainments, and when he appeared in chapel this morning he looked fatigued, but was otherwise in fine spirits.

Mr. Clemens, attired in a Yale scholastic gown, led the graduating procession in its march to the stage, and conferred the diplomas upon the graduates. All the exercises were made as brief as possible. The distinguished humorist gave the audience a treat of humorous stories, personal anecdotes, and humorous remarks at the expense of the other distinguished visitors, in whose company he received the degrees.

The conferring of the degrees was especially interesting, each of the ones thus honored responding with a few remarks appropriate to the occasion. Before the degree of Doctor of Laws was formally conferred upon Mark Twain, Gardner Lathrop read a statement introducing the author to the audience, containing many references to his work and characteristics of his genius.

Mr. Clemens stepped to the centre of the stage and paused. He seemed to be hesitating whether to make a talk or retire with a few remarks. Suddenly, and without a signal, the great audience arose as one man and stood in silence at the feet of the man who wrote "Tom Sawyer." Mr. Clemens bowed and remained silent. Then the audience began a peculiar chant, spelling slowly the word Missouri, with a pause between each letter. It was a solemn sound, and the effect was strongly impressive.

The humorist said that he was in doubt as to whether a speech was expected or only a few remarks. He was not left in doubt very long. With

*Reprinted from *New York Times*, June 5, 1902, p. 2.

one will the audience demanded a speech and were so insistent that it would have been extremely difficult to decline, but it is doubtful if Mark Twain wished to do so.

His speech was playful, satirical, and at times pathetic, including personal anecdotes, funny stories of a great variety and much that was serious, and all told with great earnestness. He referred with much feeling to his recent visit to his old home and friends, and said that though it had cost him an aching heart, he would not have missed experiencing those sacred emotions even if he could have avoided them. He touched humorously upon the matter of his degree and said that while he fully deserved the honor and was glad to get it, he was very much afraid that it might have aroused jealousy among his enemies.

He said that when he received his degree in an Eastern college as a Doctor of Literature much jealousy of a most reprehensible nature was created among those who envied his intellect and ability, and that one man wrote to him asking him what he knew about literature. Another man wished to know if a Doctor of Literature meant a man who was able to "doctor" his own literature, and others asked similar mean questions which only proved their jealousy of spirit and envy of a deserving man.

Mr. Clemens referred to Mr. Lathrop, who had read such a glowing eulogy of the humorist, as "the Ambassador," and expressed his regret that the latter had neglected so splendid an opportunity to tell the real truth instead of contenting himself with compliments.

Mr. Clemens told a watermelon story that greatly amused his audience, and a few jokes on Secretary Wilson and others that were highly characteristic of the humorist. Though he began his talk rather sadly, he was in a merry mood before he had completed. He finally launched forth into a eulogy on himself delivered so seriously and with such a straight face that the audience were almost tempted to take him at his word and refrain from laughing when the laugh came in.

"Since I have been in Missouri," said the speaker, "I have distributed more wisdom than ever before, and I am sure that much good will result from my visit. I have had many honors conferred upon me, but I deserved them all. I sometimes suspect when you confer these honors you mean it as a sort of hint that I have been with you long enough. Some of the Eastern colleges seemed to be rather in a hurry about getting me out of the way, and began conferring honors upon me years ago, but as I stated before, I deserve them all, and am always willing to accept anything in the way of honors that you have to offer."

Mark Twain's Farewell?

Anonymous*

It is reported that Dr. Clemens, after the variegated and admirable speech recently made by him on receiving his latest degree, announced that it was his last appearance as a speaker in public.

We must all hope that it is only the first of a long series of last appearances. Probably there is no genius now known to the English-speaking world who can impart such vitality to a pleasantry of ripe age as can Mark Twain. Let us trust that he is illustrating this happy facility in the present instance and that his announcement is but an incident in the continuous exercise of his unique and precious function in this generation. We have many humorists of more or less distinction in "occasional" talk. There are some who have aspired to association, and even to rivalry with him. Some have approached him on a few of the many sides he has turned to a delighted public. No one has attained his rank. No one is so familiar and so uniformly surprising. Of no one can we be so sure that he will be funny and so utterly at a loss to predict what form or direction his fun will take. It would be a great pity if at future entertainments his "turn" should be missing.

Every one will read with pleasure the accounts of Dr. Clemens's material prosperity, and hope that they are far short of the fact. He has proved his possession of that rarest claim to fortune—the capacity to face deprivation and hard work for the satisfaction of his own conscience and his emancipation from even indirect responsibility for losses incurred through him. His title is very clear to the best that can possibly come to him. And, of course, he is entitled to repose if he wishes it. But it is hard to connect his retirement from the public stage with the notion of repose. He has borne his part with such ease and apparent spontaneity, it has seemed so much more natural for him to talk in his own way than to keep silent, that one can imagine his self-repression only as an act of self-denial. It would certainly be unkindness to the public for whom he has so long been indulgent. We prefer to regard his announced intention as a practical joke, which, like most practical jokes, has in it an element of cruelty.

*Reprinted from *New York Times*, June 7, 1902, p. 8.

A Toast to Mark Twain!

Henry Van Dyke*

Good friends, whose hearts to-night have heard
    The welcome of our host,
At his request I bring you here
The best provision of good cheer:
A rare, delightful, juicy bird,
    Alive,—yet on a toast.
The bird,—how shall I tell you half
    The wonders of his worth?
He's full of wit, and knows the way
To sing a new song every day
That makes you smile within, or laugh
    In full, side-shaking mirth.

And yet this laughter leaves no sting
    Of bitterness behind:
It does not mock, despise, deride,—
'Tis fun that has a tender side,
And feels for every living thing,—
    'Tis friendly, free, and kind.
No parrot is this bird, though he
    Can talk beside the best;
He's no repeater: every tone
And every word is all his own:
With wild originality,
    He tells the oldest jest.

He's gay as any buck can be,
    He's wise as any owl,
And, like the Phoenix, he survives
The fires that wreck less noble lives.
Yet you will find his record free
    From everything that's foul.

*Reprinted from *Harper's Weekly*, 46 (December 13, 1902), 1944.

He's travelled far: on every land,
Men know his world-wide name:
Italian, French, and German folks,
And even Scotchmen praise his jokes;
Best best he loves his native land
    And sings her spreading fame.

His six-and-sixtieth year they say
    This very night departs;
So let us leave this talk of birds,
And speak in simple Saxon words,—
Before the moment flies away,—
    The love that fills our hearts.
With memories old, with wishes new
    We crown our cups again:
And here's to you, and here's to you!
    With love that ne'er shall wane!

And may you keep, at sixty-seven,
The joy of earth, the hope of heaven,
And fame well earned, and friendship true,
    And peace that comforts every pain,
And faith that fights the battle through,
And all your heart's unbounded wealth,
And all your strength and all your health.—
Yes, here's a hearty health to you,
And here's to you, and here's to you,
    A health to you, Mark Twain.

Happy Pessimist Is Mark Twain

Anonymous*

Mark Twain to Date

Taking the pledge will not make bad liquor good, but it will improve it. Anybody who has taken the pledge will know that any kind of liquor tastes good after a few days.

It is not best to use our morals on week days—it gets them out of repair for Sundays, and we ought never to do wrong when people are looking.

Don't part with your illusions; when they are gone, you may still exist, but you have ceased to live.

Every person is a moon, and has a dark side which he never shows to anybody.

Do your duty today and repent tomorrow, which is what you do almost every time.—Mark Twain.

It is noble to be good—it is still nobler to make others good, and much less trouble.—Col. T. W. Higginson

These inspiring aphorisms given above, all fresh from the notebooks of Mark Twain, except the last, which was excogitated on the spur of the moment by Col. Thomas Wentworth Higginson, were published yesterday for the first time at the residence of Mr. Sumner B. Pearmain, 388 Beacon street, where Mr. Clemens gave a delightful talk two hours in length to the representatives of the Boston newspapers. The mere conjunction of the two veteran litterateurs, the one a confirmed pessimist, as he calls himself, at 70, the other as persistent an optimist at 82, was a literary event of some magnitude, but it took enlarged shape as the contrasted minds struck fire from their collisions of wit and banter, or drew richly from each other's stores of world experience.

Mr. Clemens, who never looked in better health, started his talk, made up half of reply, half of monologue—all of it characterized by his keen logical faculty for thinking out his idea to the end—by reminding the newspaper men that since beginning with his pen at 14, he had never been able to regard himself as really out of journalism.

As to my age, he went on, that does not affect me, nor does my gray

*Reprinted from *Boston Herald*, November 6, 1905, p. 4.

hair, for it was gray at 50; the only thing I suffer from now as regards health is dyspepsia.

It is, indeed, a long time to look back to my earlier books, and I still receive letters about them. One man says he's got all my works on his shelves, but regrets having ever read them, and is willing to tell me why if I will ask—stamped envelope enclosed. Then there is another of my recent correspondents, whose communication I prize, indeed, for while he says complimentary things, he doesn't give his name and address.

In the interval succeeding this remark, the newspaper men, having obtained possession of the letter, found in it an account of the career of a successful man of business, whose first start in self-culture came through reading "Huckleberry Finn," the work of an author whose characteristics the writer summed up as "freedom from tradition, independent judgment, humor and wholesomeness."

After talk about the letters had subsided, Mr. Clemens reviewed the reform movement now sweeping over the country. He smiled at the "Mc-Curdy centres" now being discovered, wishing that attempts had been made to find out and emphasize the empty spaces.

"And as to pessimism," said he, "any man who is a pessimist before he is 48 knows too much, but any man who has passed 48 and is not a pessimist shows thereby that he knows too little."

Col. Higginson here interjected: "But wait till you get beyond the seventies."

Mr. Clemens: "I am a pessimist, you know, and cannot change. But we have one asset in our country, and it is the finest asset we have. Whenever a condition becomes intolerable, the people will rise up and stamp it out. They did that in Philadelphia. At present look what is happening. We furnished to Europe the sentiment of liberty with our revolution—now we are furnishing Europe with graft."

The subject of copyright then came up, and found Mr. Clemens emphatic in condemnation of present arrangements.

"It irritates me," he said, "to find that Germany gives an author copyright during his lifetime and for 50 years after, and that France and Russia do the same. Indeed, there are no highly civilized countries that do not grant this period as a right except England, Labrador and America. Consider what that means in our day. We who boast of our civilization don't go in copyright as far as even Russia, which of late has been under so much criticism. As to my first books," and here there was a touch of regret in Mr. Clemens' manner, "they will fall in six years from now, for they will reach their 42d year. The excuse made in England and America is that an author has had enough when he has had 42 years' income from his books, and that the government having protected him for that period, the people of the country are entitled to the book."

Col. Higginson here asked: "But don't you think the publishers of a book have an advantage even after the copyright has expired, since they know the market better than any one else?"

"Yes," replied Mr. Clemens, "but the people of the country don't obtain the book for nothing, for no publisher is going to publish it unless he gets a profit out of it. So far as I am myself personally concerned, I do not care, because I am old enough not to be much interested in copyrights. Why, only the other day—and it is a striking thing to consider—I read that the trade mark does not require anything of anybody, and is given for a perpetuity. You don't, for example, have to specify what your patent medicine is made of, yet the government, with its eyes shut, accepts this poison, if it is a poison, and gives a man a trade mark which is perpetual. That the government should do this, and yet should limit the producer of a book to 42 years, does not seem fair.

"As to the obstacles in the way of change, the only one I ever heard of was when, in 1889 or 1890, being in Washington on copyright matters, a congressman told me that his constitutents had the impression—the superstition—that when a book lost its right of protection, people were going to get that book cheaper than before. It was for this reason, therefore, that the congressman could not venture to get copyright extended. That shows how men work upon a theory. The congressman probably never placed the matter before his constituents. I myself never heard a constituent who made any such an objection. Now, I am going down to Washington in a few days to see what they are doing there about copyright. We are trying to do something, and we authors hope to bring about for the United States an extension of the time to the lifetime of the author and for 50 years after. I ought to say that American literature has grown in spite of these obstructing conditions, until today there are issued in this country from 6000 to 7000 books a year. The production in Germany is 24,000, though I suppose that includes pamphlets."

A possible objection to the argument here came from Col. Higginson.

"Is it not, after all," he reasoned, "the community who gives the author his education, his opportunity, his subjects, his illustrations, his stimulus? Is it just for him to argue as if the thing were all on his side? If I were in Congress, I don't think I should vote for such a bill as you suggest, Mr. Clemens. I think it is giving the author and his children too much in consideration of what the public has given him. I think he ought to be willing, even proud, to give a large part of his labor for nothing."

"You see," interrupted Mr. Clemens, "I was born in a more selfish atmosphere than you, colonel."

"You are in Boston now," urged the limner of "Cheerful Yesterdays."

"But," retorted the author of "The Innocents Abroad," "I have not absorbed its atmosphere. I should look at it," continued Mr. Clemens, "in this way. When before the House of Lords in England on this question, I asked what objection there was to make the change to 'lifetime and 50 years after,' and they said: 'You can't have property in an idea. A book is an idea. That is too much in the air.' But I asked them if they could name any property in this world that was not an idea. The whole basis of any piece of property is an idea, and not any more or less of an idea than is a book. I don't see why the people of a country should take an author's work from him on the plea that they have given him the materials. That occurs in every sort of business, but business-men don't give up their property on that account, and I don't think it should be required of an author."

The conversation here drifted toward a subject on which Mr. Clemens feels strongly, and to which he has given much attention. A chance allusion to Russia, while enabling him to make an explanation, showed how frankly pessimistic he is as to the likelihood of the Russian people freeing themselves from the autocracy.

"I did feel," said he, "on hearing the news of peace that another great defeat of the Russian armies would have assured freedom at home. I was afraid that peace at that time was going to fasten the shackles still more firmly on the Russian nation. When we heard recently of the new concessions made by the Emperor I began to think that, after all, peace had come at the right time. But I do not feel so sure of that now, because the later news shows that the Czar has not granted anything valuable, but has kept all the power in his own hands. Inasmuch as he grants legislative privileges without putting the army and navy and the treasury in the hands of a legislature, what he really grants amounts to nothing. Just as soon as he can quiet those people down and get them again into orderly shape he is going to take away again the few little privileges he has granted. While the army and navy and the treasury are in the hands of the Emperor nothing is really accomplished, though I admit there has been a great advance in thought and feeling among the Russian people. If the Russian army were to side with the people then a revolution would come."

The last subject discussed by Mr. Clemens was the Congo.

"I notice," said he, "that King Leopold has received the report of his commission, but that report, saying that everything had been done satisfactorily is very different from the report of the missionaries. The members of the King's commission are interested persons—one of them is brother of his private secretary—and their report will do the King more harm than good. Leopold is too well known as a domestic person and a family person, as a King, to get his evidence, or the evidence of any commission of his, accepted by an intelligent public. The missionaries, who go out at the risk of their lives, are much better witnesses than he. Leopold sits at home and drinks blood.

"The condition of things in the Congo is atrocious, as shown by the photographs of children whose hands have been cut off. Leopold thinks this can go on because the Congo is a distant, out-of-the-way country. But once we can get England and America to investigate and take this matter up, something will be done. We Americans are especially interested, because it was our recognition of the flag there that led to recognition by other powers."

Sonnet to Mark Twain

William Dean Howells*

A traveller from the Old World just escaped
  Our customs with his life, had found his way
To a place up-town, where a Colossus shaped
  Itself, sky-scraper high, against the day.
A vast smile, dawning from its mighty lips,
  Like sunshine on its visage seemed to brood;
One eye winked in perpetual eclipse,
  In the other a huge tear of pity stood.
Wisdom in chunks about its temples shone;
  Its measureless bulk grotesque, exultant, rose;
And while Titanic puissance clothed it on,
  Patience with foreigners was in its pose.
So that, "What art thou?" the emboldened traveller spoke,
And it replied, "I am the American joke.
I am the joke that laughs the proud to scorn;
  I mock at cruelty. I banish care,
I cheer the lowly, chipper the forlorn,
  I bid the oppressor and hypocrite beware.
I tell the tale that makes men cry for joy;
  I bring the laugh that has no hate in it;
In the heart of age I wake the undying boy;
  My big stick blossoms with a thornless wit,
The lame dance with delight in me; my mirth
  Reaches the deaf untrumpeted; the blind
My point can see. I jolly the whole earth,
  But most I love to jolly my own kind,
Joke of a people great, gay, bold, and free,
I type their master-mood. Mark Twain made me."

*Reprinted from *Harper's Weekly*, 49 (December 23, 1905), Supp., p. 1884.

Mark Twain at Seventy

[Hammond Lamont]*

The most significant thing about the dinner to Mark Twain on December 5 was the greeting from forty of the leading men of letters of England. No other American author, we are confident, could receive such a tribute. In the opinion of foreigners, Mark Twain is the greatest of living American writers. An interesting side-light is thrown on his fame by an incident in Kipling's first visit to America, some fifteen years ago. Mark Twain was the man of whom Kipling had heard, and whom, above others, he wished to see. In the interval since then his reputation has grown, both at home and abroad. Bret Harte, whose name was often coupled with his, is dead. No one is left to dispute his preëminence, or even to compare with him.

He did not, however, come into his own at once. People were suspicious of him because he was not born and bred to the literary traditions of Boston, New York, or Philadelphia. Nor did he, when at last he had fairly started on his career, accept the conventions of his generation and conform to the standards of either of these three centres of culture. He was not reared with Hawthorne, Lowell, Longfellow, and Holmes; and consequently New England pitied him. He never attended the so-called "Knickerbocker School"; and New York saw at once that he suffered much from lack of early advantages. True, his essays and sketches used to appear in the staid pages of the *Atlantic*, but they were a horrible shock to the dowager duchesses of Boston. The *Atlantic*, however, was erratic. It not only tolerated Mark Twain, but for a time it was edited by a man named Thomas Bailey Aldrich, who had not graduated from Harvard, indeed had never attended college, and who was therefore not a member of the Brahmin caste. These literary pariahs, however, occasionally get on in spite of deficiencies in taste and education. Mr. Aldrich, for example, managed to write some things that people have condescended to read. Indeed, one of his stories, "Marjorie Daw," so took the fancy of a budding author that, changing the name of the personages of the tale, he kindly offered to sell it to the *Evening Post*. What is worth

*Reprinted from *Nation*, 81 (December 14, 1905), 478–79.

stealing must have some merit. Mark Twain's success has been more dazzling than Mr. Aldrich's—and with good reason.

He knows America and knows it whole. Born in Missouri seventy years ago, he saw every type of man, woman, and child, white and black, that lived in the vast Mississippi Valley. As pilot on a Mississippi steamboat he made the acquaintance of the pioneers from New England, New York, Pennsylvania, and the Western Reserve, who pushed across the prairies and filled the vacant lands of Illinois, Iowa, Wisconsin, Minnesota, Nebraska, and Kansas. He was scarcely less at home in the Gulf States, for which the Mississippi was the great highway. As Territorial secretary of Nevada and editor of the Virginia City *Enterprise*, he knew at first hand the mining camps of the Pacific Coast, the gamblers, the railway builders, and the politicians. He has dwelt for many years in the East. He has travelled extensively. He has read widely. With some native talent to start with, he has in the slow course of time picked up almost as good an equipment for literary work as a man will get in four years at Harvard or Columbia.

He has not devoted himself to carving cherry-stones according to academic rules, but to the best of his ability he has written books to read. Delicate questions of usage have not troubled him any more than they troubled Shakespeare or Defoe; he has had larger problems on his mind. We do not, we trust, undervalue choice, exact, and even academic English. A careless, sloppy style is not virtue. Misusing words and taking the edge off their meaning is the favorite amusement of fools. But Mark Twain has had stories to tell—big ones and good ones. His swift, racy style—words of the people as the people understand them—smelling of the soil, is as excellent in its kind as the classic sentences of Hawthorne. In 'Huckleberry Finn' and 'Tom Sawyer' he had matter enough to last an ordinary novelist a lifetime. That, after all, is the essential. The manner, we admit, is not that of the late Walter Pater in 'Marius the Epicurean.' It is—if the two writers be at all commensurable—far better.

Yet it is the bulk of Mark Twain's work, rather than the admirable handling of details, that gives it power. To say nothing of his ventures into historical romance—he has shown us on an extensive scale surpassingly vivid pictures of many phases of our life. "Here," cry his European eulogists, "is America as it is or was." They are right. 'Huckleberry Finn' is a cross-section of Missouri and lower Illinois. You may rise from the perusal, feeling that you have actually lived there, that you know intimately a whole social stratum of antebellum days, and that you have enjoyed one of the most entertaining and moving tales in our language. The episode of that feud between the Grangerfords and the Shepherdsons, with the men running along the river-bank, shooting at the swimming boys, and shouting "Kill them! kill them!" grips the memory like those stirring scenes where Crusoe came upon the footprints of the savages and the outlaws stormed the castle of Front de Boeuf.

In saying this we mean that Mark Twain is a much greater man than the humorist of 'The Jumping Frog.' That he is a humorist of the first rank no discriminating person has dreamed of denying for the last thirty years. But he is a humanist as well, if we accept the term in its broader sense— one versed in human affairs. His humor has served to keep clear and steady his vision of human relations, has helped him to pierce the sophistries of politicians, and to test the fleeting fashions of a day by eternal principles, has closed his ears to the passing cries of party, and enabled him to stand with courage, and to lift a voice that carries far, for justice and mercy to all men, of all colors, in all lands.

Mark Twain's Clothes

Anonymous*

Mark Twain, in a cream-colored suit in December, strikes an unusual note in the scheme of things. His argument that men dress too dolefully is worth considering. As long as a man is warm enough, what matters it whether he wears outside the clothes of summer or winter hue? Imagination plays a great part in adjusting our habits and it has undoubtedly caused the abandonment by most men of all the tones of garb which are usually associated with the warm season. Scientists will tell you that white clothes are better to wear in summer because they reflect rather than absorb the heat. But this argument does not hold good in winter as a reverse proposition. Indeed, if black clothes in summer allow the heat of the sun to penetrate to the body, do not black clothes in winter allow the heat of the body to escape to the outer air?

Mark Twain takes a sensible view of this matter even though he is a professional humorist. He is, in truth, endowed with an unusually large store of common sense. Perhaps that is why he is so successful as a humorist. It often happens that the funniest things in the world are those that are sensible. And one of the prime qualities of American humor is its appeal to the understanding. Therein, argue some patriots, lies the essential difference between the American and the British brands of humor.

If we begin to wear white clothes in winter, thus upsetting our sartorial traditions, we may possibly progress to other departures from the conventional garb of men. There are those who sigh for the good old days of picturesque costumes, knee-breeches, silk stockings, ruffled shirts and all that. Now and then the followers of a sport will undertake to blaze their way through the prime laws of haberdashery and inject a little color into our man-scape. But the hoi polloi are usually impatient with these innovators, and treat them as "dudes" and cranks.

Maybe the illustrious example of Mark Twain, who has a grip on the American sympathies that is enjoyed by few other men, not excepting statesmen and actors, will cause a more lenient attitude on the part of the great body of the people toward the advocates of more picturesqueness in our garb. We need something to liven us up in these stern and strenuous days, and perhaps the immortal Mark has given us a valuable cue.

*Reprinted from *Washington* (D.C.) *Evening Star*, December 8, 1906, Pt. 1, p. 4.

Mark Twain

Anonymous*

Wit is the champagne of life, humor the Burgundy; champagne is the joy and jag of youth, Burgundy the stay and swig of age; champagne uncorked fizzes and flattens, Burgundy improves with years. Age cannot wither, nor custom stale the heart and humor of Mark Twain; the cask grows old, but the wine grows riper in flavor and richer in bouquet with the years.

Mark Twain has confounded the Dulness which declares that humor is fatal to success, by reaching the years of indiscretion—seventy—crowned with success and still humorous. The snows of winter are on his head; but the sweetness of spring, the sunshine of summer and the mellowness of autumn are on his tongue and in his heart. He defies Time and mocks Convention.

Cruelty and greed, wrong and oppression, humbug and pretension he has hated and harried, and he has laughed them out of court and lashed them into outer darkness.

Paid a dollar a word by philanthropic publishers, he declines to be garrulous in an age of gabble; yet for the glory and gain of Letters he will waste words, and cast pearls before swine, to save the bacon of authors and the rights of writers, and risk his reputation even at Joe Cannon's mouth.

Good-humor is rarer than good health, sanity than sense, serenity than sentiment; but this merry old philosopher, who has punctuated life with laughter and sweetened it with honesty, goes down the shadowed road like vagrant sunshine, blessed with health, sense and sentiment, and adorned with humor, sanity and serenity. Well may the lucre-laden lunatic who lingers reluctant for the Reaper ask of Dulness and Greed, "What is Success?"

Death is no respecter of persons; he loves and leaves this Shining Mark.

God *save* the Mark!

---

*Reprinted from *Life*, 49 (January 31, 1907), 160–61.

Mark Twain

William Lyon Phelps*

During the last twenty years, a profound change has taken place in the attitude of the reading public toward Mark Twain. I can remember very well when he was regarded merely as a humorist, and one opened his books with an anticipatory grin. Very few supposed that he belonged to literature; and a complete, uniform edition of his "Works" would perhaps have been received with something of the mockery that greeted Ben Jonson's folio in 1616. Professor Richardson's "American Literature," which is still a standard work, appeared originally in 1886. My copy, which bears the date 1892, contains only two references in the index to Mark Twain, while Mr. Cable, for example, receives ten; and the whole volume fills exactly 990 pages. Looking up one of the two references, we find the following opinion:

> But there is a class of writers, authors ranking below Irving or Lowell, and lacking the higher artistic or moral purpose of the greater humorists, who amuse a generation and then pass from sight. Every period demands a new manner of jest, after the current fashion. . . . The reigning favorites of the day are Frank R. Stockton, Joel Chandler Harris, the various newspaper jokers, and "Mark Twain." But the creators of "Pomona" and "Rudder Grange," of "Uncle Remus and his Folk-lore Stories," and "Innocents Abroad," clever as they are, must make hay while the sun shines. Twenty years hence, unless they chance to enshrine their wit in some higher literary achievement, their unknown successors will be the privileged comedians of the republic. Humor alone never gives its masters a place in literature; it must co-exist with literary qualities, and must usually be joined with such pathos as one finds in Lamb, Hood, Irving or Holmes.

*Reprinted from *North American Review*, 185 (July 5, 1907), 540–48; Phelps signed himself as Lampson Professor of English at Yale University. Reprinted in Phelps's *Essays on Modern Novelists* (New York: Macmillan, 1910).

It is interesting to remember that before this pronouncement was published, "Tom Sawyer" and "Huckleberry Finn" had been read by thousands. Professor Richardson continued: "Two or three divisions of American humor deserve somewhat more respectful treatment," and he proceeds to give a full page to Petroleum V. Nasby, another page to Artemus Ward and two and one-half pages to Josh Billings, while Mark Twain had received less than four lines. After stating that, in the case of authors like Mark Twain, "temporary amusement, not literary product, is the thing sought and given," Professor Richardson announces that the department of fiction will be considered later. In this "department," Mark Twain is not mentioned at all, although Julian Hawthorne receives over three pages!

I have quoted Professor Richardson at length, because he represents an attitude toward Mark Twain that was common all during the eighties. Another college professor, who is to-day one of the best living American critics, says, in his "Initial Studies in American Letters" (1895), "Though it would be ridiculous to maintain that either of these writers [Artemus Ward and Mark Twain] takes rank with Lowell and Holmes, . . . still it will not do to ignore them as mere buffoons, or even to predict that their humors will soon be forgotten." There is no allusion in his book to "Tom Sawyer," or "Huckleberry Finn," nor does the critic seem to regard their creator as in any sense a novelist. Still another writer, in a passing allusion to Mark Twain says, "Only a very small portion of his writing has any place as literature."

Literary opinions change as time progresses; and no one could have observed the remarkable demonstration at the seventieth birthday of our great national humorist without feeling that most of his contemporaries regarded him, not as their peer, but as their Chief. Without wishing to make any invidious comparisons, I cannot refrain from commenting on the statement that it would be "ridiculous" to maintain that Mark Twain takes rank with Oliver Wendell Holmes. It is, of course, absolutely impossible to predict the future; the only real test of the value of a book is Time. Who now reads Cowley? Time has laughed at so many contemporary judgments that it would be foolhardy to make positive assertions about literary stock quotations one hundred years from now. Still, guesses are not prohibited; and I think it is not unlikely that the name of Mark Twain will outlast the name of Holmes. American Literature would surely be the poorer if the great Boston Brahmin had not enlivened it with his rich humor, his lambent wit and his sincere pathos; but the whole content of his work seems slighter than the big American prose epics of the man of our day.

Indeed, it seems to me that Mark Twain is our foremost living American writer. He has not the subtlety of Henry James or the wonderful charm of Mr. Howells; he could not have written "Daisy Miller," or "A Modern Instance," or "Indian Summer," or "The Kentons"—books of which every American should be proud, for they exhibit literary quality of an exceedingly high order. I have read these books over and over again, with constantly increasing profit and delight. I wish that Mr. Howells might live forever, and give to every generation the pure intellectual joy that he has given to ours. But the natural endowment of Mark Twain is still greater. Mr. Howells has made the most of himself; God has done it all for Mark Twain. If there be a living American writer touched with true genius, whose books glow with the divine fire, it is he. He has always been a conscientious artist; but no amount of industry could ever have produced a "Huckleberry Finn."

When I was a child at the West Middle Grammar School of Hartford, on one memorable April day, Mark Twain addressed the graduating-class. I was thirteen years old, but I have found it impossible to forget what he said. The subject of his "remarks" was Methuselah. He informed us that Methuselah lived to the ripe old age of nine hundred and sixty-nine. But he might as well have lived to be several thousand—nothing happened. The speaker told us that we should all live longer than Methuselah. Fifty years of Europe are better than a cycle of Cathay, and twenty years of modern American life are longer and richer in content than the old patriarch's thousand. Ours will be the true age in which to live, when more will happen in a day than in a year of the flat existence of our ancestors. I cannot remember his words; but what a fine thing it is to hear a speech, and carry away an idea!

I have since observed that this idea runs through much of his literary work. His philosophy of life underlies his broadest burlesque—for "A Connecticut Yankee in King Arthur's Court" is simply an exposure of the "good old times." Mark Twain believes in the Present, in human progress. Too often do we apprehend the Middle Ages through the glowing pages of Spenser and Walter Scott; we see only glittering processions of "ladies dead and lovely knights." Mark Twain shows us the wretched condition of the common people, their utter ignorance and degradation, the coarseness and immorality of technical chivalry, the cruel and unscrupulous ecclesiastical tyranny and the capricious insolence of the barons. One may regret that he has reversed the dynamics in so glorious a book as Malory's "Morte d'Arthur," but, through all the buffoonery and roaring mirth with which the knights in armor are buried, the artistic and moral purpose of the satirist is clear. If I understand him rightly, he would have us believe that *our* age, not theirs, is the "good time"; nay, ours is the age of magic and wonder. We need not regret in melancholy sentimentality and picturesqueness of bygone days, for we ourselves live, not in a material and commonplace generation, but in the very midst of miracles and romance. Merlin and the Fay Morgana would have given all their pretty skill to have been able to use a telephone or a phonograph, or to see a moving picture. The sleeping princess and her castle were awakened by a kiss; but in the twentieth century a man in Washington touches a button, and hundreds of miles away tons of machinery begin to move, fountains begin to play and the air resounds with the whir of wheels. In comparison with to-day, the age of chivalry seems dull and poor. Even in chivalry itself our author is more knightly than Lancelot; for was there ever a more truly chivalrous performance than Mark Twain's essay on Harriet Shelley, or his literary monument to Joan of Arc? In these earnest pages, our national humorist appears as the true knight.

Mark Twain's humor is purely American. It is not the humor of Washington Irving, which resembles that of Addison and Thackeray; it is not delicate and indirect. It is genial, sometimes outrageous, mirth—laughter holding both his sides. I have found it difficult to read him in a library or on a street-car, for explosions of pent-up mirth or a distorted face are apt to attract unpleasant attention in such public places. Mark Twain's humor is boisterous, uproarious, colossal, overwhelming. As has often been remarked, the Americans are not naturally a gay people, like the French; nor are we light-hearted and careless, like the Irish and the Negro. At heart, we are intensely serious, nervous, melancholy. For humor, therefore, we naturally turn to buffoonery and burlesque, as a reaction against the strain and tension of life. Our attitude is something like that of the lonely author of the "Anatomy of Melancholy," who used to lean over the parapet of Magdalen Bridge, and shake with mirth at the horrible jokes of the bargemen. We like Mark Twain's humor, not because we are frivolous, but because we are just the reverse. I have never known a frivolous person who really enjoyed or appreciated Mark Twain.

The essence of Mark Twain's humor is Incongruity. The jumping frog is named Daniel Webster; and, indeed, the intense gravity of a frog's face, with the droop at the corners of the mouth, might well be envied by many an American Senator. When the shotted frog vainly attempted to leave the earth, he shrugged his shoulders "like a Frenchman." Bilgewater and the Dolphin on the raft are grotesquely incongruous figures. The rescuing of Jim from his prison cell is full of the most incongruous ideas, his common-sense attitude toward the whole transaction contrasting strangely with that of the romantic Tom. Along with the constant incongruity goes the element of surprise—which Professor Beers has well pointed out. When one begins a sentence, in an apparently serious discussion, one never knows how it will end. In discussing the peace that accompanies religious faith, Mark Twain says that he has often been impressed with the calm confidence of a Christian with four aces. Exaggeration—deliberate, enormous hyperbole—is another feature. Rudyard Kipling, who has been profoundly influenced by Mark Twain, and has learned much from him, often employs the same device, as in "Brugglesmith." Irreverence is also a noteworthy quality. In his travel-books, we are given the attitude of the typical American Philistine toward the wonders and sacred relics of the Old World, the whole thing being a gigantic burlesque on the sentimental guide-books which were so much in vogue before the era of Baedeker. With so much continuous fun and mirth, satire and burlesque, it is no wonder that Mark Twain should not always be at his best. He is doubtless sometimes flat, sometimes coarse, as all humorists since Rabelais have been. The wonder is that his level has been so high. I remember, just before the appearance of "Following the Equator," I had been told that Mark Twain's inspiration was finally gone, and that he could not be funny if he tried. To test this, I opened the new book, and this is what I found on the first page:

> We sailed for America, and there made certain preparations. This took but little time. Two members of my family elected to go with me. Also a carbuncle. The dictionary says a carbuncle is a kind of jewel. Humor is out of place in a dictionary.

Although Mark Twain has the great qualities of the true humorist—common sense, human sympathy and an accurate eye for proportion—he is much more than a humorist. His work shows very high literary quality, the quality that appears in first-rate novels. He has shown himself to be a genuine artist. He had done something which many popular novelists have signally failed to accomplish—he has created real characters. His two wonderful boys, Tom Sawyer and Huckleberry Finn, are wonderful in quite different ways. The creator of Tom exhibited remarkable observation; the creator of Huck showed the divine touch of imagination. Tom is the American boy—he is "smart." In having his fence whitewashed, in controlling a pool of Sabbath-school tickets at the precise psychological moment, he displays abundant promise of future success in business. Huck, on the other hand, is the child of nature, harmless, sincere and crudely imaginative. His reasonings with Jim about nature and God belong to the same department of natural theology as that illustrated in Browning's "Caliban." The night on the raft with Jim, when these two creatures look aloft at the stars, and Jim reckons the moon laid them, is a case in point.

> We had the sky up there, all speckled with stars, and we used to lay on our backs and look up at them, and discuss about whether they was made or just happened. Jim he allowed they was made, but I allowed they happened; I judged it would have took too long to *make* so many. Jim said the moon could a *laid* them; well, that looked kind of reasonable, so I didn't say nothing against it, because I've seen a frog lay most as many, so of course it could be done. We used to watch the stars that fell, too, and see them streak down. Jim allowed they'd got spoiled and was hove out of the nest.

Again, Mark Twain has so much dramatic power that, were his literary career beginning instead of closing, he might write for us the great American play that we are still awaiting. The story of the feud between the Grangerfords and the Shepherdsons is thrillingly dramatic, and the tragic climax grips one by the heart. The shooting of the drunken

Boggs, the gathering of the mob and its control by one masterful personality, belong essentially to true drama, and are written with power and insight. The pathos of these scenes is never false, never mawkish or overdone; it is the pathos of life itself. Mark Twain's extraordinary skill in descriptive passages shows, not merely keen observation, but the instinct for the specific word—the one word that is always better than any of its synonyms, for it makes the picture real—it creates the illusion, which is the essence of all literary art. The storm, for example:

> It was my watch below till twelve, but I wouldn't a turned in anyway if I'd had a bed, because a body don't see such a storm as that every day in the week, not by a long sight. My souls, how the wind did scream along! And every second or two there'd come a glare that lit up the white-caps for a half a mile around, and you'd see the islands looking dusty through the rain, and the trees thrashing around in the wind; then comes a *h-wach!*—bum! bum! bumble-umble-um-bum-bum-bum-bum—and the thunder would go rumbling and grumbling away, and quit—and then *rip* comes another flash and another sockdolager. The waves 'most washed me off the raft sometimes, but I hadn't any clothes on, and didn't mind. We didn't have no trouble about snags; the lightning was glaring and flittering around so constant that we could see them plenty soon enough to throw her head this way or that and miss them.

"Tom Sawyer" and "Huckleberry Finn" are prose epics of American life. The former is one of those books—of which "The Pilgrim's Progress," "Gulliver's Travels" and "Robinson Crusoe" are supreme examples—that are read at different periods of one's life from very different points of view; so that it is not easy to say when one enjoys them the most—before one understands their real significance or after. Nearly all healthy boys enjoy reading "Tom Sawyer," because the intrinsic interest of the story is so great, and the various adventures of the hero are portrayed with such gusto. Yet it is impossible to outgrow the book. The eternal Boy is there, and one cannot appreciate the nature of boyhood properly until one has ceased to be a boy. The other masterpiece, "Huckleberry Finn," is really not a child's book at all. Children devour it, but they do not digest it. It is a permanent picture of a certain period of American history, and this picture is made complete, not so much by the striking portraits of individuals placed on the huge canvas, as by the vital unity of the whole composition. If one wishes to know what life on the Mississippi really was, to know and understand the peculiar social conditions of that highly exciting time, one has merely to read through this powerful narrative, and a definite, coherent, vivid impression remains.

By those who have lived there, and whose minds are comparatively free from prejudice, Mark Twain's pictures of life in the South before the war are regarded as, on the whole, nearer the truth than those supplied by any other artist. One reason for this is the aim of the author; he was not trying to support or to defend any particular theory—no, his aim was purely and wholly artistic. In "Uncle Tom's Cabin," a book by no means devoid of literary art, the red-hot indignation of the author largely nullified her evident desire to tell the truth. If one succeeds in telling the truth about anything whatever, one must have something more than the *desire* to tell the truth; one must know how to do it. False impressions do not always, probably do not commonly, come from deliberate liars. Mrs. Stowe's astonishing work is not really the history of slavery; it is the history of abolition sentiment. On the other hand, writers so graceful, talented and clever as Mr. Page and Mr. Hopkinson Smith do not always give us pictures that correctly represent, except locally, the actual situation before the war; for these gentlemen seem to have "Uncle Tom's Cabin" in mind. Mark Twain gives us both points of view; he shows us the beautiful side of slavery—for it has a wonderfully beautiful, patriarchal side—and he also shows us the horror of it. The living dread of the negro that he would be sold down the river, has never been more vividly represented than when the poor woman in "Pudd'nhead Wilson" sees the water swirling against the snag, and realizes that she is bound the wrong way. That one scene makes an indelible impression on the reader's mind, and counteracts tons of polemics. The peculiar harmlessness of Jim is beautiful to contemplate. Although he and Huck really own the raft, and have taken all the risk, they obey implicitly the orders of the two tramps who call themselves Duke and King. Had that been a raft on the Connecticut River, and had Huck and Jim been Yankees, they would have said to the intruders, "Whose raft is this, anyway?"

Mark Twain may be trusted to tell the truth; for the eye of the born caricature artist always sees the salient point. Caricatures often give us a better idea of their object than a photograph; for the things that are exaggerated, be it a large nose, or a long neck, are, after all, the things that differentiate this particular individual from the mass. Everybody remembers how Tweed was caught by one of Nast's cartoons.

Mark Twain is through and through American. If foreigners really wish to know the American spirit, let them read Mark Twain. He is far more American than their favorite specimen, Walt Whitman. The essentially American qualities of common sense, energy, enterprise, good humor and Philistinism fairly shriek from his pages. He reveals us in our limitations, in our lack of appreciation of certain beautiful things, fully as well as he pictures us in coarser but more triumphant aspects. It is, of course, preposterous to say that Americans are totally different from other humans; we have no monopoly of common sense and good humor, nor are we all hide-bound Philistines. But there is something pronounced in the American character, and the books of Mark Twain reveal it. He has also more than once been a valuable and efficient champion. Without being an offensive and blatant Jingo, I think he is well satisfied to be an American.

Mark Twain is our great Democrat. Democracy is his political, social and moral creed. His hatred of snobbery, affectation and assumed superiority is total. His democracy has no limits; it is bottomless and far-reaching. Nothing seems really sacred to him except the sacred right of every individual to do exactly as he pleases; which means, of course, that no one can interfere with another's right, for then democracy would be the privilege of a few, and would stultify itself. Not only does the spirit of democracy breathe out from all his greater books, but it is shown in specific instances, such as "Travelling with a Reformer"; and Mark Twain has more than once given testimony for his creed, without recourse to the pen.

At the head of all American novelists, living and dead, stands Nathaniel Hawthorne, unapproached, possibly unapproachable. His fine and subtle art is an altogether different thing from the art of our mighty, democratic, national humorist. But Literature is wonderfully diverse in its content; and the historian of American Letters, in the far future, will probably find it impossible to omit the name of Mark Twain, whose books have warmed human hearts all over the world.

Mark Twain the Humorist

Hamilton W. Mabie*

The name under which Mr. Samuel L. Clemens has written for many years, and which has become so much a part of him that one has to remind himself that it was assumed, was a stroke of genius. It is unique, and sets him in the environment and amid the vital circumstances which he, and he alone, has brought into literature. In him the Mississippi Valley found a reporter entirely and instinctively at one with its attitude toward life, its bearing in the presence of new conditions, its turn of thought and manner of speech. La Salle was the first man to make the voyage of the great stream to which a host of smaller streams are tributary; but Mark Twain was the first man to chart, light, and navigate it for the whole world. He has written many books of humorous invention and fresh, audacious spirit since the publication of "The Adventures of Tom Sawyer," "The Adventures of Huckleberry Finn," and "Life on the Mississippi River," but the heart and soul of his work are revealed and preserved in these earlier books, and by them he will stand or fall.

He is the most widely known American writer of his time. In the interest and attention of foreign readers he ranks with Cooper, Mrs. Stowe, and Poe; among Americans none is better known by other peoples save Washington, Lincoln, and President Roosevelt. To this host of readers beyond the sea and to the host of readers at home he is known chiefly as a humorist; but it may be suspected that fifty years hence, when his unique personality and laughter-provoking manner and mental attitude have become traditions, there will emerge a reputation based securely on a little group of books which many of those who are familiar with his later works have never read.

When Mark Twain was born, the first great tide of emigration, which had gathered itself in quiet places along the Atlantic seaboard, and sent manifold streams through the passes of the Alleghanies, and fertilized the vast central valley of the continent, had touched the edges of the plains; and the man of prophetic mind, discerning the significance of its high-water marks, might have foreseen the second great wave which, after the close of the Civil War, was to sweep from the prairies across the

*Reprinted from *Outlook*, 87 (November 23, 1907), 649–53.

Plains to the Pacific and obliterate the Great American Desert that stretched, like a vast blight, across the old school maps. St. Louis was so small a town that Mark Twain has somewhere remarked that he could have bought it for a million dollars if he had happened to have the money at hand; there were great lonely wastes which later were to be fertile and populous; but when the creator of Tom Sawyer was a boy in Hannibal, Missouri, the Mississippi Valley was under human control, the river was crowded with craft of many kinds, and a unique habit of life had been developed along its banks. Of this primitive and powerful outgo of human energy and activity the river was both the occasion and the shaping force. The majesty of it appealed to the earliest voyagers, but its magnitude can only be seen by the imagination; for it drains half a continent, is fed by fifty-four navigable streams and by several hundred more of sufficient depth to float craft of light draught. It penetrated and opened up to trade and travel the very heart of the continent; it was separated by many days' hard travel from the early settlements on the seaboard; news of the older world was slow in getting to the river population, and they were not much influenced by it.

The cry "Westward Ho," heard on the Thames in Shakespeare's time, had summoned the adventurous, the restless, the lawless, from the older communities north and south and sent them into the immense section drained by the Mississippi. The East from which they came was still in the provincial stage of its growth, with its eyes toward Europe; the Southwest that was to be soon detached itself from the ideas and interests of the older world and boldly gave itself up to the work at hand and to the manner of life which its new conditions and tasks rapidly fashioned. The earlier immigrants had brought with them a complete stock of religious and social standards, which were gradually subdued to the new soil; the men of the Mississippi Valley were deeply affected by certain fundamental ideas of conduct, but they were very little embarrassed by external conventions of manner, dress, or speech. They developed the primitive virtues of courage, resourcefulness, self-reliance, a sense of reality impatient of the circumlocutions of formality, a speech which gained in vigor and vividness what it lost in breadth of expression. Men went straight at the fact, and brushed aside everything that hindered the shortest and swiftest hitting of the nail on the head. On the river a vast and appalling profanity was developed, but it was less a matter of conscious irreverence than of surplus imagination and a primitive instinct for the picturesque. A few oaths are binding, many are loosening; and the profanity of the Mississippi Valley was largely "giving the imagination a loose." Conditions were hard and work was harder; vocabularies were limited and, beyond the demands of routine activity, inadequate; exigencies of all kinds evoked a variety and force of expression to which the resources of profanity were equal. In the Far East cursing is a solemn and elaborate ritual of imprecation, casting the shadow of a terrible blight on one's remotest ancestors and projecting it over one's farthest descendants. It shadows one's entire racial career. In the Mississippi Valley, on the other hand, cursing was mainly an illicit use of picturesque language, or a reckless excursion into the realms of humor. Life was essentially fraternal and kindly; a broad, genial humor underlay and enfolded it, and much of the profanity was fundamentally humorous. Its interest lay in the striking effects of broad contrasts; it reveled in audacious comparisons, far-fetched similes, epithets that overflowed with suggested insult.

The life of the river and of the communities that were tributary to it was probably as democratic as any the world has known. The squire, who was usually of Virginia or Kentucky descent, and was believed to be "worth" twenty-five or thirty thousand dollars, but, as a matter of courtesy, was credited with the possession of fifty thousand, was looked up to in a way, but without a particle of subservience. Every other man in the community was as good as he, only less fortunate. There was thrift, but very little greed; great wealth was unknown, but it was easy to make a living. Everybody was religious, but the current form of religion, although bristling with theoretical difficulties, was of a very comfortable sort and full of adaptations to local conditions. In Hannibal, when Mark Twain was a boy, the Presbyterians, Baptists, and Methodists were, he says, "the three religious disorders." He heard Presbyterian preaching for family reasons, but he went to the Methodist Sunday-school because "the terms were easier." There was a good deal of profanity, drinking, and loafing, but the more sophisticated forms of immorality were unknown. Certain points of conduct were also points of honor; the statute of limitations ran against legal but not against moral responsibility for debts; there was a spirit of universal kindliness and a charity which enfolded even the town drunkard, and treated him not as an outcast but as a ward of the community and an illicit local institution. He was a weaker brother, whose sins were condoned because he belonged to the family. Society in the Mississippi Valley in Tom Sawyer's time was a pure democracy, in easy circumstances, free from anxiety, charitable of everything except cowardice and meanness, taking life comfortably, with a broad margin of humor. It was as free from introspection as if Puritanism had never brooded over its sins and worried about its soul; it was as unconscious of traditional standards and classical models as Adam and Eve in the Garden of Innocence, and it led a happy-go-lucky life with serene trust in the good faith of Providence and in the square deal at the hands of the ruler of the universe. The lighthearted industry and contagious force which mastered the perils of the river and gave it a vast neighborliness are thrown into striking relief by the somber and sordid temper and the tragic conditions of life on the Volga as they have been drawn in black and white by Gorky.

Of this old-time life under conditions which will never be reproduced, Mark Twain was the interpreter and recorder, and long after he has ceased to be remembered as a fun-maker he will remain the historian in a vital dialect of the early Mississippi Valley. The facts of his career are well known and not important for the purposes of this article. He was born in the thirties, and spent his boyhood and youth in the little town of Hannibal, Missouri, as his friend John Hay was born in the little town of Warsaw, Ohio. Commenting on these facts at a dinner given in his honor several years ago, Mark Twain said incidentally that there was something in the air of the West at that time which made great men! He had little formal education, but his opportunities of training in the secrets and crafts of the human boy have never been surpassed. He learned how to set type, but his heart was on the river, the romance of which no imaginative boy who lived on its banks escaped. He reached in time the zenith of every boy's ambition: he became a pilot. He was in the war for a short time, but he was not "with Grant;" he went to Nevada and became a reporter of extraordinary audacity of invention; later he tried mining; visited the Sandwich Islands; and gave his first lecture in San Francisco. The "Jumping Frog of Calaveras" appeared about this time and was widely read. Then came the excursion to the Orient, and the vastly entertaining letters to newspapers at home, which presently appeared in that classic of American exaggeration, "Innocents Abroad." The humor of contrasts—the uttermost modern against the innermost antique, the most radical and free-spoken Americanism against the most sacred and traditional Europeanism—was so striking in this volume that it escaped at once the limitations of one language and appeared with astonishing celerity in half a dozen tongues. Mark Twain became what the newspapers call a world-figure.

From the oldest world he passed, in "Roughing It," to the newest; from the tomb of Adam to the far Western frontier. The record of a second visit in Europe bore fruit in "A Tramp Abroad." Then came work of a very original and unique character, "Old Times on the Mississippi," "Tom Sawyer," and "Huckleberry Finn." In these books Mark Twain was dealing at first hand with a life which he had lived and which had so long been part of him that in transcribing and reporting it he gave the full force and flavor of his personality. "The Prince and the Pauper" was a surprise to those who regarded him as a mere fun-maker; and "The Yankee at the Court of King Arthur" was a disappointment to those who knew that a vein of pure gold of idealism ran through his nature. "Pudd'nhead Wilson" was a mine of odd wisdom as well as a picture of a life; while "The Personal Recollections of Joan of Arc" struck the highest note of reverence, and was in some respects the most extraordinary tribute ever paid to a marvelous character and a romantic career.

Mark Twain has so long been a humorist of national significance that, when the world suddenly realized the rugged integrity and splendid courage of the man, it realized as well that it had seen the author of "Tom Sawyer" from one point of view only, and that it was dealing with a profoundly serious man. The instant girding of his loins to bear the weight of a heavy indebtedness, at a time of life when he might have been easing his load, the setting forth on a journey round the world to meet self-assumed obligations, the full payment of a great sum of money—these constitute an Odyssey of wandering full of honor; the heroic struggle and victory of an honest man.

Mark Twain is so much a world-figure and so entirely the product of the old-time Mississippi Valley life, with its vast friendliness and its unconventional intimacy, that the extraordinary frankness and detail of the autobiography which he is now publishing need not disturb the more reticent and circumspect; like those very early ancestors of ours whose diaries he had edited, he has nothing to conceal or be ashamed of, and the material which he is storing up with a prodigal hand will enrich some future biographer beyond the dreams of avarice. It is a long way from Hannibal, Missouri, to Oxford, from the apprentice pilot on a Mississippi steamer to the scarlet and gray of the Doctor of Letters of a great and venerable university, and the record of it, in its final form, will be an American document of high value.

The free, unconventional life of the Mississippi Valley of Tom Sawyer's town was an Iliad in shirt-sleeves, and there was grave question in the minds of some people whether such a stage of society was a proper subject for literary presentation; whether it was not too rudimentary for art. Mr. Howells, who is a humorist of very delicate and charming quality, has described Hannibal, Missouri, as "a loafing, out-at-elbows, down-at-heels, slave-holding Mississippi town;" and Mark Twain's records amply confirm the general accuracy of this description loosely applied to a whole section. Mr. James is reported as saying that one must be a very rudimentary person to enjoy Mark Twain. This is quite true; as true as that one must be a very sophisticated person to enjoy Mr. James. Provincialism is not a matter of locality but of attitude, and the provincialism of the Boulevard des Italiens is quite as pure a product of local ignorance as that of a frontier mining town. Extreme sophistication and extreme rudimentariness are alike interesting, significant, and partial.

In his records of old-time life on the greatest of American waterways Mark Twain deals with those facts of experience which, stripped of the accidents of dress and manners, are the supreme concern of the artist because they furnish the richest and most suggestive material. Into the unconventional, lawless, devil-may-care activity and overflowing high spirits of such a stage of development only a boy could enter, and in the stories of Tom Sawyer and Huckleberry Finn Mark Twain has penetrated to the innermost recesses of that life, and, with its crudity, profanity, and reckless indifference to conventions, has made us aware of its wholesome courage, its gay audacity, its indomitable temper, its contempt for artificiality, its superstitions, and its homespun idealism of courage, loyalty, and comradeship. Under an immense pretension of loafing it was a hard-working life; under an aspect of overflowing humor it was in dead earnest. Not until one understands that in the Mississippi Valley humor was the language of a brave, generous, and laborious people can one estimate the work of Mark Twain at its true value; not until one recognizes that the author of "Tom Sawyer" is a profoundly serious man at heart will he get any real insight into his significance as a figure in American literature or into his work as a vital contribution to that literature.

Mark Twain is not a mere fun-maker, like Artemus Ward and John Phoenix; he is, in his time and way, a true humorist—a man, that is, who sees life, not irresponsibly and superficially, but in its broadest and most fundamental contrasts. Cervantes, Molière, Shakespeare, and Carlyle were great humorists; Gilbert and Sullivan were fun-makers. It was not lack of seriousness which made the old-time people of the Mississippi Valley humorists; it was ease of spirit, surplusage of cheerfulness, a sense of being on good terms with Providence in an inexhaustible country, a prevailing disposition to put a friendly mask on the fact of Fate. This is a fundamental attitude toward life, full of character, rich in eccentricity of speech and manner, redolent of that originality and spontaneity which have always been the joy of the great artists. What rich adventures of the spirit Shakespeare would have had in the Mississippi Valley of Mark Twain's boyhood!

Mark Twain's material was not of the classic kind; and his manner fits his material; that is the proof of his calling and election as a writer. He not only sees with the eye of the artist—which differs chiefly from the eye of the artisan in its ability not to see that which is of no consequence—but his phrase travels straight to the imagination of his reader, and conveys a fresh, vital, and vivid impression; it is a genuine transference of perception, and not a mere arrangement of adjectives.

His power of characterization, of suggesting what is unseen by what is visible, is illustrated in a passage from "Life on the Mississippi:"

> The face of the water, in time, became a wonderful book—a book that was a dead language to the uneducated passenger, but which told its mind to me without reserve, delivering its most cherished secrets as clearly as if it uttered them with a voice. And it was not a book to be read once and thrown aside, for it has a new story to tell every day. Throughout the long twelve hundred miles there was never a page that was void of interest, never one that you could leave unread without loss, never one that you would want to skip, thinking you could find higher enjoyment in some other thing. There never was so wonderful a book written by man; never one whose interest was so absorbing, so unflagging, so sparklingly renewed with every reperusal. The passenger who could not read it was charmed with a peculiar sort of faint dimple on its surface (on the rare occasion when he did not overlook it altogether); but to the pilot that was an *italicized* passage; indeed, it was more than that, it was a legend of the largest capitals, with a string of shouting exclamation points at the end of

it; for it meant that a wreck or a rock was buried there that could tear the life out of the strongest vessel that ever floated. It is the faintest and simplest expression the water ever makes, the most piteous to a pilot's eye. In truth, the passenger who could not read this book saw nothing but all manner of pretty pictures in it painted by the sun and shaded by the clouds, whereas to the trained eye these were not pictures at all, but the grimmest and most dead-earnest of reading matter.

Such writing as this involves the literary instinct and art in a high degree. Mark Twain confesses without shame that there is a great deal of literature which does not interest him, much of which he has not read; he confesses to a love of history and biography, but for poetry and fiction he has no liking. He probably thinks of himself as plain man and not at all as Man of Letters, very much as Shakespeare did. But his art lies beyond the reach of all save the few to whom the gift of style is intrusted. He has that feeling for words in their first estate, when they are still warm with human association and belong to the family instead of the Academy, which is the exclusive possession of the masters of speech. He has never been on good terms with the dead languages, but his intimacy with living speech is so great that he uses it with the assurance of original proprietorship. He writes vividly, with a kind of vibrating energy, with precision, and with the freshness and audacity of a man who is not afraid of the authorities, because he obeys the law of his own nature. The telling phrase which has made him at times a master of the difficult art of description has made him also a master of the art of characterization; boys and men and women stand out in his stories in the old clothes which a less artistic writer would have exchanged for their Sunday wear.

Mark Twain has written much that has only a heightened comic newspaper quality and interest, and it may be suspected that a good deal of his popularity rests on such fun-making as the "Jumping Frog" and upon those speeches which, at their best, are mirth-provoking monologues reinforced by a striking personality and a voice solemnly evoking a laughter which seems alien to its fathomless seriousness. No one will question his right to a vogue which is without a parallel in the experience of American writers; but there is a reputation before him which will rest on a surer basis. When the fun-making has been forgotten, the humorist will come to his own; the man of the fine sense of honor and the deep underlying seriousness, who saw life in its broad contrasts and was on good terms with every sort and fashion of man, who lived the life of a great thoroughfare when it was thronged with boys and men of a new type, and reported them with a fidelity and reality born of a true catholicity of spirit, will emerge as one of the little group of creative writers on this continent.

Mark Twain

Archibald Henderson*

> I've a theory that every author while living has a projection of himself, a sort of eidolon, that goes about in near and distant places and makes friends and enemies for him out of folk who never knew him in the flesh. When the author dies this phantom fades away, not caring to continue business at the old stand. Then the dead writer lives only in the impression made by his literature; this impression may grow sharper or fainter, according to the fashions and new conditions of the time.—Letter of Thomas Bailey Aldrich to William Dean Howells, December 23, 1901.

Despite the average American's complacent and chuckling satisfaction in his country's possession of that superman of humor, Mark Twain, there is room for serious doubt whether a realization of the unique and incomparable position of Mark Twain in the republic of letters has fully dawned upon the American consciousness. On reflection, the number of living writers to whom can justly be attributed what a Frenchman would call *mondial éclat* is startlingly few. It was not so many years ago that Rudyard Kipling, with vigorous, imperialistic note, won for himself the unquestioned title as militant spokesman for the Anglo-Saxon race. Today, Bernard Shaw has a fame more world-wide than that of any other literary figure in the British Isles, and his dramas are played from Madrid to Helsingfors, from Budapest to Stockholm, from Vienna to St. Petersburg, from Paris to Berlin. Since Ibsen's death, Tolstoi exerts unchallenged the profoundest influence upon the thought and consciousness of the world—not so much by his intellect as by the passionate integrity of his moral aspiration. But, in a sense not easily misunderstood, Mark Twain has a place in the minds and hearts of the great mass of humanity throughout the civilized world which, if measured in terms of affection, sympathy, and spontaneous enjoyment, is without a parallel.

The robust nationalism of Kipling challenges the defiant opposition of foreigners; while his reportorial realism offends many an inviolable canon of European taste. With all his incandescent wit and radiant comic irony, Bernard Shaw makes his most vivid impression upon the upper strata of society; while his legendary character is perpetually standing in

*Reprinted from *Harper's Monthly*, 118 (May, 1909), 948-55.

the light of the serious reformer. Tolstoi's works are Russia's greatest literary contribution to posterity; yet his extravagant ideals, his unrealizable hopes, in their almost maniacal mysticism, continue to detract from his fame. If Mark Twain makes a more generally popular appeal, it is because the instrument of his appeal is the universal solvent of humor. That *eidolon* of which Aldrich speaks—a compact of good humor, robust sanity, and large-minded humanity—has diligently "gone about in near and distant places," everywhere making warm and lifelong friends of folk of all nationalities who have never known Mark Twain in the flesh. The stevedore on the dock, the motorman on the street-car, the newsboy on the street, the riverman on the Mississippi—all speak with exuberant affection of this quaint figure in his white suit, ever wreathed in clouds of tobacco smoke. In one day an emperor and a *concierge* vie with each other in tributes of admiration and esteem for the man and his works. It is Mark Twain's imperishable glory, not simply that his name is more widely known than that of any other living man, but that it is remembered with infinite and irrepressible zest.

Not without wide significance in its bearing upon the general outlines of contemporary literature is the circumstance that Mark Twain served his apprenticeship to letters in the high school of journalism. Rudyard Kipling awoke the world with a start by the crude, almost barbaric cry of his journalese; and Bernard Shaw acquired that trenchant and forthright style, which imparts such an air of heightened verisimilitude to his plays, in the ranks of the new journalism. "The writer who aims at producing the platitudes which are 'not for an age, but for all time,'" says Bernard Shaw, "has his reward in being unreadable in all ages; while Plato and Aristophanes trying to knock some sense into the Athens of their day, Shakespeare peopling that same Athens with Elizabethan mechanics and Warwickshire hunts, Ibsen photographing the local doctors and vestrymen of a Norwegian parish, Carpaccio painting the life of St. Ursula exactly as if she were a lady living in the next street to him, are still alive and at home everywhere among the dust and ashes of many thousands of academic, punctilious, most archaeologically correct men of letters and art who spent their lives haughtily avoiding the journalist's vulgar obsession with the ephemeral." Mark Twain began by studying the people and period he knew, in relation to his own life; and in writing of his time *à propos* of himself, succeeded in telling the truth about humanity in general and for any time. If it be true that the intellectual life of America for the most part takes its cue from the day, while Europe derives hers from history, then Mark Twain is a typical product of American literature as defined by Johannes V. Jensen: "journalism under exceptionally favorable conditions." Whatever modicum of truth may lurk in this definition, certain it is that Mark Twain is the greatest genius evolved by natural selection out of the ranks of American journalism.

Crude, rudimentary, and often coarse as much of his early writing was, it bore upon it the fresh stamp of contemporary actuality.

While Mark Twain has solemnly averred that humor is a "subject which has never had much interest" for him, it is nothing more than a commonplace to say that it is as a humorist and as a humorist only that the world persists in regarding him. The philosophy of his early life was what George Meredith has aptly termed the "philosophy of the Broad Grin"; and Mark Twain has had a great struggle to "live down his past." Mr. Gilbert Chesterton once said that "American humor, neither unfathomably absurd like the Irish, nor transfiguringly lucid and appropriate like the French, nor sharp and sensible and full of the realities of life like the Scotch, is simply the humor of imagination. It consists in piling towers on towers and mountains on mountains; of heaping a joke up to the stars and extending it to the end of the world." The partial and somewhat conventional foreign conception of American humor is admirably descriptive of the cumulative and sky-breaking humor of the early Mark Twain. Then no exaggeration was too absurd for him, no phantasm too unreal, no climax too extreme. After a while he learned on the platform that the unpardonable sin is to "sell" an audience, and in the study that "comic copy" will never win real fame.

In spite of these wholesome lessons learned through actual experience, Mark Twain has had to pay in full the penalty of comic greatness. The world is loath to accept a popular character at any rating other than its own. Whosoever sets to himself the task of amusing the world must realize the almost insuperable difficulty of inducing the world to regard him as a serious thinker. *"C'est une étrange entreprise que celle de faire rire les honnêtes gens,"* says Molière; and the strangeness of the undertaking is no less pronounced than the rigor of its obligations. Mark Twain began his career as a professional humorist and fun-maker; and the man in the street is not easily persuaded that the basis of the comic is not uncommon nonsense, but glorified common sense. The French have a fine-flavored distinction in *ce qui remue* from *ce qui émeut*; and if *remuage* was the defining characteristic of *A Tramp Abroad, Roughing It,* and *Innocents Abroad,* there was much of deep and genuine emotion in *Life on the Mississippi, Tom Sawyer, Huckleberry Finn,* and *Pudd'nhead Wilson.* Think of that admirable passage in which he portrays the marvellous spell laid upon him by that mistress of his youth, the great river:

> The face of the water in time became a wonderful book—a book which was a dead language to the uneducated passenger, but which told its mind to me without reserve, delivering its most cherished secrets as if it uttered them with a voice. And it was not a book to be read over and thrown aside, for it had a new story to tell every day. . . . There was never so wonderful a book written by man. . . . When I had mastered the

language of this water, and had come to know every trifling feature that bordered the great river as familiarly as I knew the letters of the alphabet, I had made a valuable acquisition. But I had lost something, too. I had lost something which could never be restored to me while I lived. All the grace, the beauty, the poetry, had gone out of the majestic river. . . . A day came when I began to cease from noting the glories and the charms which the moon and the sun and the twilight wrought upon the river's face; another day came when I ceased altogether to note them.

Even to-day, though long since dissociated in fact from the category of Artemus Ward, John Phoenix, Josh Billings, and Petroleum V. Nasby, Mark Twain can never be sure that his most solemn utterance may not be drowned in roars of thoughtless laughter. "It has been a very serious and a very difficult matter," Mr. Clemens lately remarked to me, "to doff the mask of humor with which the public has always seen me adorned. It is the incorrigible practice of the public, in this or in any country, to see only humor in a humorist, however serious his vein. Not long ago I wrote a poem, which I never dreamed of giving to the public, on account of its seriousness; but on being invited to address the women students of a certain great university, I was persuaded by a near friend to read this poem. At the close of my lecture I said: 'Now, ladies, I am going to read you a poem of mine'—which was greeted with bursts of uproarious laughter. 'But this is a truly *serious* poem,' I asseverated—only to be greeted with renewed and, this time, more uproarious laughter. Nettled by this misunderstanding, I put the poem in my pocket, saying, 'Well, young ladies, since you do not believe me serious, I shall not read the poem,' at which the audience almost went into convulsions of merriment."

Humor, it must be remembered, is a function of nationality. The same joke, as related by an American, a Scotchman, an Irishman, a Frenchman, carries with it a distinctive racial flavor and individuality of approach. Indeed, it is open to question whether most humor is not essentially local in its nature, requiring some specialized knowledge of some particular locality. After reading George Ade's *Fables in Slang*, Mr. Andrew Lang was driven to the desperate conclusion that humor varies with the parallels of latitude, a joke in Chicago being a riddle in London! If one would lay his finger upon the secret of Mark Twain's world-wide popularity as a humorist, he must find that secret primarily in the universality and humanity of his humor. Mark Twain is a master in the art of broad contrast; incongruity lurks on the surface of his humor; and there is about it a staggering and cyclopean surprise. But these are mere surface qualities, more or less common, though at lower power, to all forms of humor. Nor is Mark Twain's international reputation as a humorist to be attributed to any tricks of style, to any breadth of knowledge, or even to any depth of intellectuality. His hold upon the world is due to qualities not of the head, but of the heart. I once heard Mr. Clemens say that humor is the key to the hearts of men, for it springs from the heart; and worthy of record is his dictum that there is far more of feeling than of thought in genuine humor.

Mark Twain has a remarkable feeling for words and their uses; and the merit of his style is its admirable adaptation to the theme. And though Mr. Henry James may have said that one must be a very rudimentary person to enjoy Mark Twain, there is unimpeachable virtue in a rudimentary style in treatment of rudimentary—or, as I should prefer to phrase it, fundamental—things. Mark Twain has always written with utter individuality, untrammelled by the limitations of any particular sect of art. Style bears translation ill; in fact, translation is not infrequently impossible. But, as Mr. Clemens once pointed out to me, *humor has nothing to do with style*. Mark Twain's humor has international range, since, constructed out of a deep comprehension of human nature and a profound sympathy for human relationships and human failings, it successfully surmounts the difficulties of translation into alien tongues.

Mark Twain is a great figure, not because he is an American, paradoxical and even unpatriotic as this may sound, but because he is America's greatest cosmopolitan. He is a true cosmopolitan in the Higginsonian sense in that, unlike Mr. Henry James, he is "at home even in his own country." Above all, he has sympathized with and admired the citizens of every nation, seeking beneath the surface veneer the universal traits of that nation's humanity. It is a matter, not of argument, but of fact, that he has made far more damaging admissions concerning America than concerning any other nation. He disclaims any "attitude" toward the world, for the very simple reason that his relation toward all peoples has been one of effort at comprehension and identification with them in feeling. Lafcadio Hearn best succeeded in interpreting poetry to his Japanese students by freeing it from all artificial and local restraints, and using as examples the simplest lyrics which go straight to the heart and soul of man. And his remarkable lecture on *Naked Poetry* is the most signal illustration of his profoundly suggestive mode of interpretation. In the same way Mark Twain as humorist has sought the highest common factor of all nations. "My secret, if there is any secret," Mr. Clemens said to me, "is to create humor independent of local conditions. Though studying humanity as exhibited in the people and localities I best knew and understood, I have sought to winnow out the encumbrance of the local. *Humor, like morality, has its eternal verities*. Most American humorists have not been widely famous because they have failed to create humor independent of local conditions not found or realized elsewhere."

It must be conceded that the history of literature furnishes forth no great international figures whose fame rests solely upon the basis of humor, however human, however sympathetic, however universal that humor may be. Behind that humor must lurk some deeper and more serious implication which gives breadth and solidity to the art-product. Genuine humor, as Landor has pointed out, requires a "sound and

capacious mind, which is always a grave one." There is always a breadth
of philosophy, a depth of sadness, or a profundity of pathos in the very
greatest humorists. Both Rabelais and La Fontaine were reflective
dreamers; Cervantes fought for the progressive and the real in pricking
the bubble of Spanish chivalry; and Molière declared that, for a man in
his position, he could do no better than attack the vices of his time with
ridiculous likenesses. Though exhibiting little of the melancholy of Lincoln, Mark Twain has much of the Yankee shrewdness and bed-rock common sense of Franklin; and commingled with all his boyish and exuberant
fun is a note of pathos subdued but unmistakable. That "disposition for
hard hitting with a moral purpose to sanction it," which George Meredith
pronounces the national disposition of British humor, is Mark Twain's
racial hereditament; and it is, perhaps, because he relates us to our
origins, as Mr. Brander Matthews has suggested, that Mark Twain is the
foremost of American humorists. It is impossible to think of him in his
maturer development as other than a moralist. His impassioned and
chivalric defence of Harriet Shelley, his eloquent tribute to the Maid of
Orleans, his philippic against King Leopold and the atrocities in the Congo, are all, in essence, vindications of the moral principle. *Was it Heaven
or Hell?* in its simple pathos, and *The Man That Corrupted Hadleyburg*,
in its shrieking irony, present that same transvaluation of current moral
values which marks the age of Nietzsche, of Ibsen, of Tolstoi, of Zola, and
of Shaw. In her unfinished biography of him, Mark Twain's little daughter Susy credited him with being "as much of a pholosopher [sic] as
anything"; and insists that "he is more interested in earnest books and
earnest subjects to talk upon than in humorous ones." Mr. Clemens' first
essay on a philosophical subject—doubting the existence of free will and
declaring that every man was under the immitigable compulsion of his
temperament, his training, and his environment—was too heretical for
the Hartford Club of orthodox religionists to which he belonged; and so
was never read. But in the last thirty years he has amplified his original
conception into a philosophical and ethical system; and to-day his injunc-
tion for right living is best concretized in these words: "Diligently train
your ideals upward and still upward toward a summit where you will find
your chiefest pleasure in conduct which, while contenting you, will be
sure to confer benefits upon your neighbors and the community." As
Lassalle once said, "History forgives mistakes and failures, but not want
of conviction." In Mark Twain posterity will never be called upon to
forgive any want of conviction.

Mark Twain is a great humorist—more genial than grim, more good-
humored than ironic, more given to imaginative exaggeration than to intellectual sophistication, more inclined to pathos than to melancholy. He
is a great story-teller; and he has enriched the literature of the world with
a gallery of portraits so human in their veracious likeness as to rank them
with the great figures of classic comedy. He is a remarkable observer and

faithful reporter, never allowing himself, in Ibsen's phrase, to be "frightened by the venerableness of the institution"; and his sublimated journalism reveals a mastery of the naively comic thoroughly human and democratic. He is the most eminent product of our American democracy; and, in profoundly shocking Great Britain by preferring Connecticut to Camelot, he exhibited that robustness of outlook, that buoyancy of spirit, and that faith in the contemporary which stamps America in perennial and inexhaustible youth. Throughout his long life he has been a factor of high ethical influence in our civilization; and the philosopher and the humanitarian look out from the twinkling eyes of the humorist.

But, after all, Mark Twain's supremest title to distinction as a great writer inheres in his mastery in that highest sphere of thought, embracing religion, philosophy, morality, and even humor, which we call sociology. Mr. Bernard Shaw once remarked to me that he regarded Poe and Mark Twain as America's greatest achievements in literature; and that he thought of Mark Twain primarily, not as humorist, but as sociologist. "Of course," he added, "Mark Twain is in much the same position as myself: he has to put matters in such a way as to make people who would otherwise hang him believe he is joking!" And Mark Twain once said that whenever he had diverged from custom and principle to utter a truth, the rule has been that the hearer hadn't strength of mind enough to believe it. There is a "sort of contemporaneous posterity" which has registered its verdict that Mark Twain is the world's greatest living humorist; but there is yet to come that greater posterity of the future which will, I dare say, class Mark Twain as America's greatest sociologist in letters. He is the historian in art of a varied and unique phase of civilization on this continent that has passed forever. And it is inconceivable that any future investigator into the sociological phases of that civilization can fail to find priceless and unparalleled documents in the wild yet genial, rudimentary yet sane, boisterous yet universally human writings of Mark Twain.

It is a far cry from the steamboat on the Mississippi to the Italianate villa, from the overalls of the river pilot to the gray and scarlet of the Oxford gown. And in recalling the various vicissitudes of his varied life the mind irresistibly reverts to that day when Mark Twain, at the age of sixty, accompanied by his wife, set forth to retrieve his fallen fortunes. When the publishing-house in which he was interested, against his advice and through no fault of his own, continued a policy which led to ruin, Mr. and Mrs. Clemens discovered that even if they sacrificed all their effects they could pay the creditors only about forty cents on the dollar. But Mrs. Clemens' passion for morals manifested itself, and they agreed together that at any cost they must pay nothing less than dollar for dollar. With her courageous company, Mr. Clemens began his career a second time, setting off on a tramp abroad which has ended in "Stormfield" and autumn peace. With obligations satisfied, business integrity magnificently maintained, and fortune made, Mr. Clemens has earned that dignified and honorable leisure for congenial work and humanitarian service it was the tragic fate of Sir Walter Scott never to realize. Nothing can disturb the even tenor of his care-free existence—not even that direst of all terrors to the man of letters, the expiration of copyright. For he has incorporated the very name of *Mark Twain*!

Twain Pokes Fun at Union Station and Pities City

Anonymous*

When Mr. Samuel Langhorne Clemens, better known as Mark Twain, America's foremost living author, is left in the seclusion of his room in his palatial New York home tonight he is going to pray that the people of Baltimore may soon procure a union station really worthy of the name. He said he would.

Mr. Clemens shook the city's mud from his feet this morning, caught a 10:40 o'clock train for New York over the Pennsylvania Railroad and is scheduled to arrive there this afternoon. He was accompanied by Mr. Albert Bigelow Paine, the man who has been engaged to write his biography.

The poor accommodations at Union Station caused the humorist to depart from Baltimore in a sorrowing mood. Had he not seen the station, he declared (humorously, of course) there would have been no occasion for prayer, and he could have trusted Baltimoreans to take care of themselves. But now that he has seen with his own eyes the small, inadequate building used as a station by the Pennsylvania Railroad to accommodate the great Baltimore public, he just felt that it would be the basest ingratitude on his part not to intercede in their behalf.

"Poor Baltimore! Poor Baltimore!" remarked Dr. Clemens, sympathetically, as he strolled by one of the small gates at the station and witnessed 100 persons struggling to get to their proper trains. "It's too bad that she hasn't a better station. Why don't the people say something? Why don't they speak their minds? Yes, it's too bad. And this for Baltimore."

The humorist was numbered among the 100 persons, more or less, who attempted to jam through the gate to the New York express train. He finally did get through by making a center rush, which verified the fact that he once played football in the old college days. When he managed to wriggle his way through the gate he knocked the ashes from the black cigar he was smoking and took one deep breath for relief.

"My, but that was a squeeze," he remarked to Dr. Paine. "This city deserves something better. How does Baltimore stand it? Possibly she isn't

*Reprinted from *Baltimore Star*, June 11, 1909, pp. 1, 12.

but remains sitting holding her hands. She should arise and do some kicking.

"And look at the tracks," he said sarcastically. "Every chance of getting hurt. But, then, I suppose all the passengers, or prospective passengers, have their lives insured. But that's no way to send people to incoming and outgoing trains. Why don't they let the passengers climb over the roof and slide down poles to the track on which their train is standing? Now, that is rather an odd way, but, to me, it is less dangerous. A slide is easier than a run and especially when the latter is attended with the danger of being hit by a locomotive while running.

"Ah, but wouldn't it be better," exclaimed Dr. Clemens, growing serious, "if the Pennsylvania Railroad would construct stairs leading down to the trains? That would remove all danger. Yes, why don't they give Baltimore a better station? Other cities have much better stations. Why not Baltimore?"

Dr. Clemens was a busy man prior to his departure. He was one of the first to arise at the Hotel Belvedere, and up to the time he was ushered into his cab which conveyed him to the station, hadn't a minute to spare.

The first thing he did when he awoke was to look out the window to see if it was raining. Much to his surprise he discovered that it was not and that a few streaks of mellow sunshine were attempting to stream through the window of his room.

"That sunshine was a surprise to me," he remarked as he came down on the elevator and walked leisurely about the hotel lobby, puffing away at a cigar. "I thought it did nothing but rain in Baltimore. I did not know that Baltimoreans ever saw the sunshine.

"And I wonder," he continued, while a smile broke over his countenance, "if my visit is responsible for this rain. While I was in Sydney, Australia, there hadn't been any rain for six weeks, and the Christian people began praying for rain. They prayed night and day, and finally one day, after supplications had been offered for about a month, a shower came up which lasted for about two hours. Now take me, for instance, one who is referred to as an infidel. I come here to Baltimore and produce more rain than those Christian people in Australia could in weeks of fervent prayer. Funny, isn't it?"

After finishing his cigar, the humorist was escorted to the dining-room, where he breakfasted with Mrs. James Nunnally and her daughter, Miss Nunnally, the latter being the young woman responsible for Dr. Clemens' visit to Baltimore. From the dining-room he returned to his room and later departed for the station.

At Union Station Dr. Clemens was the center of attraction, although he endeavored to keep out of public gaze as much as possible. With Dr. Paine keeping close by, the humorist sought the rear platform and promenaded up and down it until train time. Dr. Paine saw that every fancy was gratified. Turning around Dr. Clemens happened to see the scales standing by.

"I want to weigh," he said, "to see how well Baltimore has been feeding me."

Stepping upon the scales, Dr. Paine dropped a penny in the slot and the indicator pointed to 150 pounds.

"Well, well," Dr. Clemens exclaimed, "I have gained one pound. They do feed well here, and I will go back home in good shape."

Inside the waiting room the humorist was approached by a bevy of pretty girls from the Carter school, in Catonsville. The girls wanted to bid him farewell and had taken an early car for Baltimore. Dr. Clemens shook each one by the hand and told them how he had enjoyed his visit.

"My visit to Baltimore," he said, "has been most delightful, and I especially enjoyed the exercises at Catonsville yesterday. It was the sanest commencement I ever witnessed. I mean by that the girls were not required to read long, tiresome essays. No, there was none of that. The exercises were splendid.

"Then Baltimore is such a delightful place, too," he continued, "and her people, well, we haven't their equal. The city appeals to me because of its delightful Southern atmosphere. I am a Southerner, and that is why I like to come to Baltimore. I was born in Missouri, and some of my happiest years were spent right in the South."

Dr. Clemens discussed the charge of plagiarism slightly, the only important thing coming from him being the announcement that Messrs. Harper & Co. were now printing an edition of the book "Is Shakespeare Dead," which will give the Greenwood people credit for the excerpts taken from the book in England.

"I think," he remarked, "that I have explained the situation to the satisfaction of the public, but I don't mind saying that in the future full credit will be given for all quotations from the Greenwood book. It was my intention that this should be done in the edition heretofore published."

Dr. Clemens is taking a great deal of interest in the biography that is being written of himself by Dr. Paine. Every now and then he reviews what has already been written, but the author declares it will be many, many years before the public sees it.

"It will be a long time," he declared, "because I am not going to die until I am at least 100 years old, or possibly older. Why, I am a boy, and Dr. Paine will have to wait several years before he can finish the closing years of my life. He has already written some of the biography, but not all, and he can't conclude his work until I am put under the ground. I am making no promises when that will be."

Dr. Clemens referred lightly to his belief, he stating that it was the general impression that he did not believe in a God. All on this score he would say was that he believed in a great intellectual force which ruled this great universe. He emphatically stated that he did not concur in the belief of some that this big world came here by chance.

Dr. Clemens is not contemplating writing any more new books just at this time. He will remain in New York for a few days, and will then go to his home at Redding, Ct., where he will remain all the summer.

Mark Twain: Personal Impressions

Henry M. Alden*

There are no impressions of Mark Twain that are not personal. The world is full of them, as it is full of his memories, which he has generously been communicating for nearly half a century; so that those who attempt to give 'personal recollections' of him must seem like gleaners in the field he has himself well harvested. Nobody can tell anything about him better than he can tell it himself, nor half so well. Therefore, people have come to expect directly from him the record of his experiences and impressions, whether strange or familiar.

It would be far from true to say of Mark Twain that he has always been writing his autobiography. No writer, not even Rabelais, has shown such powers of invention, and none has exercised them more effectively for universal entertainment. That means a kind of story telling which, whatever of spiritual significance may be involved, is outwardly projected, objective, wholly concrete in its presentment. Its object is entertainment—it may be more than that, but that at least it must be. This is the story teller's art from the time of Cheops to our own, and Mark Twain is a consummate master of the art, as no modern novelist is or can be. Yet all his stories are autobiographical in a way, and his personality is involved in direct ratio with his personal detachment. He may tell what he has experienced; he may narrate what has occurred within his observation only; or he may pass beyond the scope of both experience and observation into the region of speculation—to King Arthur's Court, to the Garden of Eden, or to France in the time of Joan of Arc. Here are three degrees of personal detachment; but more of the author's real personality is liberated in the field of observation than in that of experience, and still more of it in that of speculation. There is more of Mark Twain and of his art in *The Man Who Corrupted Hadleyburg* than there is in the *Tom Sawyer* stories or in *Roughing It on the Mississippi*. But they all have that detachment and clean projection, that antique fashion of the story teller's art, and the perfect illusion it is the business of that art to produce and maintain, which from the beginning have distinguished the Masters of Entertainment.

*Reprinted from *Book News Monthly*, 28 (April, 1910), 579–82.

Of course, Mark is most acceptable to the great public when he appears in his own person. It is true that he first won popularity through his writings. That was due mainly to his imagination, which was first of all a vivid sensibility to the wonders of Nature and of the human mind—a sensibility abundantly fed in his childhood on the banks of the Mississippi, and most varied in its diet during the subsequent years of his nomadic youth. It was tuned to a high pitch—to a note of altitude and expansion such as Walt Whitman had caught in his first trip across the continent. The note, which was not only one of grandeur but one of Argonautic adventure, affected Whitman, who was a poet, in one way, Bret Harte, who was a novelist, in another, and Mark Twain, who was at once a native-born philosopher and story teller, in still another and far different way. He abided with this splendid Western note, as these others did not, made the most of its inspiration in every way, in every degree of its variety, and rose to its full measure. Then, because he had imagination, he carried it an octave higher. When he had exhausted the Mississippi, the Amazon haunted his dreams. He saw nothing great or strange but that he imagined something greater and stranger—to the very limit of romantic surprise. His temperament added to his vast imaginative investment a quaint presentment, so that, while primarily a speculative philosopher, he was incidentally a humorist. Where Poe would have engendered terror, he created laughter.

Now, a man who has written stories that inevitably provoke laughter and are of the kind that suggest direct speech—being wholly unliterary, however much they belong to literature—has given hostages to fortune and must personally appear when called for, whether he wishes to or not. But I am sure that Mark likes it—indeed. I should not envy the man who did not enjoy such immediate comradeship with all classes of people. He seems all the more human because he not only enters into the spirit of the common festivity, but is inclined to meet his audience more than half way, heightening the quaintness of his personal demeanor or costume to suit the quaintness of the whole affair. His peculiar intonation, which is not affected, but native to him, contributes very materially to the harmony. He has, by virtue of the world's wider acquaintance with him than with any other author, been given the freedom of the world, and he is pleased to have made so extensive an acquaintance with it, not excluding Oxford! Everything has helped on—and the press has done its full share—this dramatic projection of Mark Twain's personality. There is only one other instance in literary history of such a projection. That was the case of Lord Bryon. But how different! Any reader's imagination will supply the contrast.

One sees in Mark Twain's case the evident compulsion, however genially complied with, of the openly dramatized personality. The thoughtful critic who knows what, at its best, that personality means for literature, in creations of eternal value, sees also the limitations put upon it by the popular demand, and no one knows better what these are than Mark Twain himself. His riper genius, with ever deepening insight into the human heart, long ago made a demand upon him contradictory to that inflexible popular dictate which holds the artist absolutely to his earliest traits, however accidental these may have been and however inadequate to the expression of his mature purpose. When one has given to the world the priceless boon of laughter, the world will willingly take from him only that offering. That is the obvious sacrifice. There are others not so obvious, but more regrettable. We shall not fail for lack of seriousness. The most pitiful of all failures is the inadequate revelation of a wonderful personality.

If Mark Twain were a professional humorist, himself limited to the conditions imposed by an indiscriminate and undiscriminating majority of his admirers, it would not matter if he should follow the lines of least resistance and be carried anywhither by the crowd. But he has abundantly shown that kind of versatility which is not facile, but comes of reaction and seeks difficulty. Look at his story of Joan of Arc, behind which lay thirteen years of earnest, passionate study. There is no greater masterpiece in American literature. Read his essay in appreciation of Mr. Howells. We have had no better criticism of the novelist's art of expression than that. All thoughtful readers have caught the profound spiritual implications of some of his short stories, like *The Man Who Corrupted Hadleyburg* and *Was It Heaven or Hell?* All these show the finest lines of his art, of his humor, of his large but delicately sensitive personality. In how many ways he is haunted by psychical suggestion—as when, after describing the inerrant course laid by the sleeping pilot, he asks: "If sleep can veil such intuition, what might not death veil?" Telepathy is but one of his spiritual enchantments.

Literature has lost much in not having had more of Mark Twain's imaginative creations on this higher plane, where grotesque extravagances are displaced by spiritual pregnancies of the largest significance and yielding the most wonderful surprises. And he has been as one divided against himself between his better genius and that outward compulsion to which he has yielded so much because of his good nature and democratic companion-ability. Sometimes he has felt the sharpness of the penalty, when he would fain have made more of the comradeship of an audience, admitting it to an almost sacred confidence, and was, at the first broaching of it, prevented by an outburst of anticipative laughter!

But I recall a different case, when, at dinner celebrating his birthday, though not on the exact date—only men being present, and all of them his personal friends—after having recounted in his most humorous vein, many vivid and laughter-provoking early experiences of his in the West, he spoke of his approaching departure to Italy with his wife, in terms that clearly indicated his apprehensions as to her health, and his hopes of its restoration through the change of scene and climate, concluding with these words: "This is *her* birthday."

I thought then of this homely side of the man's nature, of which the world at large knew scarcely anything; I thought of what he had suffered, in reverses of fortune, in private griefs and solicitudes, and how these sorrows had developed those sweeter traits of the man's personality which bind all men more closely to him, and which should yield new graces and values to his imaginative work.

Years before, I had seen him in his Hartford home. Up in his billiard-room, in the twilight, he chatted familiarly about his little ones—two of his girls were then quite young. The family circle was as yet unbroken. I do not know what storms may even then have been gathering, threatening material security, but I think those Hartford years must have been the happiest of Mark Twain's life. All know what followed—bankruptcy, the brave struggle to pay all creditors in full, seventeen years of homelessness, the loss of all but one member of his family, and that one married, till, at the opening of the present year—his seventy-fifth—we behold him utterly alone, though closely pressed about by the whole world's sympathy.

One thing he has never lost, even in the most restless moments of his life—his love of children. Wherever I have seen him, where these little ones were, he has sought them out, as if finding in them a restful solace—a refuge from all worldly conceits and masks and even from the grandeurs of his own imagination. What delicate entertainment he offers them, subduing his naive grotesquery to meet their dainty imaginings, is their secret and his. His latest sketch—that of Marjorie Fleming—betrays something of it.

Surely the last vintage of such a life must be the most exquisite. The *Autobiography* is yet to be completed. From the glimpses hitherto published—such, for instance, as he has given of "Susy's Diary"—we may hope for rare disclosures of the more intimate side of his nature; also for disclosures equally rare of his speculation concerning life and the world. For little Susy was right when she said of him: "He is as much of a philosopher (*sic*) as anything."

Mark Twain *the* Humorist

Clarence H. Gaines[*]

When we read Mark Twain, we laugh, smile, are surprised, intensely interested, touched; and we call this man the prince of humorists—as undoubtedly he is—because our predominant feeling is the sense of being royally amused. Humor is hard to define; it is not merely wit plus an appreciation of human foibles, nor "playful fancy"—whatever the dictionary may tell us. It is nothing like so simple as that. The trouble is that we are always prone to regard it as a single faculty, born in a man or acquired by him, when what we really mean by it is the united effect of many of his faculties upon *us*. That is why the quality eludes hard and fast definition, and why there are so many kinds of it. But if humor is all that cheers and invigorates, and entertains and dispels care—if it can make us sad without being depressed, and indignant without being bitter—if humor can do all this (as in its best estate it certainly can), then we know what we mean when we say that Mark Twain is the greatest of humorists. That, doubtless, is what the world means by so calling him, and, rightly understood the compliment is not so inadequate as at first blush it may appear.

But if we take a narrow and superstitious view of humor, we shall never learn to understand Mark Twain. We shall never know how he, more than almost any other English-speaking man, has been able to "add to the gaity of nations." We have had humorists and humorists in this country of ours. But Max Adeler, Petroleum V. Nasby, John Phenix, even Artemus Ward and Bill Nye, have become traditions. One quotes them, or misquotes them, but one does not often read them. Why could not these men do for us all that Mark Twain has done? It is an impertinent inquiry, and we may as well push it still further. Oliver Wendell Holmes was a humorist, and a very subtle and effective one too. Why could not Dr. Holmes do all that Mark Twain has done? It sounds like an insane question; yet we shall never be able to answer it so long as we are content with merely saying of each man that he was a humorist. Plainly, we must explain the humor by the man, and not the man by his humor. Dr. Holmes was an essayist—a man of wide ideas, much book-learning, keen

[*]Reprinted from *Book News Monthly*, 28 (April, 1910), 583–88.

221

observation; he delivered his own message in his own way, and we love him for it. What we mean by his humor is largely the Oliver-Wendell-Holmes quality in everything he wrote. We can't define it much more exactly, because it is too complicated—"Style is the man." And it is the tremendous Mark-Twain quality in everything that Samuel L. Clemens has written which gives it its immense hold upon the heart and the imagination. This may seem like reasoning in a circle, yet really it is not. It is merely to say that humor in its best and broadest sense is not a simple thing, but the complex effect of a man's personality. Only, the peculiarity of the present case is that we might use "Mark Twain" as a good, practical, working synonym for "humor" and "humorous" in their widest meaning without any noticeable lack of precision on propriety.

The man himself, we know, hasn't too much reverence for theories, so we must beware how we apply them to him. We shall do better if we take up, more or less casually, several of his books. Suppose the choice falls upon *Huckleberry Finn*. It is funny, certainly; there is more real, honest laughter in it, perhaps, than in any other book of equal length in the world. But that isn't all. It is also one of the best stories we have ever read. It is, in fact, just what we *mean* by "a good story." And yet—this is the strange part of it—try as we may, we cannot separate the humor from the quality that makes the story so extremely interesting. The two elements—if they *are* two—work together in perfect harmony. We turn, say, to *The Prince and the Pauper*, and there is humor in that too—plenty of it. But what strikes one principally is the fact that he is dealing with one of the most beautifully imagined and livingly real of historical novels. Just here we begin to ask ourselves how both stories could possibly have been written by the same man. And yet it is even glaringly apparent that the Mark Twain of *The Prince and the Pauper* is the Mark Twain of *Huckleberry Finn*. Both these tales have the same unquenchable Mark-Twain quality in them. So has the *Personal Recollections of Joan of Arc*—which makes one cry half the time; so have *Pudd'nhead Wilson* and *The Gilded Age*, and all the rest. What binds them all together is that deep-lying and characteristic quality which we somewhat inadequately term "humor" because it delights us. If there were a word that meant humor and humanity and storytelling imagination all in one, that would be a good word to use in describing Mark Twain. But it is in vain that we try to analyze him. He defeats us by being so various in his activities, yet so entirely and serenely himself, whether he is writing *Life on the Mississippi* or *A Connecticut Yankee at King Arthur's Court*. Apparently he uses the same power to make us laugh and to make us weep.

That extraordinary tale, *Tom Sawyer, Detective*, is as Mark-Twain as any of them—which seems the more remarkable when we reflect that it is, first of all, a genuine detective story, and a highly improbable and exciting detective story too. The plot is even excessively incredible, because, as the author tells us, it happens to be true. The story is funny (though it nearly touches upon tragedy), yet the amazing thing, after all, is the fact that this altogether unbelievable romance has an air of sober truth, a kind of homespun reality, about it that is utterly convincing. Here, perhaps, we come as close to one secret of Mark Twain's power as we are ever likely to get: he uses humor to make things *real*, instead of employing it, as so many writers do, to make matters appear more grotesquely improbable than they are by nature. This is not to say that he never does the other thing. On the contrary, no one is better skilled in the delicate art of piling up circumstantial falsifications to a precarious and outrageous height—the immortal story of the Old Ram in *Roughing It* at once suggests itself—but this is the author in his least serious mood. These fantasies do not weaken our faith. If Mark Twain should say that Tom Sawyer was carried up to heaven in a fiery chariot, we should all believe him. Unquestionably he would make that somewhat odd occurrence seem perfectly natural. He would cause Tom Sawyer to act just as he *would* act in the circumstances—and we should believe him.[1]

Of course, there are other elements of his art which one may, as it were, isolate and describe. There is his perfect skill in what may be called the rhetoric of humor. By sheer adroitness in the arrangement of words and phrases he produces the impression of entire naturalness and gets the utmost effect from his ideas. Like the best of extemporary speakers (which he is, among other things), he has constant regard for the psychology of his audience. One proof of this quality is the fact that every one of his books may be read aloud with increased pleasure: that is a hard test. Then, there is his consummate dexterity in arranging surprises, and, still more important, his mastery of the vernacular—the plain speech of untutored men, so much more subtle, so much harder to use with effect, than the grosser kinds of dialect. All these contribute to that delightful, humorous (or Mark-Twain) quality; yet, of course, they quite fail to explain the man. Another might have them all, and yet not be Mark Twain. A deeper trait is implied in the fact that so much of his writing appeals equally to children and to grown-ups. We need not affirm that this is a characteristic of all great literature; but it is true at least of Homer and Chaucer and the *Morte d'Arthur*, and a few of the finest things we possess.

It may be personal bias, but it seems to the present writer, at least, that Mark Twain's latest story—his *Captain Stormfield's Visit to Heaven*—is nearly the most perfect thing he has ever written: so much of him expressed in so short a space. His longer works represent his experience; this expresses a ripened character: it is a pure and potent draught of Mark Twain. I cannot pretend to analyze its composition; but if it is lacking in the "body" of fact, it has an imaginative—yes, a spiritual—quality which one scarcely finds elsewhere in the same degree, except, perhaps, in *Eve's Diary*. I pass over the circumstance that the tale is full of rollicking fun, for that is obvious. The first point that forces itself upon the attention is perhaps that characteristic Mark-Twain magic of doing the seemingly impossible. *Captain Stormfield's Visit to Heaven* is the most impossible story ever written, and the most probable. One believes in the Captain and his adventures from beginning to end. Then, one cannot but remark upon the greatness of a humorous imagination that "has fun with" (no other expression will do) such portentous things as stars and comets and the awful interstellar spaces. The story is all done upon the same cosmic scale; yet its human note never falters. When Captain Stormfield arrives, he finds himself at the wrong gate, and when the clerk questions him he cannot locate himself in space. So the clerk investigates:

> He got a balloon and sailed up and up and up in front of a map that was as big as Rhode Island. He went on up till he was out of sight, and by and by he came down again and got something to eat and went up again. To cut a long story short, he kept on doing this for a day or two, and finally he came down and said he thought he had found that solar-system, but it might be fly-specks. So he got a microscope and went back. It turned out better than he feared. He had rousted out our system sure enough. He got me to describe our planet and its distance from the sun, and then he says to his chief:
> "Oh, I know the one he means, now, sir. It is on the map. It is called the Wart."
> "Says I to myself, 'Young man, it wouldn't be wholesome for you to go down *there*, and call it the Wart.' "

This is the humor of immensity, and it is genuine humor. It is as fine in its way as Kipling's *Deep Sea Chantey* or *Tomlinson*, only this is the Mark Twain and not the Kipling of it. But the most significant fact about *Captain Stormfield's Visit to Heaven* is its pathos. Inevitably one feels it underneath the laughter. In this story Mark Twain has gathered together all the old orthodox traditions regarding the next world, that men have believed in, and lived upon, and sworn by, and suffered by and for—and if he criticizes them in the light of common sense, he treats them very tenderly. He preserves every essential feature, for he sympathizes, as only a great mind can, with the human longing that lies behind every article of the old literal faith. Captain Stormfield's Heaven is a very homelike place. Religious feeling would not suffer in the least if it should be accepted literally. Nothing—not even harps and halos and palm branches—is denied those who enter there. All in all, it is hardly possible to read *Captain Stormfield* without tears; and this is the truth about that remarkable book; it has a deep religious feeling, salted with strong common sense, and whosoever takes it for profane or irreverent is not wise.

Humor—the more one studies Mark Twain, the more one sees how endlessly it expands, merging itself with other qualities of greatness. We see this in Mark Twain's universal appeal. Shakespeare himself could hardly have reached universality without his humor. The same truth is borne in upon us when we consider the man's undaunted attitude toward life. Plainly, without humor we can scarcely maintain that cheerful courage which is so fundamental a virtue. Again, it is proved to us by his justice. Without humor, how can one, as the saying is, "give the Devil his due," and how can one scourge folly and meanness without pettiness? One cannot understand children without humor; Tom Sawyer and Huck Finn show us that. Without it, one cannot even be acceptably frank; one needs the Falstaffian art of making fun of oneself. And, to state the crowning paradox of this wonderful Mark-Twain quality: While Samuel Clemens has jested more tremendously than any of his contemporaries, he is perhaps the sincerest writer in America. So that, on the whole, one does him the greatest injustice ever to call him (merely) a humorist.

Note

1. In point of fact, do we not all feel the need of some sort of apotheosis for Tom Sawyer and Huck Finn? The story always leaves them at a point where we wish to know the sequel. Yet we never learn what *became* of them—surely no common fate. It seems likely that they are living in Never-Never Land with Peter Pan—but this is only conjecture.

Mark Twain

Anonymous*

It will be many a day before the people of the United States forget Mark Twain, the man. Since far back in the 70's he had been one of our national celebrities, and perhaps the greatest of the clan, beaming, expansive and kindly: a star at all great public feasts; the friend of Presidents and millionaires, of archbishops and actors, welcome everywhere and always in good humor, a fellow of infinite jest. As the years passed his picturesque figure grew more and more familiar and lovable. Every town of any pretensions knew him. He was in ceaseless motion, making a speech here, taking a degree there, and always dripping fun. The news that he was to be present was enough to make a success of anything, from a bacchanal of trust magnates to a convocation of philologists.

So much for the Mark Twain of banquet hall and popular fancy. He will recede slowly, but recede he must, for there is something pitifully insubstantial about fame of that sort. The new generation will have its own philosophers and its own comedians, and their pressing reality will make poor Mark's white dress suit, his chrysanthemum of white hair and his eternal cigar grow faint and wavering. Oldsters will chuckle and wag their heads when they think of him, but as a living figure he will sink into the past. In that human certainty, however, there is no need for mourning, for there remains the Mark Twain of literature, in stature vastly above the post-prandial wit—a Mark Twain whose place among the immortals is generally conceded—a Mark Twain whose life work as satirist, humorist and philosopher is measured in the estimation of many critics by that of Cervantes, Thackeray and Fielding, Aristophanes and Molière.

There is great temptation, of course, to overestimate a man in the presence of his death, but here, we believe, there is no such extravagance. More than 15 years ago the true rank of Samuel Langhorne Clemens began to impress itself upon the more discerning of his contemporaries. It was the late Sir Walter Besant who first made earnest and effective protest against the popular tendency to regard him as a funny man, and as a funny man only. To show the absurdity of this error, Sir Walter entered

*Reprinted from *Baltimore Sun*, April 22, 1910, p. 6. It is likely that the editorialist was H. L. Mencken.

upon an elaborate analysis of "Huckleberry Finn," as one who might claim expert knowledge of the literary craft and its problems, pointing out its marvelously accurate characterizations, its vivid picture of a civilization, its Homeric sweep and throb. Here, said Sir Walter, was a literary feat of the first magnitude, for a grown man had entered into the soul of a boy and looked at the world through that boy's eyes. The result, he thought, was the greatest novel ever written by an American, if not the greatest ever written in English.

Enthusiasm seemed to color this revolutionary judgment, but it won unexpected support and in unexpected places. The English critics, strangely enough, were the first to say aye with hearty good will. While we were still roaring over "The Jumping Frog," as over some masterpiece of empty clowning, they were comparing "A Connecticut Yankee" to "Don Quixote" and "Gulliver's Travels," and setting up "A Tramp Abroad" as unique and incomparable. The Germans followed the English and the French came after, and then at last we Americans began to realize that a truly great man was among us—a man who would be remembered when some of our Presidents were forgotten. In 1891, when Yale University made Mr. Clemens a doctor of letters, this turn of the tide was publicly marked. He lost, after that, nothing of his popular vogue, but he began to gain the less noisy but more lasting fame of an artist of world rank. Honors came thick and fast, and in 1907, when he was called to Oxford to receive the doctorate of that ancient university, England received him with almost royal pomp.

The Mark Twain of the last phase was little more than a shadow of the Mark Twain who wrote "Huckleberry Finn." There was still abundant foolery in him, but his old Rabelaisian joy in the human comedy seemed to be gone. He no longer got beneath the surface; he was no longer the universal satirist, dealing with broad types and touching the heart as well as the midriff. He was old, and maybe a bit weary. But the world will not take account of these weak echoes of his former self when it comes to reckon his worth, any more than it considers "Lovell the Widower" when it judges Thackeray. He must be estimated by his best, as Cervantes and the others are estimated. And that best will give delight so long as the English of today remains a living tongue.

Let us take leave of him here. The time is not one for elaborate essays. He had the great human qualities. Reading him, one came to love him, as one loves Chaucer, Fielding and Ben Jonson. For all his war upon shams and frauds, there was a vast benevolence in him, a genial tolerance, a deep human note. Truly a great man has gone from among us.

Chief of American Men of Letters

Anonymous*

MARK TWAIN IS DEAD.

It would be hard to frame four other words that could carry a message of personal bereavement to so many Americans.

He was easily the chief of our writers, by the only valid test. He could touch the emotional centre of more lives than any other.

He was curiously and intimately American. No other author has such a tang of the soil—such a flavor of the average national mind.

Europeans who complain that we denied Walt Whitman, misunderstood Emerson and have admired only those who write in old world fashions should be satisfied at least with Mark Twain, and with our unwavering taste for him.

He was our very own, and we gathered him to our hearts.

In ages to come, if historians and archaeologists would know the thoughts, the temper, the characteristic psychology of the American of the latter half of the nineteenth century, he will need only to read "Innocents Abroad," "Tom Sawyer," and "Huckleberry Finn."

Mr. Clemens's books were the transcripts of his life. And that life was the kind of life that the average American man of his time has believed in and admired.

He was the man that rose from the ranks without envy or condescension.

The man that hated dogmas and philosophies and loved a flash of intellectual light.

He was the man that cared much to get rich, yet would sweat blood to pay his debts.

The man of boundless optimism, who has never troubled to understand the great tragedies of nations.

The deepening sense of the twentieth century—with its feeling that there are social problems that cannot be resolved by pleasantries—has somehow left our dear prophet, with all his delicate and tender ironies and his merry quips, a little in the rear.

Mark Twain was never fortunate in his polemics. He was not effec-

*Reprinted from *New York American*, April 22, 1910, p. 20.

tive as the champion of a cause. What he wrote of the Congo was hardly more creditable or convincing than his crusade against Mrs. Eddy.

He had no natural acerbity, and consequently no real talent for satire.

His genius was full of bravery and brightness and the joy of life.

And in the strength of his serene and laughing spirit generations of Americans will go forth to do deeds that he himself could never have conceived.

Mark Twain: An American Pioneer in Man's Oldest Art, Whose Death Is Mourned by the World at Large

Anonymous*

Happy among creative artists is the humorist. He strikes as deep into life as his neglected brothers who deal in pain and tragedy. But he alone carries the people with him. He has their good will, while he interprets their life to them. And only at his death is there sadness because of him. The more he made them merry, the richer the grief. And there are few peoples to-day on the earth where there is no sense of loss because MARK TWAIN died. He would have been seventy-five years old in November, and in the final months had suffered much pain.

Printer's devil and Mississippi pilot, cub reporter, pioneer, miner, and tramp royal, he knew life, and got the rough stuff out of which to spin his cloth of gold from reality itself. He had lived the life from necessity, and then wrote it out.

His sense of the vast innate humor of things was beaten into the fiber of him by the Nevada years, when he was territorial secretary in the State of Nevada. Those were great days. It was a life that couldn't stand the swiftest theatrical show for ten minutes running, but in its panting restlessness clamored for poker and drink and dancing and barbaric music. Partly a glorified picnic, full of easy nuggets and dramatic high lights, and then again tragic and bitter, where sweat and blood dropped free.

A Western man has said of him: "A good many people think MARK TWAIN is a natural-born humorist. He isn't. He simply described the things he saw in Nevada and got the habit."

The tumult of that life never forsook him. It passed into the color and startling suddenness of his prose. A land that was unexpected and vast, and men who were irreverent, ironic, fearless and sincere, what was left to do but hive the honey from those unreaped fields?

In the teeth of the schools, he broke away from the gentle reminiscent New England tradition, and struck out a trail as new and sure as that of ABRAHAM LINCOLN in statecraft. He was an American in every line of his mirthful copy, and it was a generation before the critics caught up and knew it for literature, and ANDREW LANG called it Homeric.

*Reprinted from *Collier's*, 45 (April 30, 1910), 10.

Leaping into the public eye with the overburdened life of the Calaveras frog who couldn't jump because of his meal of buckshot, he hit his public yet harder with "Innocents Abroad," which showed the ignorant and unashamed American tourist thrust upon the shrines of Europe, who forthwith dramatizes his own innocence, and is unaware of COLUMBUS, but weeps at the grave of ADAM. He finds the old masters a clutter of paint, and refuses to be moved by the cant of embryo Cookists. He turns a fresh, untroubled face on Europe, and asks that it make its own impression sincerely and first-hand.

That manhandling of the holy places and hoar traditions was the key to MARK TWAIN, who faced life itself in the same naked way. Background, and atmosphere and the accumulations of convention were non-existent for him, who asked them only to give up their reality and what of vital spark they still possessed for him. This trait of the unabashed accounted for some of his more doubtful ventures, as when he entered the lists of the Shakespeare controversy.

The books which will safeguard his fame longer than a library of solemn and academic tomes are "Tom Sawyer" and its greater sequel "Huckleberry Finn," wherein the boy in literature is first discovered and celebrated. All the Boytowns and Bad Boys since owe a goodly debt to the clean sweep of those adventures, where boys whitewash fences, run away from home, and exhibit their naked souls in a leaping narrative, brimmed with undying laughter, and poignant with such touches of pathos as the unsuspected deafness of poor black Jim's little girl. The humor of those early books persists through many languages, and is little time-worn by forty years.

To see things with fresh eyes, and find nothing sacred simply because other men had removed their shoes—it was in this spirit that he invaded the medieval realm, and plucked the comic out of the forest rides of knights and ladies and the renowned jousts. He called it "A Yankee at the Court of King Arthur." He had already written "The Prince and the Pauper" to show that tenderness and reverence could be accorded.

In his "Joan of Arc" he dealt tenderly with the lovely lady in proof that he knew how to kneel as well as strike.

He made a few swift sorties into literary criticism in the same masculine, forthright way—notably in his bitter attack on SHELLEY for the treatment of the poor drowned HARRIET, and in the paper on COOPER, whom he pilloried for committing the 57 varieties of literary sin in plot construction and style.

He did not flinch from facing the popular good will, which was so largely his, and attacked the national policy of imperialism in his eloquent "To Them That Sit in Darkness," and the acrid drive at General FUNSTON. FUNSTON thought of replying, and the author in the pride of conscious power, advised him to beware or he would hand him out some "man-talk."

He was free of prejudices, and wrote a fine, strong article on the Jews, where the unfailing sympathy of it included some earnest criticism.

The external facts are few after the early hard years which grounded him in reality. The books sold like "The Pilgrim's Progress." His lectures were always thronged.

In old age he met a sudden financial loss to himself—and to those who had invested with him in a publishing house of his founding—by a recurrence of energy on the lecture platform, which cleared every cent of the indebtedness. He exactly repeated the intrepid and honorable feat of WALTER SCOTT, which had enriched literary history for a hundred years.

In his later years he was moved by the pathos of life—the ceaseless striving game. His manner was affectionate and playful, and the impression of him on the spirit was tender and pathetic. He was simple and offhand, never forcing the note. His conversation was made up of short, easy words, never aiming at wit or cleverness. Sometimes, too, there was music on his lips, as when, on his birthday celebration, he spoke of Pier 70, and the laughter and songs of the young men in the streets at midnight, no more to be heard.

With the fearless poise of the head of white hair, he would be watched by a theater audience more closely than the star actor on the stage. Ten thousand men rose to their feet when he entered the open-air auditorium at the Yale bicentennial.

Mark Twain

Anonymous*

The report of Mark Twain's death on the 21st of April, this time not "greatly exaggerated" but sadly and literally true, was the occasion of heart-felt grief to the entire nation, we may almost say to the whole world. No American of our time was more widely known; no other American writer lately among the living had endeared himself to so large and cosmopolitan an audience. His life, ended midway in its seventy-fifth year, had been rich in human experience, had fulfilled the season of mellow fruitfulness, and had given literary expression, as few other lives have done, to the qualities of buoyancy and independence so characteristic of the typical American temperament. It was also a life which, in its personal aspects, revealed the qualities of manliness and sympathy, was admirable in its public and private relations, and bore with fortitude the buffets of ill-fortune. These are tests of character which few men can suffer without some show of weakness; his character they served only to sweeten and strengthen.

Mark Twain's life may be divided into two nearly equal parts. Of the first part, which includes his boyhood days, his experiences as a journeyman printer and editor, his brief career as a Mississippi pilot, his briefer career as a Confederate soldier, and his adventures in the mining-camps and rude settlements of the West, we have the most vivid of records in his books—in "Tom Sawyer" and "Huckleberry Finn" and "Roughing It," and in the countless short stories and sketches which began with "The Jumping Frog" and are probably not yet at an end, for only a part of the work which he humorously styles his "Autobiography" has been put into print. Those early days left him with a fund of recollections upon which his drafts were honored—as was similarly the case with Bret Harte—for long years after the experiences themselves had become old (although not unhappy) far off things. As the recorder of these phases of pioneer life which he knew at first hand, and of which he almost alone has preserved for us the very form and pressure, we are immeasurably in his debt. There are few things that we know as well as what it was to be a boy in a Missouri country town, a futile skirmisher in the early days of the Civil

*Reprinted from *Dial*, 48 (May 1, 1910), 305–07.

War, and a traveller on the lower Mississippi, few bygone types that are as real to us as the miners and stage-coach drivers and politicians and bar-room loafers of the untutored West of the midcentury. The writings in which these things have been preserved for us are Mark Twain's best, because they are his raciest and least self-conscious.

The next best group of his books is provided by "The Innocents Abroad," "A Tramp Abroad," and "Following the Equator," the three extensive records of unconventional travel. Yet in these the touch of sophistication is seen, and becomes progressively pronounced with each succeeding narrative. The second is not as good as the first, and the third is distinctly weaker than the second, more artificial in its conception and more forced in its humor. When the author transplanted himself to the East for permanent residence in the seventies, he abandoned the primal sources of his inspiration, and never developed others of comparable importance. Going farther and farther afield in search of fresh material, he illustrated anew the myth of Antaeus, and displayed a pitiable weakness. Over some of his later flounderings in the alien elements of literary criticism, history, and metaphysics, it were best discreetly to draw a veil. There was in him a streak of the Philistine which might have remained undetected had he "kept to his last," but which was sharply revealed when he infringed upon the domain of intellectual and scholarly concerns.

The present is not, however, the best occasion for dwelling upon Mark Twain's limitations, or for emphasizing the ephemeral character of a considerable part of his work. A fair share of that work, at least, stands upon a level so high as to be in no danger of passing out of sight. Up to an advanced point in his career, he grew steadily in power and wisdom; his sympathies became ever broader and deeper, and his expressive faculty kept pace with the larger demands that were made upon it. From the exuberant journalist who gave us entertainment in his earlier days he developed into something like a sage to whom we came to look no less for counsel than for amusement. We learned to detect in his homely speech the movings of a fine spirit, instinct with the nobler promptings of democracy, hating shams and ostentatious vulgarity, gentle and gracious in its quieter moods, but fanned to burning indignation when facing some monstrous wickedness, such as the corruption of our political life, or the dastardly act of the American soldier in the Philippines who betrayed his rescuer and shamelessly boasted of the shameful deed, or the infamy of the royal libertine who distilled a fortune from the blood of the miserable natives of the Congo. Even more than by his strictly literary work, he earned our gratitude for the brave words which he spoke upon such themes as these, words that cleared the moral atmosphere and made us see things in the light of naked truth.

Nor should we, in our tribute to the man, forget the silent heroism with which he endured loss of fortune in his advancing years, and shouldered the burden of a debt incurred by the rascality of his associates, a debt for which he was only indirectly responsible, and which he might have evaded without serious impairment of his reputation. The strenuous labors of the years of lecturing and writing which enabled him to discharge in full the shadowy obligations which he then assumed took their toll of his vitality, but won for him an esteem higher than is ever the reward of the artist alone. This action ranks with the similar examples set by Scott and Curtis; it is one of those shining deeds that reveal the man himself, in contradistinction to the works by which most men of creative genius are contented to be known.

The attitude of criticism toward Mark Twain as a writer has undergone a slow but complete change during the past thirty years. From being thought of simply as a "funny man," of the kin of Josh Billings and Artemus Ward, he has gradually come to be recognized as one of our foremost men of letters. This is a profoundly significant transformation of opinion, and to account for it fully would require a more careful analysis than we here have space to undertake. The recognition has been unduly delayed, partly because so much of his output has been utterly unworthy of his best self, and partly because his work in its totality is of so nondescript a character. The conventional way to distinction in literature is by the fourfold path of the poem, the play, the novel, and the essay. Occasionally, also, an historian compels literary recognition. But Mark Twain was neither a poet nor a playwright nor an historian. He was hardly a novelist, either, for his share in "The Gilded Age" does not seriously count, and his work in the form of fiction is not remarkable as story-telling pure and simple. If we are to group him at all, it must be with the essayists, using that term elastically enough to include with him our own Irving, and such Englishmen as Swift and Carlyle. We must either do this, or fall back upon the *sui generis* solution of the problem. Again, if we make a subdivision of the essayist class for the humorists alone, we encounter the difficulty offered by our obstinate association of that term with mere fun-making and the appeal to the lighter interests of human nature. Obviously, our subdivision must take yet another step, and admit that, on the one hand, there are humorists who make us laugh and have hardly any other influence over us, and humorists who are also creative artists, and critics of life in the deeper sense, and social philosophers whose judgments are of weight and import. If we are to classify Mark Twain at all, it must be with the latter distinguished company; and his title to kinship with the three English writers above mentioned, and even with such alien prototypes as Aristophanes and Rabelais and Cervantes, is at least not scornfully to be put aside.

The Death of Mark Twain

Anonymous*

Samuel L. Clemens died on April 21 after a brief illness at the age of seventy-four. A great career, characteristically American, was then clos-ed. Literature, humor, humanitarianism, intellectual and moral progress suffered a severe loss.

Many glowing tributes have been paid to Mark Twain since his death by men and women of distinction, both of Europe and America. It is a source of satisfaction to know that in his rather sad old age, a period of personal bereavement and loneliness, Mark Twain knew that he had the affection, gratitude, admiration of legions of readers, young and old. He had been signally honored by Oxford and English literary and educated bodies; he had won ample recognition not as a "mere humorist" but as one of the most original and gifted men of letters of America.

Mark Twain's humor, rich and delicious as it was, was always fun-damentally serious. It was the humor of a deep thinker, a gentle but penetrating observer, a philosopher who loved mankind while seeing all its weaknesses. Mark Twain was racy, playful, whimsical, extravagant; but he was never guilty of deliberate coarseness, and as President Taft has remarked, "he never wrote a line that a father could not read to a daughter." And this in spite of the fact that he wrote much about rough men, hard and primitive conditions, pioneering, the taming of nature and the lower elements in man. He was breezy, vital, candid, colloquial, "western;" but the civilization, ideas and manners he expressed and ex-pounded were essentially sound. Geniality, charity, unselfishness, in-formed and inspired every utterance.

Mark Twain wrote in several styles and contributed to several forms of literature. He is best known, perhaps, for his earliest works, "Adven-tures of Tom Sawyer," "Huckleberry Finn," "Jumping Frog," etc., and certainly his studies of boy nature are wonderfully acute and entertain-ing. But he wrote excellent history, biography, criticism, disguised philosophy. "Is Shakespeare Dead?" the latest work, dealt with the con-troversy over the authorship of the plays attributed to "the immortal bard," and was keen and suggestive, if not original or scholarly. "Joan of

*Reprinted from *Chautauquan*, 59 (June, 1910), 9–10.

Arc" and "Christian Science" were notable books of their respective kinds. It was impossible for Mark Twain not to be humorous, stimulating, inimitable, but in his most exuberant and irrepressible moments of mirth-making he was no boisterous jester.

The cause of political morality, freedom, human equality, honest government, democracy had in him a staunch and courageous defender. He took a deep interest in the social and industrial reforms of the day, and supported children's theaters, social settlements and similar welfare work. He was an enemy of snobbery, solemn pedantry, cant and corruption in public and commercial life. His death removed a salutary, beneficent force, a rare, if not unique, personality.

Serious Humorists

[Simeon Strunsky]*

Mark Twain's memory may suffer from a certain paradoxical habit we have fallen into when passing judgment on the illustrious dead. The habit consists in picking out for particular commendation in the man what one least expects. If the world thinks of him as a great humorist, the point to make is that at bottom he was really a philosopher. If his shafts struck at everybody and everything, the thing to say is that he liked best what he hit hardest. If one of his books sold five thousand copies, the attempt is made to base his future fame on the comparatively unknown book. The motive behind such reasoning is commendable enough. It is the desire not to judge superficially, the desire to get at the "real" man behind the mask which all of us, according to tradition, wear in life. It is a praiseworthy purpose, but, in the hands of the unskilled or the careless, a perilous one. And worse than either is the intellectual snob whose business it is constitutionally to disagree with the obvious. We make no attempt to classify the writer who has declared that Mark Twain, when he wrote "Innocents Abroad," was terribly in earnest; that he set out to satirize and was funny only because he could not help it. This represents the extreme of a tendency that is made manifest on every side, to turn Mark Twain into everything but what he was—a great compeller of laughter.

One gets dreadfully weary of such topsy-turvy criticism. There are times when one would like to believe that Napoleon will be remembered because he won Austerlitz and Marengo, and not because he divided up France into a vast number of small peasant holdings; that Lincoln was a great man because he signed the Proclamation of Emancipation and wrote the Gettysburg address, and not because he kept his temper under criticism and in adversity. It is well to try to pierce behind the veil of Maya, but no amount of analysis can do away with the popularly accepted beliefs that mothers are primarily maternal, that actresses' talents lie in the direction of the stage, that joyful people laugh, and that people who make wry faces are either pessimists or dyspeptics. What use is there in trying to make a serious book out of the "Innocents Abroad," when we know well that the Mark Twain who wrote it was primarily a fun-maker?

*Reprinted from *Nation*, 90 (June 30, 1910), 645–46.

For ourselves, we confess that we have been unable to find any grave purpose in the "Jumping Frog of Calaveras." We recall the Hawaiian stranger whom Mark Twain kissed for his mother's sake before robbing him of his small change. We recall the horse he rode in Honolulu; it had many fine points, and our traveller hung his hat upon one of them. We recall that other horse behind which he went driving one Sunday with the lady of his choice; it was a milk-dealer's horse on week-days, and it persisted in travelling diagonally across the street and stopping before every gate. These adventures are easy to recall, but the hidden serious purpose within them remains hidden from us.

The serious element in Mark Twain the man and the writer, it would, of course, be futile to deny. His hatred of sham, his hatred of cruelty, his hatred of oppression, appear in the "Innocents Abroad," as they do in his "Connecticut Yankee" and in his bitter assaults on the Christian Scientists and the American missionaries in China of the Boxer days. But to say that Mark Twain was a great humorist because he was an intensely serious man is not true, whatever truth there may be in the formula that humorists are humorists because they are men of sorrow. We would reverse the formula. We would say that humorists are often sad because they are humorists, and that from much laughing the rebound must necessarily be towards much grief. If it is commonly asserted that the humorist laughs because of the incongruities of life, it is, nevertheless, just as safe to maintain that the man born to laughter will be driven by his instincts to search for incongruities. There was no fundamental pessimism in Mark Twain. As Mr. Howells brings out in his chapter of reminiscences in the last *Harper's*, Mr. Clemens had the soul of untamed boyishness. He was boyish in his exuberance of manner, in his taste for extraordinary clothes, and in his glee at earning a great deal of money:

> The postals [announcing his share of the daily profits from the "Gilded Age"] used to come about dinner-time, and Clemens would read them aloud to us in wild triumph. $150—$200—$300, were the gay figures which they bore, and which he flaunted in the air before he sat down at table, or rose from it to brandish, and then, flinging his napkin into his chair, walked up and down to exult in.

One thing there was in Mark Twain that was not apparently boyish or simple. Mr. Howells asserts positively that in his later years Twain believed neither in the Christian theology, in God, nor in immortality:

> All his expressions to me were of a courageous renunciation of any hope of living again, or elsewhere seeing those he had lost. He suffered terribly in their loss, and he was not fool enough to try ignoring his grief. He knew that for that there were but two medicines; that it would wear itself out with the years, and that meanwhile there was nothing for it but those respites in which the mourner forgets himself in slumber. I remember that in a black hour of my own when I was called down to see him, as he

thought from sleep, he said, with an infinite, an exquisite compassion, "Oh, did I wake you, did I *wake* you?" Nothing more, but the look, the voice, were everything; and while I live they cannot pass from my sense.

Here at last we have the disillusion that is said to dwell in the innermost soul of the great humorist. But here, too, we seem to feel that the gray vision of the future was with him not a cause, but a result. When the buoyant soul sinks back upon itself it is apt to feel the riddle of life very keenly indeed.

Mark Twain as Our Emissary

George Ade*

Mark Twain had a large following of admirers who came to regard themselves as his personal friends. Many of them he never met. Most of them never saw him. All of them felt a certain relationship and were flattered by it. Men and women in all parts of our outspread domain, the men especially, cherished a private affection for him. They called him by his first name, which is the surest proof of abiding fondness. Andrew Jackson was known as "Andy"; Abraham Lincoln was simply "Abe" to every soldier boy; and, as a later instance, we have "Teddy." Some men settle down to a kinship with the shirt-sleeve contingent, even when they seem indifferent to the favor of the plain multitude.

Mark Twain never practised any of the wiles of the politician in order to be cheered at railway stations and have Chautauquas send for him. He did not seem over-anxious to meet the reporters, and he had a fine contempt for most of the orthodox traditions cherished by the people who loved him. Probably no other American could have lived abroad for so many years without being editorially branded as an expatriate. In some sections of our country it is safer to be an accomplice in homicide, or a stand-patter in politics, than it is to be an "expatriate." When Mr. Clemens chose to take up his residence in Vienna he incurred none of the criticism visited upon Mr. William Waldorf Astor. Every one hoped he would have a good time and learn the German language. Then when the word came back that he made his loafing headquarters in a place up an alley known as a *stube*, or a *rathskeller*, or something like that, all the women of the literary clubs, who kept his picture on the high pedestal with the candles burning in front of it, decided that *stube* meant "shrine." You may be sure that if they can find the place they will sink a bronze memorial tablet immediately above the main faucet.

Of course, the early books, such as "Innocents Abroad," "Roughing It," and "The Gilded Age" gave him an enormous vogue in every remote community visited by book-agents. The fact that people enjoyed reading

*Reprinted from *Century Magazine*, 81 (December, 1910), 204–06; with some revisions, reprinted in George Ade, *Single Blessedness and Other Observations* (Garden City, N.Y.: Doubleday, Page, 1922), pp. 203–10.

241

these cheering volumes and preserved them in the bookcase and moved out some of the classics by E. P. Roe and Mrs. Southworth in order to make room for "Tom Sawyer" and "Huckleberry Finn," does not fully account for the evident and accepted popularity of Mark Twain. Other men wrote books that went into the bookcase but what one of them ever earned the special privilege of being hailed by his first name?

When a man has done his work for many years more or less under the supervising eye of the public, the public learns a good many facts about him that are in no way associated with his set and regular duties as a servant of the public. Out of the thousand-and-one newspaper mentions and private bits of gossip and whispered words of inside information, even the busy man in the street comes to put an estimate on the real human qualities of each personage, and sometimes these estimates are surprisingly accurate, just as they are often sadly out of focus.

Joseph Jefferson had a place in the public esteem quite apart from that demanded by his skill as an actor. Players and readers of newspapers came to know in time that he was a kind and cheery old gentleman of blameless life, charitable in his estimates of professional associates, a modest devotee of the fine arts, an outdoor sportsman with the enthusiasm of a boy, and the chosen associate of a good many eminent citizens. When they spoke of "Joe" Jefferson in warmth and kindness, it was not because he played "Rip Van Winkle" so beautifully, but because the light of his private goodness had filtered through the mystery surrounding every popular actor. William H. Crane is another veteran of the stage who holds the regard of the public. It knows him as a comedian, and also it knows him as the kind of man we should like to invite up to our house to meet the "folks." The sororities throb with a feeling of sisterhood for Miss Maude Adams because the girls feel sure that she is gracious and charming and altogether "nice."

Mark Twain would have stood very well with the assorted grades making up what is generally known as the "great public" even if he had done his work in a box and passed it out through a knot-hole. Any one who knew our homely neighbors as he knew them and could tell about them in loving candor, so that we laughed at them and warmed up to them at the same time, simply had to be "all right." Being prejudiced in his favor, we knew that if he wanted to wear his hair in a mop and adopt white clothing and talk with a drawl, no one would dare suggest that he was affecting the picturesque. He was big enough to be different. Any special privilege was his without the asking. Having earned 100 per cent of our homage he didn't have to strain for new effects.

His devotion to the members of his family and the heroic performance in connection with the debts of the publishing house undoubtedly helped to strengthen the general regard for him. Also, the older generation, having heard him lecture, could say that they had "met" him. Every one who sat within the soothing presence of the drawl, waiting to be chinked up on every second sentence with a half-concealed stroke of drollery, was for all time a witness to the inimitable charm of the man and the story-teller.

The knowledge of his unaffected democracy became general. No doubt the housewives loved him for his outspoken devotion to home-cooking. Has any one told in public the anecdote of his tribute to a humble item in the bill of fare? It was a dinner party in Washington. Senator Hearst was giving the dinner, and Mark Twain was the guest of honor. Here were two transplanted westerners who knew more about roughing it than ever appeared in a book. As the high-priced food was being served to them, they talked longingly of the old-fashioned cookery of Missouri. The Senator wondered if there was any real corned beef and cabbage left in the world. Mark Twain spoke up in praise of the many old-time dishes, reaching his climax when he declared that, in his opinion, "Bacon would improve the flavor of an angel!"

Furthermore is it not possible that much of the tremendous liking for Mark Twain grew out of his success in establishing our credit abroad? Any American who can invade Europe and command respectful attention is entitled to triumphal arches when he arrives home. Our dread and fear of foreign criticism are still most acute. Mrs. Trollope and Captain Marryat lacerated our feelings long ago. Dickens came over to have our choicest wild flowers strewn in his pathway and then went home to scourge us until we shrieked with pain. Kipling had fun with us, and for years after that we trembled at his approach. George Bernard Shaw peppers away at long range and the "London Spectator" grows peevish every time it looks out of the window and sees a drove of Cook tourists madly spending their money.

It is a terrible shock to the simple inlander, who has fed upon Congressional oratory and provincial editorials, when he discovers that in certain European capitals the name "American" is almost a term of reproach. The first-time-over citizen from Spudville or Alfalfa Center indicates his protest by wearing a flag on his coat and inviting those who sit in darkness to come over and see what kind of trams are run on the Burlington. The lady, whose voice comes from a point directly between the eyes, seeks to correct all erroneous impressions by going to the table d'hote with fewer clothes and more jewels than any one had reason to expect. These two are not as frequently to be seen as they were twenty years ago but they are still gleefully held up by our critics as being "typical."

Probably they are outnumbered nowadays by the apologetic kind—those who approach the English accent with trembling determination and who, after ordering in French, put a finger on the printed line so that the waiter may be in on the secret.

There are Americans who live abroad and speak of their native land in shameful whispers. Another kind is an explainer. He becomes fretful and involved in the attempt to make it clear to some Englishman with a cold and fish-like eye that, as a matter of fact, the lynchings are scattered over a large territory, and Tammany has nothing whatever to do with the United States Senate, and the millionaire does not crawl into the presence of his wife and daughters, and Morgan never can be King, and citizens of St. Louis are not in danger of being hooked by moose. After he gets through the Englishman says "Really?" and the painful incident is closed.

Every man is handicapped and hobbled when he gets out of his own bailiwick. The American is at a special disadvantage in Europe. If he cannot adapt himself to strange customs and social regulations, he thinks that he will be set down as an ignoramus. If he tries to nullify or override them he may be regarded as a boor or a barbarian. Once in a while an American, finding himself beset by unfamiliar conditions, follows the simple policy of not trying to assimilate new rules or oppose them, and merely goes ahead in his own way, conducting himself as a human being possessed of the usual number of faculties. This odd performance may be counted upon to excite wonder and admiration. Benjamin Franklin tried it out long ago and became the sensation of Europe. General Grant and Colonel Roosevelt got along comfortably in all sorts of foreign complications merely by refusing to put on disguises and to be play-actors. But Mark Twain was probably the best of our emissaries. He never waved the starry banner and at the same time he never went around begging forgiveness. He knew the faults of his home people and he understood intimately and with a family knowledge all of their good qualities and groping intentions and half-formed plans for big things in the future; but apparently he did not think it necessary to justify all of his private beliefs to men who lived five thousand miles away from Hannibal, Missouri. He had been in all parts of the world and had made a calm and unbiased estimate of the relative values of men and institutions. Probably he came to know that all had been cut from one piece and then trimmed variously. He carried with him the same placid habits of life that sufficed him in Connecticut and because he was what he pretended to be, the hypercritical foreigners doted upon him and the Americans at home, glad to flatter themselves, said, "Why, certainly, he's one of us."

INDEX

This index is centered on Mark Twain. A heading such as "artistry" or "style" applies primarily to his own writings. Books, stories, and essays by Twain are also integrated with the main alphabetical listing.